"This book is a highly compelling study of Freud and Schelling in search of the philosophical soul of psychoanalysis and the psychoanalytic heart of philosophy. Freud's declared scientism veils an approach in which reality engages with the world necessarily by way of fantasy; Schelling's philosophy implies that we can know reality, which includes ourselves, only through an engagement with its strange uncanniness. In this beautifully written book, Fenichel reveals a new way to make philosophy and psychoanalysis converse."

Russell Grigg, author of *Lacan, Language and Philosophy*

"If nihilism, as Nietzsche stated, is the 'uncanniest of guests,' it is so not because it unveils the uncanny but because it covers it over, even to the point of dissolving it completely with the help of one benzodiazepine or the other, the pharmaceutical take on modernity's distinctive blend of dull everydayness and the self-evidence of reason. This bold and ambitious book represents Teresa Fenichel's gritty determination to combat nihilism by rehabilitating the oldest but most difficult form of therapy. Championed by practitioners from Freud to Julia Kristeva, it can be characterized as the simple resolve to live in the truth, and above all in the truth of truth's flaming center, the sheer uncanny fact that being is. That truth is what is at issue here is the justification for Fenichel's decision to interpret Freudian psychoanalysis through the lens of Schelling's metaphysics of the unconscious. Uncanny truth is not, however, the last word, for the mystery of life is that it brings with it the possibility of an uncanny belonging. Just as we belong to one another in love, we belong to everything that exists in the shared fragility of a mortality that is always a blessing and a curse."

Joseph P. Lawrence, author of *Schellings Philosophie des ewigen Anfangs*

Schelling, Freud, and the Philosophical Foundations of Psychoanalysis

Schelling, Freud, and the Philosophical Foundations of Psychoanalysis provides a long-overdue dialogue between two seminal thinkers, Schelling and Freud. Through a sustained reading of the sublime, mythology, the uncanny, and freedom, this book provokes the reader to retrieve and revive the shared roots of philosophy and psychoanalysis.

Teresa Fenichel examines the philosophical basis for the concepts of the unconscious and for the nature of human freedom on which psychoanalysis rests. Drawing on the work of German philosopher F. W. J. Schelling, the author explores how his philosophical understanding of human actions, based as it was on the ideas of drives, informed and helped shape Freud's work. Fenichel also stresses the philosophical weight of Freudian psychoanalysis, specifically in regards to the problem of freedom and argues that psychoanalysis complicates and reinforces Schelling's basic idea: to know reality we must engage with the world empathetically and intimately.

This book also serves as an introduction to Schelling's thought, arguing that his metaphysics—particularly concerning the primacy of the unconscious and of fantasy—can be read as a therapeutic endeavor. Finally, the book offers a deep rethinking of the action and nature of sublimation through both Freud's and Schelling's texts. Fenichel suggests psychoanalytic therapy is self-interpretation—a recognition of our narratives as narratives, without for that reason taking them any less seriously. *Schelling, Freud, and the Philosophical Foundations of Psychoanalysis* will be of great interest to psychoanalysts and psychoanalytic psychotherapists as well as scholars of philosophy.

Teresa Fenichel is a visiting assistant professor at the College of the Holy Cross in Worcester, MA, USA. Her research interests include German idealism, psychoanalysis, feminist philosophy, and aesthetics.

The Psychology and the Other Book Series

The *Psychology and the Other* Book Series highlights creative work at the intersections between psychology and the vast array of disciplines relevant to the human psyche. The interdisciplinary focus of this series brings psychology into conversation with continental philosophy, psychoanalysis, religious studies, anthropology, sociology, and social/critical theory. The cross-fertilization of theory and practice, encompassing such a range of perspectives, encourages the exploration of alternative paradigms and newly articulated vocabularies that speak to human identity, freedom, and suffering. Thus, we are encouraged to reimagine our encounters with difference, our notions of the "other," and what constitutes therapeutic modalities.

The study and practices of mental health practitioners, psychoanalysts, and scholars in the humanities will be sharpened, enhanced, and illuminated by these vibrant conversations, representing pluralistic methods of inquiry, including those typically identified as psychoanalytic, humanistic, qualitative, phenomenological, or existential.

For a full list of titles in the series, please visit the Routledge website at: www.routledge.com/Psychology-and-the-Other/book-series/PSYOTH

Schelling, Freud, and the Philosophical Foundations of Psychoanalysis

Uncanny Belonging

Teresa Fenichel

Routledge
Taylor & Francis Group

LONDON AND NEW YORK

First published 2019
by Routledge
2 Park Square, Milton Park, Abingdon, Oxon OX14 4RN

and by Routledge
711 Third Avenue, New York, NY 10017

Routledge is an imprint of the Taylor & Francis Group, an informa business

British Library Cataloguing-in-Publication Data
A catalogue record for this book is available from the British Library

Library of Congress Cataloging-in-Publication Data
Names: Fenichel, Teresa, 1981- author.
Title: Schelling, Freud, and the philosophical foundations of psychoanalysis : uncanny belonging / Teresa Fenichel.
Description: Abingdon, Oxon ; New York, NY : Routledge, 2019. | Includes bibliographical references and index.
Identifiers: LCCN 2018026265 (print) | LCCN 2018027975 (ebook) | ISBN 9781351180153 (Master) | ISBN 9781351180146 (Web PDF) | ISBN 9781351180139 (ePub) | ISBN 9781351180122 (Mobipocket/Kindle) | ISBN 9780815385813 (hardback : alk. paper) | ISBN 9780815385837 (pbk. : alk. paper)
Subjects: LCSH: Psychoanalysis and philosophy. | Psychoanalysis–Philosophy. | Schelling, Friedrich Wilhelm Joseph von, 1775-1854. | Freud, Sigmund, 1856-1939.
Classification: LCC BF175.4.P45 (ebook) | LCC BF175.4.P45 F45 2019 (print) | DDC 150.19/5–dc23
LC record available at https://lccn.loc.gov/2018026265

ISBN: 978-0-8153-8581-3 (hbk)
ISBN: 978-0-8153-8583-7 (pbk)
ISBN: 978-1-351-18015-3 (ebk)

Typeset in Times New Roman
by Wearset Ltd, Boldon, Tyne and Wear

Contents

Acknowledgments

This book would never have been written or published without the love, support, and guidance of my family, friends, teachers, and students. I am forever grateful to: Nancy, Paul, Willie, Jesse, Mera, and Theo Fenichel; Dan, Kelli, Matt, Jennie, Frances, Hayyim, Renée, Nico, and Longnook Beach Volleyball; Professors Joe Lawrence, Vanessa Rumble, Richard Kearney, Fr. William Richardson, Jeff Bloechl, Alan Bass, and John Manoussakis, The *Psychology and the Other* team, and especially David Goodman. My many wonderful students at Boston College and College of the Holy Cross.

Abbreviations

AS	*Aesthetics and Subjectivity*, Andrew Bowie. Manchester: Manchester University Press, 2003.
AW	*Ages of the World* (1813), trans. Judith Norman. Ann Arbor: The University of Michigan Press, 1997.
BPP	*Beyond the Pleasure Principle*, trans. Gregory C. Richter. Buffalo: Broadview, 2011.
CJ	*Critique of Judgment*, trans. Warner Pluhar. Indianapolis: Hackett Publishing Company, 1987.
CPR	*Critique of Pure Reason*, trans. Paul Guyer and Allen W. Wood. Cambridge: Cambridge University Press, 1997.
DR	*Die Religion innerhalb der Grenzen der bloßen Vernunft*, Frankfurt am Main: Suhrkamp, 1977.
FS	*Philosophical Inquiries into the Nature of Human Freedom*, trans. James Gutmann. Illinois: Open Court, 1992.
KU	*Kritik der Urteilskraft*, Hamburg: Felix Meiner Verlag, 2001.
SE	*The Standard Edition of the Complete Psychological Works of Sigmund Freud*, ed. James Strachey, 24 vols. London: Hogarth Press.
STI	*System of Transcendental Idealism*, trans. Peter Heath. Charlottesville: University of Virginia Press, 2001.
SW	*Schellings Sämmtliche Werke*, ed. Karl Schelling, 14 vols. Stuttgart and Augsburg: J.G. Cotta'scher Verlag, 1859.
TEL	*The Essential Loewald: Collected Essays and Monographs*. Maryland: University Publishing Group, 2000.
TS	*Schillers Theoretische Schriften (Sämmtliche Werke, Fünfter Band)*.

Introduction
Twisted beginnings

The Unconscious is in fact the real psychical, as unknown to us in terms of its inner nature as the reality of the outside world and as incompletely rendered to us by the data of consciousness as the outside world is rendered by the information supplied the sense organs.
—Freud, Interpretation of Dreams

Man must be granted an essence outside and above the world; for how could he alone, of all creatures, retrace the long path of developments from the present back into the deepest night of the past, how could he alone rise up to the beginning of things unless there were in him an essence from the beginning of times? Drawn from the source of things and akin to it, what is eternal of the soul has a co-science/ con-sciousness [Mitt-Wissenschaft] of creation.
—Schelling, Die Weltalter, 1813

I have often wondered, and I still do, what it would be like to write truth-fully—to *be* true. These are the dual concerns that motivate this book. It is not settled whether there is some genuine kernel of agitation, around which all my thinking and writing have gathered, or whether there is only an empty space, crisscrossed by disparate strands. I'm not even sure whether there is a difference. What I can say is that this space or this kernel is what I call *truth*, and this process of gathering, or crisscrossing, is what I call *freedom*. I am writing to understand how it is that, for me, philosophy and psychoanalysis converge just here: in the entanglement of seeking and what is sought, in the complications of creativity and authenticity. I engage with the works of F. W. J. Schelling and Freud because I believe that they expand our idea of reality, remaking truth and knowledge in terms of empathy and vulnerability; and because, in their sensitivity to the uncanny, the mythological, and the sublime, the problem of freedom is given new force and immediacy. Psychoanalysis must remember how to shock us back into life, to renew our sense of fascination with ourselves and our world. And philosophy, as the search for wisdom, cannot survive unless it returns to its therapeutic roots.[1]

I received my first real introduction to psychoanalysis and philosophy at the New School for Social Research. I became interested in these subjects both independently and at their intersection, because I discovered in them possibilities for self-questioning, languages that could do justice to a textured reality, to an objectivity that can encompass desire, fantasy, freedom, and the unconscious. Freud's therapeutic methods and their ethical implications, namely that psychic health requires an empathetic engagement with the most radical alterity, suggested to me a way to think the kind of grounding instability that must underlie a metaphysics of freedom.[2] I focused my work on the psychoanalytic contributions of Hans Loewald—an analyst and former student of Heidegger's.[3] I found in Loewald a critique of key Freudian assertions, clinical, and metapsychological, that came from a genuine, *philosophical* appreciation.[4] Concerned that psychoanalysis can be naïvely understood as relying upon a form of "objectivity," which would be exposed as a fantasy in the therapeutic situation, Loewald argued that Freud, at times, suffered from a "neurotic" sense of reality. In other words, Freud often retreated into a fundamentally antagonistic ontology—a distorted perspective he diagnosed in his neurotic patients—rather than following through with the much more radical and nuanced alternatives that psychoanalytic treatment depends upon:

> On three levels, then, the biological, the psychological and the cultural, psychoanalysis has taken for granted the neurotically distorted experience of reality. It has taken for granted the concept of a reality as it is experienced in a predominantly defensive integration of it. Stimulus, external world, and culture, all three on different levels of scientific approach, representative of what is called reality, have been understood unquestioningly as they are thought, felt, experienced within the framework of a hostile-defensive ego-reality integration. It is a concept of reality as it is most typically encountered in the obsessive character neurosis, a neurosis so common in our culture it has been called the normal neurosis.
>
> ("Defense and Reality," p. 30)[5]

Freud could not see that the (sometimes implicit, sometimes explicit) assumption of a hostile relationship between the psyche on one side, and the pre-given world on the other, was a neurotic construction of his own making.[6]

Like Loewald, I was dissatisfied with Freud's strained insistence on the scientific status of psychoanalysis; I wanted to articulate a more radical worldview that psychoanalysis seems to demand, but that also seems to threaten the very foundations of the system. I considered Freud's reading of the uncanny and telepathy as focal points for such a questioning, and thus situated myself in the same territory that so attracted Jacques Derrida.[7] If Loewald offered insight into the *therapeutic* consequences of a more philosophically robust *theory*, Derrida helped me work toward a philosophical formulation of the therapeutic situation.

It was not until I began studying Schelling and German Idealism at Boston College, however, that I became interested in the philosophers that laid the groundwork for Freud's therapeutic project. Situated at the interstices of science and subjectivity, the post-Kantian philosophers were in fact the very well-spring of the intellectual tradition from which, and within which, Freud was able to formulate his own project.[8] In a sort of shock of recognition, I recalled that in the short paper at the center of my thesis work—"The Uncanny"—Freud had already pointed the way: it is Schelling's definition of the uncanny that he uses.[9] And there were broader similarities, too. Schelling, like Freud, has been dismissed from mainstream, academic philosophy for having made false claims to rigorous, scientific thinking; and this, in no small part, is due to the central role the unconscious played in his thought. Somewhat ironically, it was partly in response to the shadow of Schelling's once-pervasive *Naturphilosophie*— or rather to its consequently being shunned as mysticism—that Freud so rabidly defended psychoanalysis as a system of psychic determinism.[10] And yet at the same time, in reinterpreting the human through the reality and potency of the unconscious, Freud also carries on Schelling's interest in mythology as the privileged site of and access to a truth that exceeds the logic and order of consciousness.[11]

But it is in the seriousness with which they attend to human desire, the genuinely philosophical weight they accord to emotional life, that Schelling and Freud most decidedly converge: drive [*Trieb*] is Schelling's basic unit of reality, that which structures our psychic experience as well as the world we encounter. And like Freud, Schelling's drive theory collapses

under the artifice of their rationality, when dualism approaches cosmo-
logical aspirations:

> It is God's will to universalize everything, to lift it to unity with light
> or to preserve it therein; but the will of the deep is to particularize
> everything or to make it creature-like. It wishes differentiation only
> so that identity may become evident to itself and to the will of the
> deep. Therefore it necessarily reacts against freedom as against what
> is above the creature, and awakens in it the desire for what is
> creature—just as he who is seized by dizziness on a high and precipi-
> tous summit seems to hear a mysterious voice calling to him to
> plunge down, or as in the ancient tale, the irresistible song of the
> sirens sounded out of the deep to draw the passing mariner down into
> the whirlpool.[12]

The manifest opposition that characterizes Freud's and Schelling's drive
theories conceals an originary, *dizzying* ambivalence; the essential liminality of the drive is only revealed in their inevitable culmination/
collapse. That is, it is the nature of the drive both to separate out, and to
draw together, (desiring) subject and (desired) object. Or, as Schelling
puts it in the *Weltalter*, in the beginning there is desire: the will, in its
struggle to return to and reclaim itself, begets existence. Truth is not
obscured by desire, but rather emerges from it. Schelling's aesthetic
claims are no mere corollary to his metaphysics of freedom, but its very
foundation.[13]

The connection between desire and truth in Schelling, the way they
disrupt, and define each other, is evident in the call that introduces his
Weltalter:

> Perhaps he will yet come, who will sing the great heroic poem,
> encompassing in spirit (as is reputed of the seers from times gone by)
> what was, what is, and what will be. But this time is not yet at hand.
> As its harbingers, we do not wish to pluck its fruit before it is ripe,
> nor do we wish to misjudge our own. This is still a time of struggle.[14]

The aim of philosophy, Schelling suggests, is not to overcome the illu-
sions of art—it is not an antidote to the fantasies and deceptions endemic
to the human. Rather, philosophy must be devoted to maintaining a

connection (one we are always, it seems, in danger of losing) to the ecstatic pulse of creation. Schelling's interest in the philosophical "seer," the "great heroic poem" he will produce, does not imply that the "time of struggle" should one day cease; the unity of time is not some universal, redemptive event, as we will see, but an ever-present possibility—lost and gained—that is the life of a free subject. Schelling's task in the *Weltalter*, as in the *Freiheitsschrift*, is to develop a form of philosophy that can serve as an expression of and impetus to this horrific yet beautiful possibility. The mutual dependence of love and evil, which he derives from the ultimate inseparability of ontological drives toward otherness and egoity, suggests the extent to which the creations and permutations of human desire inform even Schelling's most abstract thinking.

Within psychoanalysis, it might seem that the drives serve to rectify the superficial irrationality of symptoms and dreams; that their underlying logic is the key to "decoding" the truth. I would argue, however, that this is a dangerously facile reading. The drives, as Freud repeatedly points out, are unknowable in themselves, a useful linguistic fiction that can help us interpret and recalibrate the meaning of our experience. As I intend to show, Freud's dependence on a paradigm of conflict—torn between the wish and our fear of its accomplishment—is undercut by his insistence on an essentially ambivalent and eternal unconscious. For Freud, and this supports my point, there are almost as many iterations of drive theory as there are texts—from the dualism of sexual and self-preservation drives in *Studies on Hysteria*, to the antagonism of Eros and Thanatos in *Beyond the Pleasure Principle*.[15] As with Schelling, it is this latter drive theory that I focus on, where the *duality* of the drives (and the stable identities such duality depends upon) becomes questionable. If Freud is commonly understood as a determinist, such a reading is surely belied by a system predicated on the strange interdependence and in-between status of unconscious drives. That is, in the confused convergence/antagonism of Eros and Thanatos that disrupts the very narrative of *Beyond the Pleasure Principle*, Freud recalls the essential distinction between drives and mechanical forces. In contrast to instinct [*Instinkt*], drives are the fundamental components of *psychical* reality, of the inchoate beginnings from which the oppositions between self and world can emerge.

In one among many revealing admissions concerning the provisional status of drives in *Beyond the Pleasure Principle*, an intrusion of self-doubt that speaks not only to the subject at hand but to the philo-sophical underpinnings of psychoanalysis more generally, Freud writes:

> In judging our speculation about the life and death drives, we would not be much disturbed by the fact that so many strange and unclear processes occur in them, e.g., one drive may be driven out by others, or may turn from the ego to the object, and so on. This is merely a result of the fact that we are obliged to work with *scientific termin-ology, i.e., with our own figurative language, that of psychology (or more correctly: depth psychology). Otherwise, we would be com-pletely unable to describe the processes in question; indeed, we would not even have noticed them.* The deficiencies of our descrip-tion would probably disappear, were we already able to invoke physiological or chemical terms in lieu of psychological ones. *Admit-tedly, those terms too belong merely to figurative language*—but one long familiar to us and perhaps simpler as well.[16]

Even, or perhaps especially, in dealing with what we might call the atomic theory of psychoanalysis, Freud is torn between aesthetic and scientific truth. Language—whether chemical or psychoanalytic—is not a tool separ-able from the object it discloses, adequate, or not to the truth it claims to reproduce; rather, as Freud is uniquely aware, language is most fundament-ally the capacity to shape the truth, or to make certain kinds of truth avail-able to us. Freud's drive language, with its emphasis on antagonism, is world-disclosing in this way. But it is no accident that Freud draws our attention to the limitations of language in the same text where the drives begin to take on the aspect of metaphysical principles. In the end, Freud's dualism succeeds (which is to say, is over-turned) in revealing, anew, an originary plasticity, and ambivalence that distinguishes the realm of the psychical and motivates each new theory of the drives. It is the irrepressible creativity and stubborn concealment of the drives, along with Freud's deter-mination to compulsively order their conflicts and expressions that, leads to his speculation on language and structures of representation—not the other way round. As the primary components of the unconscious, the drives must be essential to developing an account of freedom in psychoanalysis—a freedom that, like the drives, exceeds opposition.

It is this concern with freedom, particularly in relation to a fundamental aesthetics, that I found lacking in Loewald's and Derrida's readings of Freud. Ultimately, their elaborations of Freud's psychic reality remain untethered from the existential concerns they set out to transform. Though very much in line with their calls for psychoanalysis to acknowledge the *reality* of the unconscious, the *temporal* or *causal* repercussions are never fully dealt with:[17] Is there freedom in psycho-analysis? And if so, how might this transform philosophical approaches to freedom? Through my focus on the uncanny as the possible site of freedom in psychoanalytic practice and theory, I found that Schelling's middle and late texts offered insights into unconscious temporality that are essential to developing such a framework. Moreover, I began to understand Schelling's later works as themselves metaphysical and ethical elaborations of a fundamentally therapeutic system: a theory of freedom inextricably bound to its practical realization.

It should not be a surprise that it is within a text he calls *aesthetic* —"The Uncanny"—that Freud invokes Schelling; that the uncanny con-vergence of fate and omnipotence, which I argue is the domain of freedom, can be most adequately addressed as *feeling.*[18]

Where Freud finds in the uncanny the return of the repressed, I will argue that Schelling understands existence itself as uncanny. In dismant-ling the equation of truth with self-evidence, by instead deriving reason from a generative and reciprocal act, Schelling gives us a metaphysics of the uncanny. As we will see in Freud's account, it is that which *appears* identical but *is* not that most reliably results in the anxiety of the uncanny. Moreover, such logic is found not merely in our various experiences of the uncanny, but in the creative longing that allows for any and all experi-ence. In other words, the very *fact* that what is *is*—a fact we *feel* in the overwhelming freedom that marks existential crisis—profoundly broadens the scope of the uncanny.

I would like to briefly address the duplicity of the uncanny, the thera-peutic possibility where psychoanalytic fantasy and the Schellingian imagination converge. After a detailed account of one of Hoffman's tales, *The Sandman*, to which Freud attributes great uncanny effects deriving from the return of infantile fears and desires he comes to the following conclusions:

> We must content ourselves with selecting those themes of uncanni-ness which are most prominent, and seeing whether we can fairly trace them also back to infantile sources. These themes are all

concerned with the idea of a "double" in every shape and degree, with persons, therefore, who are to be considered identical by reason of looking alike; Hoffman accentuates this relation by transferring mental processes from the one person to the other—what we should call telepathy—so that the one possesses knowledge, feeling and experience in common with the other, identifies himself with another person, so that his self becomes confounded, or the foreign self is substituted for his own—in other words, by doubling, dividing and interchanging the self.[19]

It is not simply the resurgence of infantile fears that makes us anxious; as Freud points out in this passage, perfectly innocuous infantile *wishes* may also be uncanny. This suggests that it is the very structure of return—of the reappearance of groundlessness and non-presence as the root of our being—that gives rise to the uncanny. In other words, the feeling of uncanniness is dependent upon the primordial fantasy of reason: a stable identity. The uncanniness of the double is an echo of an original uncanniness, or better put, of uncanniness *as* originary. We then experience the brute reality of that which cannot show itself *as* itself—the barest structure of fantasy as that which threatens to reveal the insecurity and absence it works to conceal.[20]

This is, in truth, not far from Schelling's own account of the duplicity inherent in being, where the identity of ground and existence is always already divided by the longing for just such a union: "But the more this composure is profoundly deep and intrinsically full of bliss, the sooner must a quiet longing produce itself in eternity ... This is a longing to come to itself, to find and savor itself."[21] Schelling's *Freiheitsschrift* is an attempt to construct a system of freedom—where the structure of his system requires the thinking of a ground that *belongs* to the Absolute but is not *identical* to it:

For if, at the first glance, it seems that freedom, unable to maintain itself in opposition to God, is here submerged in identity, it may be said that this apparent result is merely the consequence of an imperfect and empty conception of the law of identity. This principle does not express a unity which, revolving in the indifferent circle of sameness, would get us nowhere and remain meaningless and lifeless. The unity of this law is of an intrinsically creative kind. In the relation of subject to predicated itself, we have already pointed out the relation of ground and consequence ... Dependence does not determine the nature of the dependent, and merely declares that the dependent entity, whatever else it may be, can only be as a consequence of that upon which it is dependent ... Every organic individual, insofar as it has come into being, is dependent upon another organism with respect to its genesis but not at all with regard to its essential being.[22]

His argument here is that in order for beings to *be*, the nature of identity must be rethought as a principle of *Unheimlichkeit*: identity eternally and primordially requires difference. The possibility of human freedom, for Schelling, is dependent upon the identity/duplicity of the Absolute—dependent upon the space opened up by the ungrounded ground (*Ungrund*) that both *is* and *is not* the Absolute. Without a fracturing, which seems horrifically, to precede and derive from the Absolute there *is* nothing: we are *anxious* in the face of identity that requires self-division and of differentiation that depends upon self-identity. Such anxiety is the essence of the uncanny, the disturbed union of the *Heimlich* and *Unheimlich*, and *that which should have remained secret and hidden becomes visible.*[23]

  The Freud I develop in this book is uncanny precisely because of this therapeutically essential and theoretically inescapable duplicity: to cure is both to disentangle reality from fantasy *and* to acknowledge fantasy at the basis of reality. The reality of redemption is a function of its remaining irreducibly yet-to-come—of our ability to remain open to and engaged with the meaningfulness we attribute to the past. In Freud's works on the uncanny and telepathy, as he hovers around the possibility of an unconscious that exceeds the individual, we can begin to see how freedom must intrude upon the scientific *Weltanschauung* of psychoanalysis. The uncanny is a disturbing confrontation with the fragility of boundary—between self and other, past and future, fantasy and reality. This is the place where Freud comes closest to articulating the incompatibility of scientific objectivity with a truth that would be properly *psychoanalytic*. It is, after all, psychoanalysis that ensures the entanglement of psychic reality—drive and wish—with all perception, memory, action, and speech. In the uncanny, then, it is not that a *particular* piece of repressed material returns to us; but rather that the very *givenness* of existence becomes questionable. We *feel* the instability of the ground show up for us personally, intimately. And, as it turns out, for Freud this feeling is always one of the expansion/contraction of identity—the very space of Schelling's egoic evil and erotic redemption. Not only do I want to argue that Schelling's late philosophy suggest the kind of metaphysics Freudian therapy depends upon; the vitality and viability of Freudian therapy also offers a genuine alternative to contemporary methods of interpreting Schelling's concerns with evil, freedom, temporality, and myth.

Freud, citing Schelling, writes "*unheimlich is the name for everything which ought to have remained ... hidden and secret but has become visible.*"[24] This is the definition to which Freud returns after a long discussion of various etymologies. Importantly for Freud, the word "*unheimlich*" is itself ambiguous, suggesting both intimate knowledge and uncomfortable mystery—at-home-ness and not-at-home-ness: "Thus *heimlich* is a word the meaning of which develops toward an ambivalence, until it finally coincides with its opposite, *unheimlich. Unheimlich* is in some way or other a sub-species of *heimlich.*"[25] The word, divided in itself, simultaneously signals both alienation and absorption: it enacts the "un-homely home" that marks the dual anxieties of life. The possibility of going "home," of return, is precluded by the language that pronounces this desire. It is not unimportant, then, that Freud's analysis of the uncanny centers on *literature*; although he is careful to point out that he uses aesthetic here in its widest sense, encompassing both feeling *and* art, it is our experience with literature that Freud focuses on.[26] His analysis is thus not *only* concerned with the feeling of the uncanny, but also and in no small part with the manner in which we must be affected in and by artistic creations:

> The story-teller has this license among many others, that he can select his world of representation so that it either coincides with the realities we are familiar with or departs from them in what particulars he pleases ... The situation is altered as soon as the writer pretends to move in the world of common reality. In this case he accepts all the conditions operating to producing uncanny feelings in real life ... He takes advantage, as it were, of our supposedly surmounted superstitiousness; he deceives us into thinking that he is giving us the sober truth, and then after all oversteps the bounds of possibility. We react to his inventions as we should have reacted to real experiences.[27]

Freud comes close here to recognizing that there is an element of deceit at the heart of our experience of art or of language more generally: the same deception that gives rise to our feeling of the uncanny. This suspension of the boundaries between truth and fantasy evoked by the artist, the presentation of reality as unreality and vice versa, is itself a *repetition* of a more primitive interaction with reality. The infantile relationship between ego and world that returns to us in the feeling of the uncanny is one of imaginary omnipotence and authentic helplessness—the anxiety, which emerges from this ambiguity marks a space in which we may feel ourselves both absolutely guilty (our thoughts become reality, we control nature) and entirely passive (victims of fate, subject to determinism). In Schellingian terms, we have either renounced freedom in choosing evil (a separation from and presumed control over nature) or do not yet belong to freedom at all (a naïve absorption in things that allows for no reflection).[28] As Schelling puts it in the *Freiheitsschrift*,

> So the beginning of sin consists in man's going over from being to non-being, from truth to falsehood, from light into darkness, in order himself to become the creative basis and to rule over all things with the power of the center which he contains ... In evil there is that contradiction which devours and always negates itself, which just while striving to become creature destroys the nexus of creation and, in its ambition to be everything, falls into non-being.[29]

It turns out that one of the consequences of accepting the Freudian unconscious is that we do not and cannot *know* the extent of our freedom or our guilt. Rather, we *feel* uncanniness: we *feel* freedom as it escapes us, as loss—which is, perhaps, the only way to feel freedom at all.

What we have the opportunity to see in these works is not so much a movement away from psychoanalysis as science, but rather toward a psychoanalytic view of reality that allows for an expansion of *what counts as science*—what *counts as real*.[30] In "The Uncanny," Freud is obviously much less concerned than in the telepathy papers that his work will threaten the tenuous link between traditional science and psychoanalysis, or call into question the supposition of an *objective* reality that is always already there. And yet, his work on the uncanny is surely a movement in this direction, echoing Freud's earlier, defining step in giving up the distinction between "real" seduction and fantasy.[31] In his treatment of the uncanny, Freud recalls the *fluidity* of the boundary, creating an undecidable space between science and fiction within which he will never be entirely comfortable.[32] The source of this feeling is a return of the repressed, an eerie reminder of unconscious, infantile wishes/fantasies that evokes a more primitive, permeable ego-reality situation. For Freud, it is psychoanalysis itself that allows us insight into that which is so familiar it is alien; into that which touches us so deeply that we can no longer recognize it as our own. In Freud's work on telepathy and the uncanny we find intimations of the *transitional* reality that paves the way for—and in fact surpasses—the opposition between fantasy and reality.

For psychoanalysis to be "in a position to create a *Weltanschauung* of its own," it must grope toward the forgotten, the unutterable, the refused; Loewald's contribution comes in no small part in critically turning Freud's discovery of unconscious processes back upon the presuppositions of a given, material reality. Freud shies away from the consequences of the *reality* of the unconscious, opening up a wider metaphysical horizon at the same moment that he reverts to the dichotomous, comfortable paradigms from which he constructed his therapeutic method. Psychoanalysis *is* a metaphysical view of the universe, and one that must be committed to articulating and transforming its interpretation of reality: it is the unique possibility of psychoanalysis to consistently question its own foundations, including the nature of scientific activity and the structure of knowledge it implies.[33]

My claim in this book is that only in reading Freud and Schelling together can we uncover their fundamental insight: to become who we are, to feel at home in existence, is to acknowledge an essential and irreducible *uncanniness*. Put differently, Schelling understands his, and indeed *the*, philosophical task to be the development of a system *of* freedom. He is not interested in a system that merely accommodates or allows for freedom, but instead recognizes that reason itself needs to be radically transformed by our finitude—by our traumatic, irreducible *existence*. It is in similar terms, appealing to a kind of knowledge that finds its integrity not in closure but in rupturing, that Jean Laplanche describes Freud's philosophy:

> For this reason, psychoanalysis—which is itself but a tiny part of our forever unfinished knowledge of the cosmos—is a body of knowledge which we might describe as "wounded," opened up from the

first by the enigma of the experience of the unconscious ... A *wounded rationalism*: this would be one of the possible formulas for referring to Freud's philosophy, in the knowledge that that very wound is a stimulating event.[34]

My contention is that psychoanalysis *is* such a system, the *wound* here understood as the very freedom that Schelling repeatedly tries to conceptualize. And it is so precisely and only to the extent that therapeutic success means a continued and increased availability to interpretation—a ceaseless creativity and regeneration. That is, the alleged determinism of psychic events is in fact built upon the underlying assumption that interpretation is never complete; that, indeed, freedom is an expression of a continued openness to the past, and psychic health is a persistent confrontation with alienation and collapse. In this way, Freud can fulfill Schelling's program. At the same time, the fundamental questions that Freud skirts are best approached through Schelling's metaphysics: Why does psychoanalysis work? How can interpretation be a therapeutic act—an act of *freedom*? Schelling tells us that the challenge in creating a system of freedom, or in bringing together the theoretical and the existential, is to unify while preserving difference. This ought to be the structure of therapeutic work: psychoanalytic interpretation is not a matter of integrating the unconscious into consciousness, and thus flattening, or disposing of it. Interpretation, *if* it is free, and freeing, must be a gathering that preserves difference. Schelling articulates in theory a system that is true to what is—a *Weltanschauung* that would not deny the concrete individuals that constitute it; Freud offers it as practice. It is psychoanalysis, as system, that begins and ends with freedom: the therapeutic task and process both center on our capacity to create meaning, to draw together but not to close off or reduce, to recreate, and refind the limits of self and reality.

I offer here an encounter with a certain trajectory of thought, a trek through the tangled paths of philosophy and psychoanalysis. We know that Freud inherited, directly and indirectly, fundamental aspects of Schelling's *Naturphilosophie*, particularly his articulation of unconscious drives. But Schelling's overarching interest in freedom seems to have been dropped. It is of course well-known that Freud often explicitly claimed an absolute psychic determinism, or rather, over-determinism; and even more often, such claims are attributed to him. The unconscious, its mechanisms ever more nuanced and detailed in Freud's metapsychology, appears to be a refutation of freedom rather than its guarantor. But in order to maintain the radical and vital unity of philosophy/theory and reality/practice that psychoanalysis enacts, Freud's supposed determinism needs to be challenged. Freud's disavowal of psychic freedom—and, indeed, of his philosophical forebears—is bound up with his near pathological insistence that psychoanalysis is a science.

The course this book takes is in no way a linear one: like the traumatic, unconscious time I deal with, there is a great deal of circling back to the beginning—to a beginning that is no longer what I thought it was. Indeed, I have learned the hard way that the uncanny shows up out of turn, always out of place. So having offered here a rudimentary sketch of the centrality of the uncanny to Freud's thought, and its relevance to Schelling's metaphysics of freedom, I go backward. Chapter 1 offers a reading of the sublime in Kant, placing Freud in an aesthetic tradition to which Schelling belongs, that "invents" the unconscious in order to protect rather than to deny freedom. I go on to suggest that Schelling's departure from Kant, particularly in terms of their reading of tragedy, prefigures the psychoanalytic *Weltanschauung*. I claim that, by way of Schelling, the Kantian sublime is transformed into the Freudian uncanny—the universality of reason into the particularity of desire.

With this development of tragedy in mind, Chapter 2 conceives of Schelling's *Freiheitsschrift* as a definitive shift toward a more dynamic and living unconscious—an unconscious inextricably linked to his system of freedom and the concept of personality, which undergirds it: to the health of this personality that, we might say, is threatened from either side by the evils of self-enclosure (neurosis) and of self-dissolution (psychosis). In Chapter 3, I argue that Schelling, like Freud, understands the fundamentally tragic dimension of all that is inherited and personal—of human life and decision. The success of this comparison in large part rests on an interpretation of Freud's concept of *Nachträglichkeit*, or the temporal spasm in which trauma becomes what it is only in relation to what comes after—too early to be acknowledged and too late to be denied. My claim is that freedom, as this unconscious temporality, depends upon a past that is neither present nor absent but eternally becoming: our ground that must also be, at every moment, of our own making. Finally, Chapter 4 is a *return* to the uncanny in literature—or, more specifically, in mythology. Here I consider the dual function of language as both symptom and cure. Schelling's reading of mythology is *literal*—claiming that mythology *means* what it *is*—and I reconsider Freud's interpretive method in similar fashion. The question of human freedom now centers on originary trauma that disturbs the very possibility of origins and identity.

Finally, my conclusion is an effort both to retrace the arc of the narrative and offer a way forward through the lens of two "omitted" themes—the imagination in Schelling and sublimation in Freud. Through these themes, which I argue are not precisely omitted after all, I hope to clarify certain important connections between fantasy and freedom that perhaps remain a bit scattered throughout the body of the work. I articulate what I understand to be the main challenges facing contemporary philosophy and psychoanalysis, and propose concrete methods for revitalizing these essential forms of engagement by way of the uncanny.

Notes

1 It is Pierre Hadot that makes this argument so beautifully and forcefully in *Philosophy as a Way of Life*.
2 From very early on in his development of psychoanalysis, Freud insists that the "normal" is in no way qualitatively different from the "neurotic," the "psychotic" or the "perverse." Part of his project entails using his treatment of the pathological both to illustrate its encroachment into the normal and to show that psychic "health" can only be an interpretive recognition of unconscious desires and fears. Paraphrasing one of the theses of a late work, *Civilization and Its Discontents*, insofar as we are civilized so too are we neurotic. And, as he writes in "The Uncanny" (1914), the work of psychoanalysis is akin to telepathic communication:

> Indeed, I should not be surprised to hear that psychoanalysis, which is concerned with laying bare these hidden forces, has itself become uncanny to many people for that reason. In one case, after I succeeded— though none too rapidly—in effecting a cure in a girl who had been an invalid for many years, I myself heard this view expressed by the patient's mother after her long recovery.
>
> (*SE* Vol. XVII, p. 243)

3 Alan Bass, *Difference and Disavowal: The Trauma of Eros* (Stanford: Stanford University Press, 2000).
4 Teresa Fenichel, "Neurotic Being and Erotic Time: Philosophic Reflections on Hans Loewald's Contributions to Psychoanalysis." *American Imago*. Vol. 70 No. 4, Winter 2013, pp. 663–698.

5 Hans Loewald, *The Essential Loewald: Collected Papers and Monographs*. New Haven: Yale University Press, 2000. Hereafter, *TEL*.

6 "Hate, as a relation to objects, is older than love" ("Drives and their Fates," *SE* Vol. XIV, p. 137).

7 See in particular: "Telepathy" in *Psyche: Inventions of the Other* Vol. 1, pp. 226–261. Eds. Peggy Kamuf and Elizabeth Rottenberg. Stanford: Stanford University Press, 2007.

8 See in particular: John Sallis's essay, "The Logic and Illogic of the Dream-Work," pp. 1–16 in John Mills, *Rereading Freud: Psychoanalysis Through Philosophy* (Albany: State University of New York Press, 2004) and *The Gathering of Reason: 2nd Edition* (Albany: State University of New York Press, 2005). See also: Richard Kearney, *On Stories* (London: Routledge, 2002) and Joe Lawrence, *Schelling's Philosophie des ewigen Anfangs* (Würzburg: Königshausen & Neumann, 1989). I have Vanessa Rumble, Joe Lawrence, Jeff Bloechl, and Richard Kearney to thank for countless wonderful conversations as well as access to published and unpublished writings alike, including Lawrence's essay "Philosophical Religion and the Quest for Authenticity" in Jason M. Worth, *Schelling Now: Contemporary Readings* (Bloomington: Indiana University Press, 2005).

9 *Standard Edition of the Complete Psychological Works of Sigmund Freud*, Vol. XVII, pp. 217–256. Hereafter, cited as *SE*.

10 It is also worth noting that some of Freud's most fundamental concepts—the constancy principle, for example—derive from inheritors of and contributors to the *Naturphilosophie* movement, like Gustav Fechner. This only adds to the sense that Freud is at pains to make a place for psychoanalysis as science, at times at the expense of fully admitting both the precedents and consequences of his work.

11 See Denis Schmidt's brief discussion of Schelling's account of the *tragic* coming to fruition in Freud in *On Germans and Other Greeks: Tragedy and Ethical Life*:

> The ultimate outcome of this modern emphasis on the issue of subjectivity in connection with the dynamics of tragedy is most clearly expressed in Freud's theory of psychological complexes. It is not by accident that when Freud chooses to name the complexes which forge and shape the development of the self, he names these forces after figures in ancient Greek tragic drama. Freud could not use figures from Shakespearean tragedy as models to exemplify such dynamics because those characters are already too clearly defined as psychological types and by forces too obviously directed at the specific subjectivity of the characters. Since the hiddenness of the complex belongs to its basic nature, those characters so profoundly alert to their own subjective life, cannot serve as models for such unconscious complexes. In the final analysis, Freud's theory of complexes needs to be seen as the final consolidation of this modern shift in the presentation of

tragedy. It is the ultimate destination of the specifically modern experience of tragedy. It is also the point at which the specifically ancient Greek character of the experience of tragedy is most obscured.

(p. 79)

12 F. W. J. Schelling, *Philosophical Inquiries into the Essence of Human Freedom*. Trans. James Gutmann. LaSalle: Open Court, 1992. Hereafter this will be cited as *FS* (*Freiheitsschrift*) and I will use the pagination from Schelling's *Sämmtliche Werke* Vol. VII, hereafter denoted by *SW*, which is also given in the former. *FS*, 58–59/*SW*, 381.

13 F. W. J Schelling, *The Philosophy of Art*, trans. Douglas Stott (Minneapolis: University of Minnesota Press, 1989).

14 F. W. J. Schelling and Slavoj Žižek, *The Abyss of Freedom: Ages of the World (2nd draft, 1813)*. Trans. Judith Norman (Ann Arbor: The University of Michigan Press, 2000). Hereafter, unless otherwise cited, this will be the draft cited as *AW*. pp. 119–120.

15 Sigmund Freud, *Studies on Hysteria*. *SE* Vol. II, pp. 1–323.

16 Sigmund Freud and Todd Defresne, *Beyond the Pleasure Principle*. Toronto: Broadview editions, 2011. Hereafter, reference will be to this edition, cited as *BPP* with reference also to page numbers from *SE* Vol. XVIII. 96/60.

17 See: Derrida's "Telepathy" and Loewald's "The Experience of Time" in *The Essential Loewald: Collected Papers and Monographs*, pp. 138–147.

18 I only recently discovered, and have not seen it mentioned elsewhere in the literature, that the only other text in which Freud mentions Schelling (and his "followers") is in the first chapter of *Interpretation of Dreams*:

> Quite apart from all the pietistic and mystical writers—who do right to occupy the remains of the once extensive realm of the supernatural, as long as it has not been conquered by scientific explanation—we also encounter clear-sighted men averse to the fantastic who use this very inexplicability of the phenomena of dreams in their endeavors to support their religious belief in the existence and intervention of superhuman powers. The high value accorded to the dream-life by many schools of philosophy, for example, by Schelling's followers [*Naturphilosophie*], is a distinct echo of the undisputed divinity accorded to dreams in antiquity; and the divinatory, future-predicting power of dreams remains under discussion because the attempts at a psychological explanation are not adequate to cope with all the material gathered, however firmly the feelings of anyone devoted to the scientific mode of thought might be inclined to reject such a notion.
>
> (*SE IV*, p. 5)

It is worth noting that, in this brief reference, Freud connects Schelling with *both* occultism and "clear-sighted" scientific explanation—thus occupying the same territory that Freud himself seeks to lay claim to in his "scientific" explanation of the dream work that follows.

19 *SE* Vol. XVII, p. 233.
20 At first, this bears a strong resemblance to Lacan's account of the uncanny as the "lack of lack"—where that which (*objet a*) simultaneously holds open and blocks off the abyss of desire is filled up, paradoxically forcing the subject into anxiety. However, although I am interested in the nature of the *loss* that appears for us in the uncanny, I do not see any deep connections between my interpretation of Freud's essay and Lacan's at this juncture. See: *The Seminar of Jacques Lacan*: Anxiety 1962–1963 Book X, trans. Cormac Gallagher (from unpublished French manuscript). In particular, Seminar VII.
21 *AW*, p. 136.
22 *FS*, p. 346.
23 Markus Gabriel suggests a similar reading of Schelling in *Mythology Madness and Laughter*, though only in passing: "This willingness to explore and even to embrace the uncanniness of existence grounded in its libidinal instability is certainly what makes Schelling extraordinarily contemporary" (p. 33). Markus Gabriel and Slavoj Žižek, *Mythology, Madness and Laughter: Subjectivity in German Idealism* (London: Continuum, 2009). Like Žižek, Gabriel's reading of Schelling is (for the most part) grounded in the Lacanian interpretation rather than in Freud's own texts, so the very sense of what "uncanny" means here needs to be—but is not—at issue.
24 *SE* Vol. XVII, p. 224. In the original version of the essay Freud attributes the definition to Schleiermacher instead of Schelling (Beach, p. 289).
25 Ibid. p. 225.
26 It is perhaps worth noting here that Lacan sees Freud's "The Uncanny" as *the* most important reflection on anxiety, which he deals with in *Seminar X*. Thus, in part, the "psychoanalytic import" of the uncanny has much to do with what can be discovered about anxiety more generally. As Roberto Harari writes in *Lacan's Seminar on "Anxiety": An Introduction*:

> The key text in understanding anxiety in its various manifestations is simply "The Uncanny," as Lacan points out so well ... As we have written elsewhere, do not expect Freud to show up for an appointment if it is to take place in a conventionally defined place. *One has to proceed very cautiously with Freud because when we believe that the texts will provide answers we expect they do not; they go to unexpected, unforeseen places.*
>
> (p. 63)

See also: *The Seminar of Jacques Lacan: Anxiety 1962–1963 Book X*, trans. Cormac Gallagher (from unedited French manuscripts).
27 *SE Vol.* XVII, pp. 249–250.
28 This dynamic of union with and separation from Nature, particularly as evidenced through art, is also evident in Schiller's *On Naïve and Sentimental Poetry*:

How is it that we are so infinitely surpassed by the ancients in everything that is natural, and yet at precisely this point we are able to revere nature to a higher degree, to cling to it more intimately, and to embrace even the inanimate world with the tenderest feelings? This is *so* because nature has disappeared from our humanity, and we reencounter it in its genuineness only outside of humanity in the inanimate world. Not our greater *naturalness* but the very opposite, the *unnaturalness* of our relationships, conditions, and mores forces us to fashion a satisfaction in the physical world that is not to be hoped for in the moral world. This is the satisfaction of that awakening urge for truth and simplicity that lies, like the moral predisposition from which it flows, in all human hearts as something indestructible and ineradicable ... This road taken by the modern poets is, moreover, the same road human beings in general must travel, both as individuals and as a whole. *Nature makes a human being one with himself, art separates and divides him; by means of the ideal he returns to the unity. Yet because the ideal is an infinite one that he never reaches, the cultured human being in his way can never become complete as the natural human being can be in his way.*

(p. 194, p. 202; my italics)

29 *SW*, p. 390.

30 Freud himself is aware, at least at some points, that there is an important reciprocity between the discoveries of psychoanalysis and revolutionary changes occurring in the sciences during his time. In *Psychoanalysis and Telepathy* (1921) he writes:

The discovery of radium has confused no less than it has advanced the possibilities of explaining the physical world; and the knowledge that has been so very recently acquired of what is called the theory of relativity has had the effect upon many of those who admire without comprehending it of diminishing their belief in the objective trustworthiness of science.

(p. 178)

31 Freud goes back and forth on the "reality" of the primal scene, for instance, as he writes in his case history of the Wolf Man:

If neurotics are endowed with the evil characteristic of diverting their interest from the present and of attaching it to these regressive substitutes, the products of their imagination, then there is absolutely nothing for it but to follow upon their tracks and bring these unconscious productions into consciousness; for, if we disregard their objective unimportance, they are of the utmost importance from our point of view ... the analysis would have to run the precisely the same course as one which had a naïf faith in the truth of the phantasies. The difference would only come at the end of the analysis, after the phantasies had been laid bare.

> We should then say to the patient: "Very well, then; your neurosis pro-
> ceeded *as though* you had received these impressions and spun them out
> in your childhood."
>
> (SE Vol. XVII, pp. 49–50)

He goes on later in the same essay:

> Let us assume as an uncontradicted premise that a primal scene of this
> kind has been correctly evolved technically, that it is indispensable to a
> comprehensive solution of all the conundrums that are set us by the
> symptoms of the infantile disorder, that all the consequences radiate out
> from it, just as all the threads of the analysis have led up to it. Then, in
> view of its content, it is impossible that it can be anything else than a
> reproduction of a reality experienced by the child.
>
> (p. 55)

32 Loewald also remarks on Freud's discomfort here. He writes in "Psychoanalysis and the History of the Individual" (1976):

> Freud hesitated to attribute reality to the mind and contented himself
> with calling the psychical a "particular form of existence," not to be con-
> fused with material or "factual" reality ... what in his view tends to
> confer a reality-like character on psychic life is the undeniable fact of the
> power of the unconscious.
>
> (p. 537)

And later in the same paper:

> In declaring them to be *psychic* processes, he took the step of investigat-
> ing them from the standpoint of man's full mental life, from the per-
> spective of man as a moral being, and not from the reductive perspective
> of modern natural science. But he never was wholly comfortable with his
> decision.
>
> (p. 542)

33 See Freud's discussion of psychoanalysis and the scientific *Weltanschauung*
in "The Question of a *Weltanschauung*," *SE* Vol. XXII pp. 158–184. He
writes: "The unified nature of the explanation of the universe is, it is true,
accepted by science, but only as a programme whose fulfillment is postponed
to the future" (pp. 158–159).
34 Jean Laplanche. *Freud and the Sexual*, trans. John Fletcher (International
Psychoanalytic Books, 2011).

Chapter 1

Sublimity

> *Everything that is hidden, everything full of mystery, contributes to*
> *what is terrifying and is therefore capable of sublimity.*
> —*Schiller, "On the Sublime"*

Despite his claims to the contrary in "The Uncanny," Freud's interest in
the *aesthetic* is in no way peripheral to the work of psychoanalysis.
Through the aesthetic, Freud explores a reality that encompasses the
unconscious, opening up a psychoanalytic *Weltanschauung* that fundamentally diverges from the scientific. Freud thus inherits a set of issues
that pervaded Schelling's middle and late philosophy, arising from
attempts to systematize a subjectivity no longer centered in consciousness. This chapter serves the function of establishing Freud's place within
a larger tradition of aesthetic philosophy, one that includes Kant, Schiller,
and the early Schelling, wherein the systematicity of reason collides with
the disruptive forces of desire and feeling in important and unique ways.
My hope is to show that for Freud and his predecessors, aesthetics
becomes *the* opportunity for reformulating the conflict between freedom
and determinism.

Kant's *Critique of Judgment*, a sustained meditation on the philosophical import of the aesthetic, opens up the problematic relationship
between *system* and *subjectivity* that will guide the Idealist project as well
as psychoanalysis. In this text, the abyss separating nature and freedom
that transcendental philosophy depends upon is given over to the unifying domain of feeling.[1] Although Kant does not posit the unconscious in
this regard, as Schelling will go on to do, he reveals a dimension of
experience that is similarly irreducible to either the determinism of nature
or the determination of reason. This aesthetic encroachment into the

Critical Philosophy, a privileging of feeling, and artistic genius that inspires the German Idealist project, implies that pleasure and pain transform the system of reason, as it were, from within:

> Hence we must suppose, at least provisionally, that judgment also contains an a priori principle of its own, and also suppose that since the power of desire is necessarily connected with pleasure or displeasure ... judgment will bring about a transition from the pure cognitive power, i.e. from the domain of concepts of nature, to the domain of the concept of freedom, just as in its logical use it makes possible the transition from understanding to reason.[2]

It is feeling, and most fundamentally pleasure and pain that, simultaneously challenges and salvages Kant's rational system. The dangerous possibility that belongs to the *Critique of Judgment* concerns this notion of "transition": The centrality of the aesthetic—particularly through returning to the bodily and natural—undermines Kant's ultimate claims in this work about the realization of freedom.

Kant's analysis of the beautiful focuses on the *harmony* of this reflective, aesthetic judgment. In the judgment of the beautiful, it is the unproblematic union of imaginative and cognitive faculties that comes to the fore. However, it is his inclusion of the sublime under the umbrella of aesthetic judgments, while at the same time insisting that the sublime has no real connection to products of nature or of art, which brings into relief the conflict between Kant's dual conceptions of freedom: the sublime, an experience of pleasure in pain and of transition more generally, is reduced to an expression of reason's superiority over and absolute rupture from nature (and the body). In this insistence, Kant minimizes the much more radical consequences of *aesthetic* freedom.

In what follows, I argue that Schiller and the early Schelling develop an aesthetics that is in fact truer to Kant's own hopes of attending to the *transition* between nature and freedom, between a concept, and its realization. Specifically, they illustrate the ways in which the insights of the *Critique of Judgment* illuminate the tensions within the Kantian conception of freedom—as imaginative, productive spontaneity on the one hand, and as repressive prohibition, and refusal of feeling and nature on the other.[3] It is with this in mind that my discussion of the Kantian sublime is followed by Schiller's elaborations of it, primarily in "Letters on the

Aesthetic Education of Man" and "Concerning the Sublime";[4] and Schelling's incorporation of these views in *System of Transcendental Idealism* and *The Philosophy of Art*.[5] These works share the basic intuition of the *Critique of Judgment* that art and aesthetics unite the sensible and the supersensible; Schiller and Schelling, however, regard the *feeling* of the sublime as the disclosure of freedom that is prior to and more fundamental than the law.

My focus here will be on tracing the different qualities and moments of this feeling, including horror and confusion, which anticipate Freud's analysis of the uncanny. Schiller and Schelling argue that freedom is not merely exercised in the constraint of desire or nature; they call for an aesthetic freedom that recognizes the human to be in excess of the *rational*. In Kant, sublimity contracts into the moment in which fear and helplessness in the face of nature disappear into reverence for the supremacy of reason. For Schiller, and to an even greater degree for Schelling, the sublime is human *activity*—it is the process of holding together alienation and integration rather than what results. The sublime is not a *failure* of the imagination but evidence of its re-inscription as the root of freedom. In similar fashion, we might consider the development from Kant to Schelling, mediated by Schiller's emphasis on wholeness and play, in terms of the role played by aesthetics more generally: whereas for Kant art and nature are symbols or tools for recognizing our dutiful, rational, universal freedom, for Schiller and Schelling aesthetic experience is an enactment of our creative, desirous, personal freedom.

The interrupted self

Kant's *Critique of Judgment*, like the reflective judgment it treats, is essentially an act of *unification*—the faculty to which feeling belongs offers a transitional space between deterministic nature in the *Critique of Pure Reason*, and rational, law-giving freedom in *The Critique of Practical Reason*.[6] Kant gives us some reason to believe that reflective judgments not only unify, but also *exceed,* and even *ground*, deterministic, and autonomous cause.[7]

Kant's explorations of aesthetic judgments in particular, a sub-set of reflective judgments, open up a connection between the supersensible and the sensible, the universal, and the individual. Through his explanation of the a priori principle of purposiveness grounding our experience of the beautiful and the sublime, Kant intimates a third way: a form of relating to the world and to ourselves that is fundamentally unlike the theoretical domination of knowing (experiences subsumed under rules of the understanding) and the practical domination of acting (feelings subsumed under the moral law). Ultimately, it is through this capacity of aesthetic judgment for bridging the personal and the universal, rather than collapsing the former into the latter, that Kant exposes the crucial question haunting his Critical Philosophy: How can the *noumenal* freedom of *The Critique of Practical Reason* express itself in and indeed alter the *phenomenal* world of the *Critique of Pure Reason*? And how could the seemingly ancillary field of aesthetics perform *the* philosophical task of bridging the *noumenal* and *phenomenal* realms?[8]

Kant distinguishes aesthetic judgments from cognitive judgments insofar as they are *reflective*, rather than *determinative*.[9] That is, these judgments do not determine their objects, or subsume particular experiences under already given concepts or laws, but rather create, or seek the universal for the particular. As a form of reflective judgment, the necessity, and universality belonging to aesthetic judgments is *not* a function of a priori concepts or intuitions; rather, the necessity and universality involved in judgments of taste is attributable to our capacity for a common experience of the ways in which the faculties of imagination, understanding, and reason relate to each other. It is *feeling*—not knowledge or duty—that initiates us into the universality of reflective judgments. Kant argues that aesthetic judgments offer a form of relating—the form of the hypothetical, of the "as if"—that allows us to feel the transition between the determinism of the first critique and the autonomy of the second. When faced with the workings of genius, or with a living organism, we realize that these opposed forms of causation are inadequate. Through aesthetic judgments of the beautiful, Kant emphasizes a notion of freedom, which not only separates us from sensible nature, but also brings us closer to supersensible nature. That is, the tension between *moral* and *spontaneous* freedom in Kant brings into greater relief the disinterested engagement proper to judgments of the beautiful. This tension, which was already evident in the *Critique of Pure Reason*, could be reformulated in terms of the distinction between the productive and reproductive imagination in that text.[10] Kant's aesthetics expose and perpetuate a pervasive fault-line in the Critical Philosophy: the need to develop a reflexive space *between* activity and passivity, whether we are talking about self-consciousness or our knowledge of objects. It is not by chance that this exposure comes about through the artwork—an object that forces us to question where its meaning lies, that dares us to distinguish truth from interpretation.

In the judgment of the beautiful, the form of an object sets in motion our powers of cognition, but in such a way that they remain in "free play" [*freien Spiele*]: our cognitive faculties do not determine their object, but are engaged harmoniously in their proper functions despite the lack of any attainable goal or end.[11] The beautiful form incites a feeling that the world is there *for us*, and this feeling of an underlying unity between subject and object *is* pleasure. This is mirrored in Kant's account of genius, where the creation of an art work—like the pleasurable play that grounds our judgment of the beautiful—is not determined by rules; the activity of rule-making itself becomes playful, creative, and spontaneous without devolving into chaos.[12] Freedom is here understood in its creative capacity, and our vocation is realized through inventing rather than obeying the law. Kant's invocation of purposiveness in accounting for the pleasure of the beautiful allows a consideration of a subject's relation to nature (and to art)—both within and external to him—that is neither reducible to the necessity of judgments of fact nor merely analogous to autonomy:

> On the other hand, we do call objects, states of mind, or acts purposive even if their possibility does not necessarily presuppose the presentation of a purpose; we do this merely because we can explain and grasp them only if we assume that they are based on a causality [that operates] according to purposes, i.e., on a will that would have so arranged them in accordance with the presentation of a certain rule. Hence there can be purposiveness without a purpose insofar as we do not posit the causes of this form in a will, and yet can grasp the explanation of its possibility only by deriving it from a will.[13]

But Kant is clear that such purposiveness remains hypothetical—that we must treat nature as if it were organized, that we approach the beautiful form as if it were meant to harmonize our cognitive powers, only in order to explain particular appearances. Although Kant points beyond the determinism of nature and the self-determination of reason through the reflective principle of purposiveness, he stops short of recognizing this as a truly *other* causality.

In the sublime, however, this pleasurable sense of purposiveness that characterizes the beautiful (and the teleological) gives way: not only does the sublime *painfully* interrupt the proper functioning of our cognitive powers, but it recalls our supersensible vocation in negative terms, violently exposing our sensible—imaginative and bodily—helplessness. The harmonious union of imagination and understanding that we feel in the beautiful is sundered in the awe of the sublime; the sense of belonging to nature that we experience as pleasure is lost. The sublime is predicated on our alienation from nature, disclosing a world that is distinctly *not* for our comprehension or pleasure.

Indeed, in his efforts to distinguish the sublime from the beautiful, Kant does not appear to see the sublime as an aesthetic judgment at all. The sublime is rarely, if at all, the product of artistic genius; and although it remains tied to reflective judgment, it is only in the failure of the imagination that we can experience it. The feeling of the sublime is only tangentially related to an object, a cue that reminds us that autonomy depends upon an insurmountable divide between freedom and nature. In contrast to his account of the beautiful, Kant's description of the sublime does not seem to tell us anything about how the supersensible and the sensible might practically affect each other. Such a vision reifies Kantian freedom as a form of *domination*—as a repression[14] of drive, nature, and individuality—while freedom as *playfulness* is relegated to the subjunctive voice, to a mere symbol of morality.[15] However, in claiming that our experience of the sublime is fundamentally the feeling of *self-consciousness*—of the internal contrast between the weakness of our flesh and understanding on the one hand, and the strength of reason on the other—Kant himself implicitly suggests an alternative approach to the sublime: What kind of freedom does such essential self-division lay bare? How might the violence of the sublime threaten the integrity of the subject? In order to respond to these questions, we need to consider in some detail what distinguishes the universality of the sublime from the universality of the beautiful. In the latter, of course, it is the shared, harmonious functioning of the imagination and understanding that is felt as pleasure. The universality of the sublime is more problematic: grounded in disruption—in the *pain* of separation and division—the sublime seems to defy unity at the most intimate level. Paradoxically, the sublime deconstructs the Kantian equation of freedom with the universality of reason.

It is in part Kant's insistence that the universality of the sublime is a function of the universality of reason that diminishes its role in art; as we will see, Schiller's emphasis on the sublime in art, and in tragedy particularly, arises from his understanding of freedom as integrative rather than repressive autonomy. Still, Kant does make gestures toward the peculiarly fractured universality of the sublime in its own right through the fragmentary completeness of poetry:

> A poet ventures to give sensible expression to rational ideas of invisible beings, the realm of the blessed, the realm of hell, eternity, creation and so on ... but then, by means of an imagination that emulates the example of reason in reaching [for] a maximum, he ventures to give these sensible expression in a way that goes beyond the limits of experience, namely, *with a completeness for which no example can be found in nature* ... Now if a concept is provided with a presentation of the imagination such that, even though this presentation belongs to the exhibition of the concept, yet it prompts, even by itself, so much thought as can never be comprehended within a determinate concept and thereby the presentation aesthetically expands the concept itself in an unlimited way, then the imagination is creative in [all of] this and sets the power of intellectual ideas in motion.[16]

Kant describes the completeness the poet uncovers as being without likeness in nature, expanding indefinitely, limitless. The completeness the poet communicates is not any determinable content, but a feeling of recognizing ourselves in the non-conceptual and incomplete. In Kant's view, the universality of the sublime and the beautiful derive from our shared cognitive powers. In the latter, it is the play between imagination and the understanding that binds us together, and in the former it is the limitlessness of reason. However, through these brief remarks on the nature of poetry, we can begin to see in Kant another vision, one that Schiller, and later Schelling acknowledge, of how it is that *we* speak the sublime—how language itself, in its very failure to translate the sublime, suggests a universality that allows us to be ourselves and to be with others. It is not only, or even primarily, the moral law that captivates us in the sublime; rather, feeling this universal lack compels us to speak, driving us to recognize and be recognized by each other and nature.

Although Kant does not offer much more on the language of the sublime, he does make strange and intriguing claims about the language of nature:

> It will be said that this construal of aesthetic judgments in terms of a kinship with moral feeling looks rather too studied to be considered as the true interpretation of that cipher *through which nature speaks to us* figuratively in its beautiful forms.[17]

Notice that Kant anxiously defends himself against the charge ("it will be said") that translating our connection to nature into moral feeling would be a denial and falsification of its excessive truth ("too studied to be ... true"). If our appreciation of the beautiful implies a familiarity with the language of nature, our capacity for the sublime would be a confrontation with the precariousness of our translation: an expression of the dialectics of chaos and order, of differentiation, and renewed integration. In "speaking," nature reveals its double aspect—as a text that ought to be read and as an expressing that exceeds all interpretations. In the face of the sublime it is thus not merely *our* dual nature that surfaces, but the duality of nature itself.

Shocked by the sublime, we suddenly find nature indecipherable and unfamiliar—our habitual forms of communication lost; and yet, it is only this discontinuity that allows us to recognize that, like all speakers, nature also gestures at the meaning kept in silent reserve. The silence that would seem to characterize the sublime, through which there is an intimation of what it is like to authentically understand and be understood, reminds us of the ways in which language serves to unify and to divide us. To name something is at once to appropriate it and to put it at a distance—it is, like freedom, simultaneously a movement away from wholeness and the struggle to recapture it in another form. It seems that in reducing our experience of the sublime to moral fortitude, and nature to a decipherable message, Kant violates the unsettling, and captivating excess of both. But this is not to say that *all* efforts at speaking the sublime must do so. It is no easy task to say just what it is that *we*, as humans, share—nor whether what we do share is inherently good.

Pain and play

Schiller's hope for aesthetics represents a departure from Kant, who opened up the aesthetic realm as a way to resolve the conflict of embodied reason, arguing that the ideas of reason ought to control and overcome nature. Though Schiller adheres to Kant's vision of the sublime as the awakening within us of the power of reason, he also offers a radical rethinking of freedom in terms of the *personal*. For Schiller, it is precisely the challenge of a new language that sublime nature announces. It is only when one "gives up trying to *explain* nature and makes this inscrutability itself the standpoint of the evaluation" that the language of the sublime, beyond knowledge, or explanation, can be heard.[18] The language of the sublime is the language of *self-differing*:

> The feeling of the sublime is a mixed feeling. It is a combination of *being in anguish* (at its peak it expresses itself as a shudder) and *being happy* (something that can escalate to a kind of ecstasy). This combination, although it is not actually pleasure, is still preferred by all noble souls over all pleasure. This synthesis of two contradictory sensations in a single feeling establishes our moral self-sufficiency in an irrefutable manner. For, since it is absolutely impossible for the same object to be related to us in two contradictory ways, it follows from the fact that *we ourselves* are related to the object in two contrasting ways, that two opposite natures must be united within us.[19]

Schiller manages to bring out the disorienting aspect of the sublime in such a way that, despite his proximity to Kant, universal reason, and morality do not do justice to the *feeling* of human freedom. The vocation to which the sublime calls us cannot be the enactment of the categorical imperative, for this would entail dissociation from an essential aspect of our being—our natural desires. It is rather wholeness, conceived as the integration of contradictory elements that, would be the true expression of human freedom. Kant argues that the sublime is within us, and yet his account of *what we are* fails to capture the precarious unity of human being. In examining the way we speak the sublime, Schiller points out that just as language allows us to know, explain, and dominate, so too does its limitation reach beyond itself toward that which resists knowledge, explanation, and domination; in the same manner, it is only through an acknowledgment of our vulnerability—our limit—that the sublime reveals our true potency. By pointedly expanding Kant's account of the sublime into our experience with art, Schiller shows that the sublime gestures toward the unspeakable from which language was born and to which it recalls us. Tragically, we listen for the whispers of *our* freedom—freedom that breaks us apart. Only through the silence and rupture of the sublime, in our stunned inability to know nature and ourselves, can we speak truthfully.

Enlarging the value of the human to include desire and division, Schiller argues that the repression of our sensual nature and the totalizing of reason are anathema to freedom. Schiller insists that Kant fails to capture *both* the depth of our identity with nature *and* the severity of our isolation from nature. Because we too are part of the natural order, the ways in which we understand ourselves to be both united with and divided from nature are essentially tied up with self-consciousness and the possibility of ethical life: for Schiller, aesthetics is not merely useful in developing our sense of freedom, as it seems to be for Kant; it is necessary. In re-appropriating the human dimension of freedom, which is not properly captured by the paradigm of law and submission, Schiller critiques the abstractness of Kant's account. It is in part due to this emphasis by Schiller on the whole or fully human being, that Schelling goes on to reformulate subjectivity and human freedom in terms of personality.[20] But where Schelling will eventually suggest that freedom itself is wrapped up in the dark and desirous unconscious, Schiller focuses on our mode of enacting that freedom, refusing the model of antagonism and constraint in favor of integration and reconciliation. Viewing Schiller's *playful* sense of freedom as a convergence not only with nature, but the beautiful and the sublime, it is clear why within Kant's dominating version these pairs must remain ever at odds.

Though Schiller seems to accept Kant's formulation of the sublime as the experience of reason's supremacy over nature and desire, he also draws us more deeply into the experience of devastation and self-division. The captivation [*ergreift*] of the sublime, rooted in contradiction, at first appears entirely removed from the pleasurable lingering [*weilen*] that belongs to the harmony of the beautiful:[21]

> In what is sublime, on the other hand, there is *no* harmony of reason and sensuousness, and the spell that captivates our minds lies precisely in this contradiction. Here the physical and the moral sides of the human being are severed from one another in the sharpest possible way, for it is precisely when confronted by such objects that the physical side feels only its limitation, while the moral side

experiences its *power*. The moral side of human nature is infinitely elevated by the very thing that forces the physical side of human nature into the ground.[22]

Schiller continues to draw out this distinction, in agreement with Kant that "not gradually (since there is no transition from dependency to freedom), but only suddenly and through a kind of shock, does something sublime tear the independent spirit loose from the net a sophisticated sensuousness uses to ensnare it."[23] As a "shock" [*Erschütterung*] and a "tear" [*reißt*], the sublime points to alienation at the root of our freedom.[24] Beauty, Kant argues, is communicable because we all have the same capacity for experiencing the harmonious, free play of imagination and understanding; since the experience of the beautiful *is* the feeling of our self-identity, we recall our shared humanity. But how does the sublime—in its silence—unify us in our peculiarly human vocation?[25]

Privileging radical division and the ensuing need for re-integration entailed in the sublime, identity is predicated on an essential lack inscribed in the foundation of human being:

> The road taken by the modern poets is, moreover, the same road humans in general must travel, both as individuals and as a whole. Nature makes a human being one with himself, art separates and divides him; by means of the ideal he returns to the unity. Yet because the ideal is an infinite one that he never reaches, the cultured human being in *his* way can never become complete as the natural human being can be in his way.[26]

The awareness of our freedom prohibits us from returning to an undivided, naïve unity; such freedom involves both the recognition of a lost wholeness—this lack that defines us—and a striving to recapture it. So although Schiller still believes that the sublime directs us toward a unity of will and action, human freedom remains irreducibly split: anguish and pleasure, fear and rapture, submission and domination. It is not surprising that the language of the sublime, for Kant as well as for Schiller, is the language of *violence*. And it is not merely the language *of* violence that permeates the sublime, but language *as* violence. Kant argues that aesthetic judgment is both subjective and universal: in our experience of the beautiful and the sublime we are subject to the demand that it is not *I* that speaks but *We*. Still, it is not altogether clear how through the disruption of the sublime we can *speak* at all—how it is that acknowledging our ruptured identity might make us whole. It would seem that the sublime calls us to a moral duty that requires an act of self-domination, to unity at the cost of repression or disavowal; Schiller's account of the sublime, particularly insofar as it converges with the beautiful, contributes to an account of freedom that isn't conditioned by violence, in offering a possibility for self-consciousness that neither denies nor succumbs to the radical disjunction that unites us.

While recognizing the chasm between nature and freedom, between passivity and activity, Schiller marks the sublime as the site of a *centering* contradiction. It is not only our power to resist nature that we experience in the sublime, but precisely because of this resistance, a vital and universal alienation: we are at a distance both from nature and from ourselves and this separation makes us existentially uncomfortable, disturbing the unity of self-consciousness that *ought* to ground our freedom. Schiller allows us a way to think of the disorienting aspect of the sublime as more than simply "a momentary inhibition of the vital forces," as more than an unfortunate prelude to the resurgence of reason and its lawfulness.[27] The sublime, in the uncertainty of its silence, opens us to freedom's paradoxical demands: there must be an infinite distance between reason and nature and yet, reason only comes to itself in and through its engagement with nature.[28] To speak this impossibility would be to deny the essential possibility of transcending it; to remain silent would be inhuman.

The experience of the sublime is a *discovery*, rather than a proof, of our freedom. For Kant, the sublime discloses the impossible distance between reason and sensibility that *ought to* lead us to recognize the supremacy of the moral law. In a clear departure from Kant, and inspiration for Schelling, Schiller suggests that the destabilizing effect of the sublime forces us to ask different sorts of questions: Can freedom be reduced to reason's constraint of sensibility? Is true integration between reason and sensibility attainable?[29] In other words, freedom is threatened from both sides—vulnerable to the twin dangers of sensibility overcoming reason and of reason suppressing sensibility.[30] As Schiller points out in his treatment of tragedy, "in aesthetic judgments we are interested, not in morality of itself, but simply in freedom, and morality can please our imagination only insofar as it makes that freedom visible."[31] Thus, in no uncertain terms, freedom exceeds our adherence to the moral law, creating a space for difference apart from opposition.[32] Where Kant tries to resolve this difference through reason's absolutism, Schiller allows us to see that real freedom entails an insoluble tension: identity that is nourished by, rather than negated in, contradiction.

If Kant focuses on the *empowering* aspect of the sublime, as an answer to the question that is freedom, we might say that Schiller emphasizes the *suffering* such questioning inspires.[33] It is the rift within us, as much as that between man and nature, which the sublime forces us to acknowledge. We can see the consequences of this shift clearly in Schiller's treatment of tragedy: while Kant limits his account of the sublime to nature, Schiller's interpretation extends into the realm of art—and particularly inter- and intra-personal relationships. Part of his motivation is to show that our involvement with tragedy involves a *feeling* of freedom that reaches beyond reason: an expression of the human as that which holds together order and chaos, necessity and freedom. In sublime art, as in nature, there needs to be a separation that provides security. We are far enough away that the stormy sea will not devour us; we are in a cozy theater thinking of dinner and not in Antigone's tomb. And yet there must also be empathy, insofar as the sublime demands an intimacy with finitude and fear that could motivate our realization of the infinite moral demand. Indeed, it is through our acknowledgment of the frightening gulf between unlimited, chaotic nature on the one hand, and limited sensibility on the other, that the sublime occurs. Tragedy, as Schiller points out, depends upon our ability to remain at a properly human *distance* from ourselves and from others. That is, the universality that belongs to our judgments of the sublime is the suffering of both human distance and proximity:

> Hence, the aesthetic power with which sublimeness of character and action take hold of us rests in no way upon reason's interest in things *being* done rightly, but rather upon imagination's interest in it *being possible* that things are done rightly. This is to say, it is in the interest of the imagination that no feeling, however powerful, be capable of subduing the freedom of the mind. This possibility lies, however, in every hardy expression of freedom and the power of the will, and only where the poet hits upon this, has he found a fitting subject matter to portray.[34]

It is not the victory of the moral law that tragedy communicates, but rather the weight of possibility—the burden of identity that remains ever in transition. Kant traces the progression of the sublime from weakness and fear, through a recovery of unbounded reason, toward a triumphant restoration of the law. For Schiller, freedom is not the capacity to overcome vulnerability, but the possibility of living with it as our own. The tragic hero is not *above* fate; acceptance of fate is a reaffirmation of his worldview that, while remaining authentic, and secure, recognizes its own vulnerability. The sublimity of tragedy is rooted in its presentation of freedom *as* suffering:

> Thus beings who declare themselves free from all *morality*, such as the evil demons painted by folk superstition or by a writer's imagination, and humans similar to them; also beings who are free from the coercion of *sensuousness*, such as we regard pure intellects, and humans who have extricated themselves from this coercion to a greater extent than human weakness permits—all these are equally unfit for tragedy. In general, the concept of suffering and of a suffering in which we are supposed to participate already determines that only *human beings* in the full sense of the word can be the object of the suffering.[35]

Taking seriously Schiller's reference to "human beings in the full sense of the word," [*Menschen im vollen Sinne dieses Worts*] the sublime would demand a radical rethinking of freedom as grounding disorientation, as identity founded in difference.[36] It is this paradoxical identity, where in acknowledging self-division we are most profoundly ourselves, that Schiller deems the "sublime spiritual disposition" [*Diese erhabene Geistesstimmung*] that "is the lot of strong and philosophical minds" [*Los starker und philosophischer Gemüter*]:

> Even the most painful loss does not drive them beyond the sort of composed melancholy that is always capable of being combined with a noticeable degree of pleasure. Only such minds, who alone are capable of *separating themselves from themselves*, enjoy the privilege of *taking part in themselves* and *feeling their own suffering* in the gentle reflection of sympathy.[37]

Although this passage points to a certain tranquility that belongs to the sublime, bringing it yet closer to the beautiful, Schiller also makes the provocative claim that "taking part" in one's own experience makes identity an integrating *activity*. To "feel" one's own suffering implies an essentially disjointed subject. Yet where Kant defines freedom as reason's power to refuse this self-separation, Schiller demands the preservation of this difference: to feel whole is to have already been divided. This notion of wholeness within the individual also informs Schiller's account of human community, marking an important departure from Kant. Schiller recognizes that, more fundamentally than the moral law, we share in suffering the division of our being: unable to exhaust what we are able to feel in what we can know and do.

The problematic notions of wholeness and totality pervade both Kant's and Schiller's works on the sublime. Kant writes that in our experience of the sublime "our imagination strives to progress toward infinity, while our reason demands absolute totality as a real idea."[38] Our realization of unbounded nature, via the limitation of sensibility, leads to an awareness of reason's limitlessness and our own supersensible freedom.[39] Schiller's concern with *human* totality involves an analogous development: the experience of the sublime moves us from the boundlessness of nature to the human desire for wholeness, for self-identity that is not self-denial. In both cases, the sublime turns us back to ourselves, suggesting another dimension to Kant's claim that the sublime is not tied to the object, but to a particular form of self-relating.[40] For Schiller this self-relating is not resolved by overcoming the sensible via the law-giving capacity of reason; it remains instead as a questioning and reaffirmation of wholeness that depends on human empathy.[41] This idea of wholeness gets lost in Kant, as his account of the sublime veers toward a disembodied freedom.[42] Schiller reminds us that the *identity* proper to human being cannot be the same as the totality of nature *or* of reason:

> It is, after all, peculiar to man that he unites in his nature the highest and the lowest; and if his *moral dignity* depends on his distinguishing strictly between the one and the other, *his hope of joy and blessedness* depends on a due and proper reconciliation of the opposites he has distinguished. An education that is to bring his dignity into harm with his happiness will, therefore, have to see to it that those two

principles are maintained in their utmost purity even while they are being most intimately fused.[43]

It is clear that Schiller understands the sublime as a disclosure of a crucial difference; however, he does not seek the essence of human freedom beyond this divided and dividing moment, but remains precariously within it.

Kant suggests a number of ways in which the sublime violates; there is the violence of nature itself in the dynamic sublime (or what Schiller calls the practical sublime)—its threat to our existence; further, Kant presents practical reason (the true site of the sublime) as an oppressive force that should conquer nature and desire alike.[44] But I would like to draw attention to Kant's intimation of a much more subtle form of violence, when he claims that in our experience of the sublime there is "a subjective movement of the imagination by which it does violence to the inner sense [*eine subjektive Bewegung der Einbildungskraft, worduch sie dem inneren Sinne Gewalt antut*]."[45] In introducing a rupture in *time*—the inner sense—Kant points to a conflict between the multiplicity of sense and the unity of comprehension that results in a specifically temporal paralysis. Kant provides us an opening to understand the *captivating pain* of the sublime: the sublime captures us—engages and stills us—because holding together difference *is* our connection to the supersensible. Although Kant sees this paralysis as preliminary, Schiller suggests that returning to the space between passivity and activity—to the site where being and becoming converge—is our highest calling:

> In order, therefore, not to be mere world, he must impart form to matter; in order not to be mere form, he must give reality to the pre-disposition he carries within him. He gives reality to form when he brings time into being, when he confronts changelessness with change, the eternal unity of his own self with the manifold variety of the world. He gives form to matter when he annuls time again, when he affirms persistence within change, and subjugates the manifold variety of the world to the unity of his own self.[46]

There is a reformulation here of the strange temporality at work in the experience of the sublime; what is for Kant a mere shock of timelessness becomes, for Schiller, time created and annulled in the reciprocity of freedom and nature, of self and world. Schiller equates the opposition between the eternal and the temporal, or being and becoming, with that between the sensuous drive and the formal drive. And rather than attributing the paralysis of the sublime to the irreducible conflict between them, he introduces a third drive that makes their reconciliation possible: the play drive, which "would be directed toward annulling time *within time*, reconciling becoming with absolute being and change with identity [*der Spieltrieb also würde dahin gerichtet sein, die Zeit **in der Zeit**, aufzuheben, Werden mit absolutem Sein, Veränderung mit Identität zu vareinbaren*]."[47] If along with Schiller we understand the sensuous drive as physical constraint (determinism), and the formal drive as moral constraint (autonomy), this would suggest that their harmony in freedom is a *reciprocal play*. Both the sensuous and the formal drive constrain us by constraining each other, and it is only through the action of the play drive that we can encounter freedom.[48]

Although Schiller argues that this intermediate drive is directed at and promoted by the beautiful, the sublime must have a place here too. Returning to the same language he uses in his account of the sublime character of tragedy, Schiller writes: "For, to mince matters no longer, man only plays when he is in the fullest sense of the word a human being, and *he is only fully a human being when he plays*."[49] Surely, the human being in the fullest sense of the world is not merely rational, but also made *whole*. While Schiller clearly connects the play drive with pleasure, the play drive also gives us access to a determinability that is not empty, and to an *uncertainty* that is beyond and prior to both pleasure and pain:

> In the aesthetic state, then, man is *naught*, if we are thinking of any particular result rather than the totality of his powers, and considering the absence in him of any specific determination ... By means of aesthetic culture, therefore, the personal worth of a man, or his dignity, inasmuch as this can depend solely on himself, remains completely indeterminate; and nothing more is achieved by it than that he is henceforth enabled *by the grace of nature* to make of himself what he will—that the freedom to be what he ought to be is completely restored to him.[50]

The plasticity of the aesthetic state is thus not "naught" it is an openness or permeability; between the activity of self-determination, and the passivity of sensual becoming, there is a possibility for identity that recognizes its need for otherness. Freedom is *not* the ability to rule over nature, but our infinite capacity to play with and suffer the limits of our responsibility. Schiller's use of the term "play" need not remain fixed by its pleasurable connotations—indeed, as Freud astutely notes, it is precisely through play that we first begin to work out our fundamental anxieties and insecurities and to respond to the unknown.[51] The sublime would represent the seriousness of play, where that same capacity to contemplate and reshape our relationship to the world and to ourselves can be as frightening as it can be freeing. It is thus not only nature, but also play, that gives the rule to art through genius.

We can see the intimate connection between Schiller's account of freedom—as the *playful* integration of the dual aspects of our being—and of self-consciousness. Schiller makes an important move beyond Kant in clarifying how the structure of the "I" relates to our human freedom. Self-consciousness, like the freedom that is its source and fulfillment, is an integration of our sensible and supersensible natures, of change, and changelessness. Moreover, it is in bringing together freedom and self-consciousness in this way that Schiller can defend his inclusion of art in the realm of sublime experience. It is not merely our separation from nature that announces itself in the sublime but, more importantly, an abyssal self-division as well. The alienation from ourselves that we experience in the sublime is thus also an essential aspect of self-consciousness—a stepping outside ourselves that allows us to become *whole*. In order to grasp the possibility of our freedom we must allow ourselves to feel this intrinsic disjunction; for, as I have suggested, this very possibility is grounded in our ability to endure—to play and to suffer—in this place of (dis-)integration.

At the limit

In Schelling's *System of Transcendental Idealism*, a work widely associated with his "Fichtean" period and considered one of his more traditionally philosophical texts, the work of art and philosophical reflection are paired together as the culminating experiences of freedom.[52] Taking up where Schiller leaves off, Schelling makes his own contributions toward a theory of aesthetic freedom. He intensifies the connection between art and freedom by developing an account of our relation to the unconscious as the essential activity of self-consciousness. Here, artistic creation and philosophy are complementary modes of expressing identity-in-difference—freedom neither collapses into Kantian constraint nor resolves itself within Schiller's harmonious human being. The structure of the book's text is itself an enactment of forging a *single* narrative through a *double* history: the phases of self-consciousness are considered alongside the philosopher's privileged observation of these phases, as Schelling deepens Schiller's insights into the distance from ourselves that characterizes the feeling of the sublime and our engagement with tragedy. In his attempt to complete the transcendental philosophy of Kant and Fichte, Schelling comes to see freedom as a holding together of difference—a relating between consciousness and the unconscious that cannot be accounted for in Schiller's form of integration.

I will suggest that there are two, interconnected ways in which Schelling approaches the reality of freedom in the *System*: (1) through the identity of the unconscious/consciousness expressed in the sublime or beautiful art product, and (2) in terms of the philosopher's approach to what must *exceed* consciousness in order for self-consciousness to be possible. Of course, the concept of the unconscious belongs to a long and varied philosophical history; I limit myself here to pointing out a certain formulation in terms of *repression*, unique to Schelling's early conception of freedom and developed in myriad ways throughout his work. To get an idea of the essential role repression plays in this regard, consider the following claim:

> Since I seek to ground my knowledge only *in itself*, I enquire no further as to the ultimate ground of this primary knowledge (self-consciousness), which, if it exists, must necessarily lie *outside* knowledge. Self-consciousness is the lamp of the whole system of knowledge, but it casts its light ahead only, not behind.[53]

Notice that, on the one hand, Schelling insists along with Fichte that self-consciousness is the bedrock of knowledge and the original, free deed of philosophy; on the other hand, Schelling hesitantly marks out space beyond knowledge ("ultimate ground")—even though he disavows it ("I enquire no further") as soon as it appears. As we will see, this logic in which the recognition or creation of a boundary already reaches out beyond the boundary is essential to Schelling's explanation of the dialectic of consciousness and the unconscious. In retracing the mutual development of self and reality, Schelling relies on the philosopher's unique ability to locate and interpret the symptoms of unconscious activity. In contrast to Kant's account of freedom *as* a form of repression, and Schiller's integrative freedom that would claim to eliminate repression, Schelling's freedom is an active, therapeutic engagement with the process of repression: this engagement is *aesthetic* insofar as it occurs in intuition, whether in the intellectual intuition of the philosopher or the sensible intuition of the artwork. As with Kant and Schiller, it is the feeling of freedom with which Schelling concerns himself. However, for Schelling, it is neither a feeling of our superiority over nature nor of our harmony with nature, but precisely the feeling of relating to the irreducibly other that discloses our freedom: the point of convergence between the beautiful and the sublime.

In order to understand this feeling of identity, Schelling maintains that we need to begin from ordinary experience: from the opposition between subject and object that would seem to refute such identity. This opposition is not—as with Fichte—merely a semblance, an error that awaits correction. Rather, Schelling immediately draws our attention to the truth of this ordinary experience, taking up a properly philosophical approach to identity that is itself grounded in a sympathetic distance, a detached attentiveness. It is toward this end that Schelling posits the distinction between the philosopher and the self that is under investigation:

> Here for the first time we may perceive very clearly the difference between the philosopher's standpoint and that of his object. We, who philosophize, know that the limitation of the objective has its sole ground in the intuitant or subjective. The *intuiting self as such* does not and cannot know this, as now becomes clear. Intuiting and limitation are originally one. But the self cannot simultaneously intuit and intuit itself as intuiting, and so cannot intuit itself as limiting either.[54]

The demand of philosophy, which "is therefore nothing else but the free imitation, the free recapitulation of the original series of acts into which the one act of self-consciousness evolves," is the bringing to light of what must have been repressed from consciousness.[55] In order for there to be consciousness, which requires opposition, or limitation, there must already have been a repression of its creative, non-oppositional ground—a repression of its origin. The self's inability to know that it is the ground of the objective is part of what it means to be a self; but because the philosopher is able to think beyond this defining limitation, some sort of encounter with this unknowability is equally essential. The viability of this philosophical dissociation depends upon the possibility of *transforming* the structure of the self—of recognizing its structure *as* self-transformation, which Schelling equates with freedom. Schelling understands philosophy as an enactment of this freedom insofar as it is the *conscious reconstruction* of *unconscious self-limitation*. Only through the philosopher's "*free* imitation" of the epochs of self-consciousness, where the philosopher dwells in the liminal as such, does the repressed become available to us as the *beyond* that such a boundary exposes. Freedom is just this capacity to reopen the boundaries of the self, to "interrupt this [unconscious] evolution" and to disentangle the transition-ality of self-consciousness from the stability of self-knowledge.[56] The philosopher approaches the repressed, then, not as an object of possible cognition unavailable to the layman, but as a limit—as an intimation of freedom grounded in vulnerability. Schelling is not claiming that from the philosophical perspective, we can finally know the self-limiting activity or shed light "behind" it; as with the Freudian model, the philosopher only gains access to the unconscious through the conflicts manifested in its symptomatic return. In this case, these traces are the distinguishing oppositional structures of each epoch of self-consciousness.

Part of what makes Schelling's approach to repression so important, in contrast to Hegelian dialectic, for example, is his insistence on a grounding activity that is not surpassed or exhausted in the development of self-consciousness; it is precisely *because* the repressed can never be entirely appropriated, because the "I" requires resistance to be what it is, that the unconscious is the impetus for consciousness and the latter's development toward freedom.[57] We would do well to return to Schelling's introductory remarks, where he relates the non-conscious productivity of nature to the conscious productivity of human freedom:

> How both the objective world accommodates to presentations in us, and presentations in us to the objective world, is unintelligible unless between the two worlds, the ideal and the real, there exists a *predetermined harmony*. But this latter is itself unthinkable unless

the activity, whereby the objective world is produced, is at bottom identical with that which expresses itself in volition, and *vice versa.*[58]

The identity Schelling points to here, between the activities resulting in nature and in freedom, suggests there is also a common form of repression; just as the productivity of nature is concealed in its inhibited products, while at the same time expressing itself through them, it must also be the case that the productivity of freedom both is withdrawn from and is realized through our actions. Repression, as a process both limiting and necessary to self-consciousness, discloses an essential aspect of our identity with nature. Schelling's notion of aesthetic freedom thus evokes an unknowable, repressed unconscious that we nonetheless must relate to. Schelling's intellectual intuition, or the grasping of the unity of consciousness and the unconscious in reflection, is ultimately one's freely relating to the self-constituting, grounding act of repression.

This idea of the repressed as inaccessible to knowledge and yet interpretable is brought into relief through Schelling's attention to the *boundary*. He argues that the development of self-consciousness depends upon both a conflict and reconciliation between the self as ideal activity or that which "goes beyond the boundary," and the self as real activity or a "becoming bounded."[59] I would suggest that this is one way to bring together Schelling's understanding of our freedom with the repressed: insofar as consciousness is a limitless demand for the construction of limits, it must exceed the opposition of "within" and "without." The original activity where Real and Ideal are posited in their identity, "both inside and outside the boundary at once," is also the original activity of repression.[60] Thus the self, essentially a *boundary* phenomenon, turns on a questioning of that which is fundamentally *transitional*—of that which, as in the return of the repressed, opens up precisely what it seems to foreclose. It is the availability of this structure—rather than any particular material that has been repressed—that characterizes intellectual intuition and the work of genius.

I will consider only briefly the way this structure is made manifest in intellectual intuition, before going on to its expression in the work of art. Schelling writes:

The *self* is such an [intellectual] intuition, since it is *through the self's own knowledge of itself* that that *very self* (the object) first comes into being. For since the self (as object) is nothing else but the very *knowledge of itself*, it arises simply out of the fact *that* it knows itself; the *self itself* is thus a knowing that simultaneously produces itself (as object). Intellectual intuition is the organ of all transcendental thinking. For the latter sets out to objectify itself through freedom, what is otherwise not an object; it presupposes a capacity, simultaneously to produce certain acts of mind, and so to intuit that the producing of the object and the intuiting itself are absolutely one; but this very capacity is that of intellectual intuition.[61]

Schelling's intellectual intuition is not a mysterious or magical revelation; rather, it is a grasping of identity rooted in duality. Although he uses the term *knowledge* here, Schelling is essentially revealing a different kind of relationship between subject and object altogether. The activity that grounds subject and object—the self *as* self-producing/knowing or intellectual intuition—is non-conceptual: it is the site where activity and passivity, knowing and feeling, are not yet opposed. It is the intuiting *of* this holding together of duality and identity that Schelling terms intellectual intuition. It is not the unconscious that is made conscious through intellectual intuition, but the boundary that unites and divides consciousness. Here, my goal is simply to point out that Schelling is primarily interested in the activity that *binds* duplicity and unity; his focus is on the status of the *boundary* itself—of the boundary *as* the paradigmatically repressed—rather than the reality or ideality it delimits.

Not only does the very positing of intellectual intuition present a marked contrast with Kant, but the freedom that is intuited through it bears little resemblance to moral obligation. Schelling implies that freedom is in fact an acknowledgment of *irreducible* resistance, distancing himself as much from Schiller's harmonious reconciliation of nature and reason as from Kant. It is really through his understanding of art as "the only true and eternal organ and document of philosophy," however, that Schelling's original contributions to aesthetic freedom are realized. Schelling contends that what is expressed sensibly in the intuition of art, and intellectually in the intuition of the philosopher, is not an object of knowledge. The unconscious is not appropriated by consciousness—nature is neither overcome by (Kant, Fichte) nor in harmony with (Schiller) reason—but grasped, in its very otherness, as its own:

> The intuition we have postulated [intuition of art] is to bring together that which exists in separation in the appearance of freedom and in the intuition of the natural product; namely *identity of the conscious and the unconscious* in the *self*, and *consciousness of this identity*.[62]

Feeling ourselves to be the *convergence* of the conscious and the unconscious—this is what art can offer us that neither practical nor theoretical philosophy can. It is important to note that it is not the unconscious *as such* that is grasped in aesthetic intuition, but rather its unity with consciousness. In contrast to Kant and Schiller, Schelling posits that the highest act of freedom is one "in which freedom and necessity are absolutely united": consciousness intuits its connection to the unconscious while allowing it to maintain its integrity *as* unconscious.[63]

The work of art is no longer a useful enjoinder toward the categorical imperative, or even a necessary moment in human progress toward moral perfection. It is quite simply the true expression of our freedom and the free expression of truth:

> If aesthetic intuition is merely transcendental [intellectual] intuition become objective, it is self-evident that art is at once the only true and eternal organ and document of philosophy, which ever and again continues to speak to us of what philosophy cannot depict in external form, namely the unconscious element in acting and producing, and its original identity with the conscious. Art is paramount to the philosopher precisely because it opens to him, as it were, the holy of holies, where burns in eternal and original unity as if in a single flame, that which in nature and history is rent asunder, and in life and action, no less than in though, must forever fly apart.[64]

Although Schelling's language here is that of identity, it is more specifically the language of identity as *opening*. Aesthetic freedom, for Schelling, is a transformative communication—a communication of truth that exists only as resistance and in transition. This is the case both for the genius that produces the work of art and the one that can receive it; there is no knowledge passed on here, but only the opening itself—an active receptivity. As "an *unconscious infinity* [synthesis of freedom and nature]," the work of art is a testament to the possibility of renegotiating the boundaries of our existence.

It is at this point in his exposition of the art product/production that Schelling invokes the sublime:

> Every aesthetic production proceeds from the feeling of an infinite contradiction, and hence also the feeling which accompanies completion of the art-product must be one of an infinite tranquility ... However, the opposition between beauty and sublimity is one which occurs only in regard to the object, not in regard to the subject of intuition. For the difference between the beautiful and the sublime work of art consists simply in this, that where beauty is present, the infinite contradiction is eliminated in the object itself; whereas when sublimity is present, the conflict is not reconciled in the object itself, but merely uplifted to a point at which it is involuntarily eliminated.[65]

Like Kant, Schelling seems to differentiate between the beautiful and the sublime in terms of the subject/object divide; as with Schiller, they are reconciled in the highest expression of freedom. Schelling suggests that while the beautiful and the sublime are present in the object as distinct forms, they are present in the subject by virtue of their identity. By asserting that the sublime does not merely belong to the subject but is transformed through it, he intimates that there is something about the sublime that complicates the correspondence or communication between subject and object as such. While it is unclear what Schelling intends in claiming that through the sublime conflict is "uplifted to a point at which it is involuntarily eliminated," it might best be understood as a disruption and recreation of the boundary between subject and object. Thus, it is not the infinite contradiction between consciousness and the unconscious that is "eliminated:" instead, the *boundaries* of this conflict—between subject and object, freedom and nature—show themselves to be neither objectively *there* nor subjectively *produced*. Schelling reminds us that the work of art, and particularly the sublime work of art, *opens up* the limits of self and world.

The mythological imagination

Foreshadowing several strands of thinking prominent in *The Philosophy of Art*, Schelling ties the unconscious to Greek mythology in *The System of Transcendental Idealism*:

To explain what we mean by a single example: the mythology of the
Greeks, which undeniably contains an infinite meaning and a symbolism for all ideas, arose among a people, and in a fashion, which
both make it impossible to suppose any comprehensive forethought
in devising it, or in the harmony whereby everything is united into
one great whole. So it is with every true work of art, in that every one
of them is capable of being expounded *ad infinitum*, as though it contained an infinity of purposes, while yet one is never able to say
whether this infinity has lain within the artist himself, or resides only
within the artwork.[66]

Again, Schelling problematizes the boundary between subject and
object—the infinity of purposes cannot be located in the producer, the art
product, nor its interpreter. In the case of mythology, Schelling suggests,
this inability to locate meaning is particularly evident. The world that
Greek mythology brings into being is at the same time so organically
whole and so inexhaustible that it exceeds the possibilities of artifice
(which needs an author) and of nature (which has none). In *The Philosophy of Art* Schelling reasserts the privileged position of art that he
began to lay out in his *System*, and in particular focuses on mythology as
its culmination. The highest expression of freedom must be transforma-
tional: a reframing of our relationship to the world that must also
destabilize us. Already provoking comparison with Freud in that
mythology becomes fundamental to our self-understanding, Schelling
also moves closer to a psychoanalytic account of the uncanny: mythology, Schelling argues, is intrinsically related to a shifting boundary
between fantasy and truth.[67] He writes, *"The world of the gods is the
object neither of mere understanding nor of reason, but rather can be
comprehended only by fantasy."*[68] Further, as we will see, Schelling's
approach to the *chaos* and *formlessness* proper to the sublime is similarly
implicated in this dialectic of *imagination* and *truth*:

For reason and fantasy limitation, too, becomes either simply a form
of the absolute or, considered as *limitation*, an inexhaustible source
of jest and play, for one is allowed to joke with limitation, since it
takes nothing away from the *essence* and is within itself nullity or
nothingness. Hence, the most brazen jesting plays about within the
world of the Greek gods with fantasy's images of the gods.[69]

The notion of playing with limitation should recall Schiller's conciliatory play drive, and indeed his works are cited quite often and at some length throughout *The Philosophy of Art*. The limitations of the gods, Schelling argues, represent the perfect union of form and formlessness: it is "precisely the *missing* characteristics in the manifestations of the gods that lend them the highest charm and yet still weave them back together into various relationships. The mystery of all life is the synthesis of the absolute with limitation."[70] In other words, it is only in the play of limitations, in playing *with* limitations, that the limitless can be felt.

The meaning of Schelling's claim that mythology is "*the necessary condition and first content of all art*" is not by any means obvious; just what makes the union of the absolute and the particular in mythology so fundamental still needs to be worked out. One approach comes through Schelling's understanding of mythology as *symbolism* and, specifically, as a *primal* symbolism: "*Representation of the absolute with absolute indifference of the universal and the particular **within the particular** is possible only symbolically.*"[71] It remains to be seen what symbolic representation is for Schelling, and how mythology can be its founding moment. Schelling defines symbolism in contrast to, or rather as a kind of indifference point between, *schematism* and *allegory*. The schema of a work of art—and here Schelling reinvigorates the Kantian term—is the artist's guiding "rule":[72]

> The schema is the rule guiding his production, but he intuits this universal simultaneously in the particular. First he will produce only a rough outline of the whole according to this intuition; then he develops the individual parts completely until the schema gradually becomes for him a fully concrete image, and the work itself is completed simultaneously with the fully determined image in his imagination.[73]

The schema of the genius suggests that what the artist imagines (the universal) is inseparable from what he produces (the particular), where each element of the production is meaningful only in its relation to a whole that is continuously created anew. As Schelling is quick to point out, language is perhaps the best example of schematism—where we "make use of merely universal designations even for the designation of the particular. To that extent even language itself is nothing more than perpetual schematization."[74] This process of rediscovering and reshaping the whole through the particular, while at the same time already having to rely on an intuition of the whole, is the essential contradiction of language: in speaking, we invoke the shared experience that emerges through and is transformed by such speaking. This will be essential in understanding Schelling's later conception of language as "faded mythology."[75]

If schematism suggests that the meaning of the whole remains beholden to its concrete expressions, Schelling tells us that allegory must be the reverse. In allegory, the artwork sheds light on the framework of meaning we already share; in schematism, such a framework is shown to be malleable, itself the product of imagination and freedom. It is as if in schematism the living quality—the capacity for transformation—belongs to the creation of meaning; in allegory, to our ability to receive it. Mythology, then, would be the living union of the universal and particular, of meaning and its instantiation. Myths do not *signify* the universal, the worldview from which they emerge, as allegory does; nor do myths *produce* the universal, a reality within which it can be meaningful, as schematism does. Rather, intention and production converge in mythology precisely because in its particularity "it itself *is* simultaneously also the universal."[76] The world of mythology is thus neither created nor given. In a departure from his discussion of freedom and the work of art in his *System*, Schelling shifts his emphasis toward the role of *meaning [Sinn]*. There is a mutual dependency between being and meaning in mythology—a living personality—that defines the symbolic. Or, as Schelling puts it, "Meaning here is simultaneously being itself, passed over into the object itself and one with it. As soon as we allow these beings to *mean* or *signify* something, they themselves are no longer *anything*" (p. 49).[77]

Although we can discover allegorical and schematic meaning in mythology, this is only because symbolism creates the space for both; indeed, the very possibilities of allegory and schematism already depend upon the union of meaning and being in symbolism, which is fundamentally expressed for Schelling through mythology:

Hence, one can also demonstrate convincingly—and I will do so in what follows—that the Homeric myth, and to that extent Homer himself, was absolutely the first element in the beginning of Greek poesy. The allegorical poesy and philosopheme, as Heyne calls it, were entirely the work of later periods. The synthesis is first.[78]

Insofar as Schelling insists that all "thinking is simple schematization" (theoretical) and that "all action, in contrast, is allegorical," (practical) the primacy of their synthesis would entail a primacy of *feeling* (of the aesthetic).

Schelling appreciates that this simultaneity of meaning and being characterizing the mythological challenges certain conceptions of freedom and sublimity. Indeed, Schelling suggests that morality "like sickness and death, only plagues mortals," and that the freedom of the gods—the freedom expressed in mythology—has nothing to do with morality at all. Equally, the sublime character of tragedy depends upon a realization that even the highest morality, the most righteous suffering, still evidences "the boundaries and limitations to which human beings are subject."[79] But the freedom of the gods, while unrelated to autonomy and obligation, is nevertheless tied up with necessity and fate; we know this through the prophesies fulfilled by Uranus, Kronos, and Zeus, their struggles no less futile than Oedipus'. The mythological world is a primordial working out of the boundaries between thinking and acting, desire and truth—freedom and necessity. As we might learn from the gods, freedom is not the absence of limitations but the capacity to play with them.

Notes

1 Immanuel Kant, *Critique of Judgment*. Trans., Werner S. Pluhar. Indianapolis: Hackett Publishing Company, 1987. Hereafter *CJ*, with pagination also from the *Akademie* edition. This is merely to say that the dualism between phenomena (as determined by the concepts of the understanding) and noumena (as produced in the ideas of reason) is problematized by the spontaneity of feeling and imagination. Kant is quite explicit in his introduction to the *Critique of Judgment* that the faculty of judgment is a *mediating* faculty between understanding (the domain of nature) and reason (the domain of freedom):

> And yet the family of our higher cognitive powers also includes a mediating link between understanding and reason. This is *judgment*, about which we have cause to suppose, by analogy, that it too may contain a priori, if not a legislation of its own, then at least a principle of its own, perhaps merely a subjective one, by which to search for laws.
>
> (p. 177)

He goes on to make it clear that just as the domains of understanding and reason must be cognition and desire, respectively, the similarly mediating domain or territory of judgment is *feeling*: "Now between the cognitive power and the power of desire lies the feeling of pleasure, just as judgment lies between understanding and reason" (p. 178).

2 *CJ*, p. 18/179.

3 See: Immanuel Kant, *Critique of Pure Reason*. Trans. Paul Guyer and Allen W. Wood (Cambridge: Cambridge University Press, 1997), p. 257/B 152. Hereafter, *CPR*.

4 Friedrich Schiller, *Essays*. Eds. Walter Hinderer and Daniel O. Dahlstrom (New York: Continuum, 2001). All citations and paginations are from this collection unless otherwise noted.

5 F. W. J. Schelling, *System of Transcendental Idealism*. Trans. Peter Heath. Charlottesville: University Press of Virginia, 1978. All paginations for the German are from Vol. III of the *Sämtliche Werke*. *The Philosophy of Art*. Trans. Douglas W. Stott (Minneapolis: University of Minnesota Press, 1989).

6 "For all of the soul's powers or capacities can be reduced to three that cannot be derived further from a common basis: the *cognitive power*, the *feeling of pleasure and displeasure*, and the *power of desire*" (*CJ* p. 18/179). Kant continues:

> Now between the cognitive power and the power of desire lies the feeling of pleasure, just as judgment lies between understanding and reason. Hence we must suppose, at least provisionally, that judgment also contains an a priori principle of its own, and also suppose that since the power of desire is necessarily connected with pleasure or displeasure.
>
> (Ibid.)

Finally, he concludes:

> judgment will bring about a transition from the pure cognitive power, i.e., from the domain of concepts of nature, to the domain of the concept of freedom, just as in its logical use it makes possible the transition from understanding to reason.
>
> (Ibid.)

7 In Henry Allison's *Kant's Theory of Taste*: *A Reading of the Critique of Aesthetic Judgment*, citing the work of Béatrice Longuenesse, the author argues that reflective judgments, and particularly the principle of purposiveness that governs them more generally, introduced in the *Critique of Judgment* offer a way to better understand the development of the schematism sketched out in the *Critique of Pure Reason*. Allison states the problem of the schemata as follows: "How, for example, could one apply the concept of causality to a given occurrence unless it were already conceived as an event of a certain kind, for example, the freezing of water?" (p. 24). Allison goes on to agree with Longuenesse's response, for the most part:

> If I understand her correctly, the gist of Longuenesse's answer is that this comparison does not begin with a blank slate. This is because the mind,

in its universalizing comparison, is guided by the very same concepts of reflection that are operative in the comparison of schemata that leads to the formation of reflected concepts. Presumably, at this level, however, the comparison leads the mind to seek similarities and differences, which can first be codified as schemata governing apprehension and then reflected as concepts. And this is possible, according to Longuenesse, because this comparison is oriented from the beginning toward the acquisition of concepts applicable in judgments.

(p. 27)

See also: Béatrice Longuenesse, *Kant and the Capacity to Judge: Sensibility and Discursivity in the Transcendental Analytic of the Critique of Pure Reason*, Charles T. Wolfe, trans. Princeton: Princeton University Press, 1998.

8   Hence an immense gulf is fixed between the domain of the concept of nature, the sensible, and the domain of the concept of freedom, the supersensible, so that no transition from the sensible to the supersensible (and hence by means of the theoretical use of reason) is possible, just as if there were two different worlds, the first of which cannot have any influence on the second; and yet the second *is* to have an influence on the first, i.e., the concept of freedom is to actualize in the world of sense the purpose enjoined by its laws.

(*CJ*, p. 14/176)

9   Judgment in general is the ability to think the particular as contained under the universal. If the universal (the rule, principle, law) is given, then the judgment, which subsumes the particular under it, is *determinative* (even though [in its role] as transcendental judgment it states a priori the conditions that must be met for subsumption under that universal to be possible). But if only a particular is given and judgment has to find the universal for it, then this power is merely *reflective*.

(*CJ*, p. 19/180)

10 As Andrew Bowie reminds us, Kant's aesthetics draws our attention to the shifting boundaries, not only between subject and object, but more fundamentally within the subject, that disturb the Critical Philosophy from the beginning:

In the "B" version of the *CPR* (1787) Kant changes the role of the imagination, in order to sustain the boundary between what we contribute to the world's intelligibility and what the world contributes, by subordinating the reproductive imagination to the functioning of the categories of the understanding. He therefore planned (but did not actually do so) to remove the famous description of the imagination as a "blind but indispensible function of the soul without which we would have no knowledge" (B p. 103, A p. 78) and replace it with the assertion that all synthesis is based on the understanding. The problems lurking in the idea of a boundary between spontaneity and receptivity become most apparent in the decisive part of Kant's account of the structure of our subjectivity, the attempt of the I to describe itself. It is this account, the "transcendental deduction of the categories," which will have a major effect on German Idealism and early Romanticism, and thus upon the history of aesthetics.

(Aesthetics and Subjectivity, 20)

11   But the way of presenting [which occurs] in a judgment of taste is to have a subjective universal communicability without presupposing a determinate concept; hence this subjective universally communicability can be nothing but [that of] the mental state in which we are when imagination and understanding are in free play (insofar as they harmonize with each other as required for *cognition in general*).

(CJ, p. 62/218)

See: Immanuel Kant, *Kritik der Ureteilskraft*. Hamburg: Felix Meiner Verlag, 2001. Hereafter cited as *KU*.

Die subjektive allgemeine Mitteilarkeit der Vorstellungsart in einem Geschmacksurteile, da sie, ohne einen bestimmten Begriff vorauszusetzen, stattfinden soll, kann nichts anderes as der Gemütszustand in dem freien Spiele der Einbildungskraft und des Verstandes (sofern sie unter einander, wie es zu einem Erkenntnisse überhaupt erforderlich ist, zusammenstimmen).

(p. 67/218)

12   *Genius* is the talent (natural endowment) that gives the rule to art. Since talent is an innate productive ability of the artist and as such belongs itself to nature, we could also put it this way: *Genius* is the innate mental predisposition (*ingenium*) *through which* nature gives the rule to art.

(CJ p. 174/307)

Genie ist das Talent (Naturgabe), welches der Kunst die Regel gibt. Da das Talent, als angeborenes produktives Vermögen des Künstlers, selbst zur Natur gehört, so könnte man sich auch so ausdrücken: Genie ist die angeborene Gemütsanlage (ingenium), durch welche die Nature der Kunst die Regel gibt.

(KU, p. 192/307)

13   *Zweckmäßig aber heißt ein Objekt oder Gemützustand oder eine Handlung auch, wenn gleich ihre Möglichkeit von uns nur erklärt und begriffen werden kann, sofern wir eine Kausalität nach Zwecken, d.i. einen Willen, der sie nach der Vorstellung einer gewissen Regel so angeordnet hätte, zum Grunde derselben annehemen. Die Zweckmäßigkeit kann also ohne Zweck sein, sofern wir die Ursachen dieser Form nicht in einen Willen*

setzen, aber doch die Erklärung ihrer Möglichkeit nur, indem wir sie von einem Willen ableiten, uns begreiflich machen können.

(*KU*, p. 70/220)

14 In Kyriaki Goudeli's *Challenges to German Idealism*, she suggests a similar conception of a peculiarly Kantian repression, only here at the most basic level of cognition in the *CPR*:

> The self can secure its unity only so long as its representations and corresponding states can be synthesized in an *a priori* way. However, these representations are already *inwardly determined* by the understanding: the legal contract turns into the domination of the understanding upon sensibility.
>
> (p. 36)

15 As Andrew Bowie argues in his *Aesthetics and Subjectivity: From Kant to Nietszche* that Kant's departure from earlier aesthetic theories, like Baumgarten's and Hamann's, involves a turn from the value of the individual or particular experience (grounded in a secure theological worldview) and toward the universal:

> Baumgarten's *Aesthetica*, and Hamann's *Aesthetica in nuce*, begin to suggest what is at stake in the emergence of aesthetics as an independent branch of philosophy. Despite their obvious differences, Baumgarten and Hamann share a concern with the failure of the rationalist traditions of the eighteenth century to do justice to the immediacy of the individual's sensuous relationship to the world which is part of aesthetic pleasure ... Aesthetic theory from Kant onwards, in contrast, often searches for the whole into which a single phenomenon can fit, once theological certainties have been abandoned, and this search is related to other ways in which modernity attempts to make the world cohere, from the political to the scientific.
>
> (p. 5)

16 *CJ*, pp. 182–183/314–315; my italics.

> *Der Dichter wagt es, Vernuftideen von unsichtbaren Wesen, das Reich der Seligen, das Höllenreich, die Ewigkeit, die Schöpfund u. dgl. zu versinnlichen ... die Schranken der Erfahrung hinaus, vermittelst einer Einbildungskraft, die dem Vernunft-Vorspiele in Erreichung eines Größten nacheifert, in einer Vollständigkeit sinnlich zu machen, für die sich in der Natur kein Beispeil findet ... Wenn nun einem Begriffe eine Vorstellung der Einbildungskraft untergelegt wird, die zu seiner Darstellung gehört, aber für sich allein so viel zu denken veranlaßt, als sich niemals in einem bestimmten Begriff zusammenfassen läßt, mithin den Begriff selbst auf unbegrenzte Art ästhetisch erweitert, so ist die Einbildungskraft hierbei shöpferisch und bringt das Vermögen intellektueller Ideen (die Vernunft) in Bewegung ...*
>
> (*KU*, pp. 202–203/314–315)

17 *CJ*, p. 167/301.

> *Man wird sagen, diese Deutung ästhetischer Urteile auf Verwandtschaft mit dem moralischen Gefühl sehe gar zu studiert aus, um sie für die wahre Auslegung der Chiffreschrift zu halten, wodurch die Natur in ihren schönen Formen figürlich zu uns spricht.*
>
> (*KU*, p. 184/301)

18 "Concerning the Sublime," p. 81. "*Wie ganz anders, wenn man darauf resigniert, sie zu erklären, und diese ihre Unbegreiflichkeit selbst zum Standpunkt der Beurteilung macht*" (*Theoretische Schriften*, Sämtliche Werke, Fünfter Band 1962. "Über das Erhabene," p. 804). Hereafter, *TS*.

19 Ibid. p. 74.

> *Das Gefühl des Erhabenen ist ein gemischtes Gefühl. Es ist eine Zusammensetzung von Wehsein, das sich in seinem höchsten Grad als ein Schauer äußert, und von Frohsein, das bis zum Entzücken steigen kann und, ob es gleich nicht eigentlich Lust ist, von feinen Seelen aller Lust doch weit vorgezogen wird. Diese Verbindung zweier widersprechender Empfindungen in einem einzigen Gefühl beweist unsere moralische Selbständigkeit auf eine unwiderlegliche Weise. Denn da es absolut unmöglich ist, daß der nämliche Gegenstand in zwei entgegengesetzen Verhältnissen zu uns stehe, so folgt daraus, daß wir selbst in zwei verschiedenen Verhältnissen zu dem Gegenstand stehen, daß folglich zwei entgegengesetzte Naturen in uns vereinigt sein müssen, welche bei Vorstellung desselben auf ganz entgegengesetzte Art interessieret sind.*
>
> (Ibid. p. 796)

20 I deal with Schelling's account of personality and its relation to freedom in the *Freiheitsschrift* in Chapter 2. See also: Sean McGrath's *The Dark Ground of Spirit*.

21 Kant writes: "*Wir **weilen** bei der Betrachtung des Schönen, weil diese Betrachtung sich selbst stärkt und reproduziert...*" (*KU*, p. 222, my emphasis). And in Schiller, "*Beim Erhabenen hingenen stimmen Vernunft und Sinnlichkeit nicht zusammen, und eben in diesem Widerspruch zwischen beiden liegt der Zauber, womit es unser Gemüt **ergreift**" (*TS*, p. 798; my emphasis).

22 "Concerning the Sublime," p. 75.

23 Ibid. p. 77/*TS*, p. 799.

24 Ibid. p. 77/799.

25 Although Schiller takes up Kant's term he does not share his definition, as I hope to show in what follows. Whereas Kant claims that "it is a law (of reason) for us, and part of our vocation, to estimate any sense object in nature that is large for us as being small when compared with the ideas of reason," Schiller emphasizes the very *human* aspect of our vocation:

> Every individual human being, one may say, carries within him, poten-
> tially and prescriptively, an ideal man, the archetype of a human being,
> and it is his life's task to be, through all his changing manifestations, in
> harmony with the unchanging unity of his ideal.
>
> ("Letters on the Aesthetic Education of Man," p. 93)

He continues, explaining what this "ideal" would consist in:

> Should there, however, be cases in which he were to have this twofold
> experience *simultaneously*, in which he were to be at once conscious of
> his freedom and sensible of his existence, were, at one and the same
> time, to feel himself matter and come to know himself as mind, then he
> would, in such cases, and in such cases only, have a complete intuition
> of his human nature ...
>
> (p. 126)

26 "On Naïve and Sentimental Poetry," p. 202/*TS*, p. 718.
27 *CJ/KU*, p. 245.

28   At this point we must remind ourselves that we are dealing with a finite,
    not with an infinite, mind. The finite mind is that which cannot become
    active except through being passive, which only attains to the absolute
    by means of limitation, and only acts and fashions inasmuch as it
    receives material to fashion.

("Letters on the Aesthetic Education of Man," p. 141)

29 Frederick Beiser also makes this point in *Schiller as Philosopher: A Re-
Examination*:

> The shortcoming of Kant's conception becomes apparent, in Schiller's
> view, as soon as we see that moral autonomy alone is compatible with a
> form of constraint. A person can do his duty for its own sake yet still feel
> an inner reluctance, a deep resistance within himself. In this case, though
> his action is autonomous, though he wills it as a rational being, the
> person is still not entirely free. While he is free as a rational being, he is
> not free as a whole being, for the simple reason that part of his self is
> under the *domination* of his reason. It is this thesis—the very idea that
> reason can dominate or create lack of freedom—that is completely alien
> to Kant's moral philosophy, and that plays a fundamental role in
> Schiller's thinking about freedom.
>
> (p. 217)

30   Reason does indeed demand unity; but nature demands multiplicity; and
    both these kinds of law make their claim upon man. The law of reason is
    imprinted upon him by an incorruptible consciousness; the law of nature by
    an ineradicable feeling. Hence it will always argue a still defective education
    if the moral character is able to assert itself only by sacrificing the natural.

("Letters on the Aesthetic Education of Man," p. 93)

31 "On the Pathetic," p. 68. *"In ästhetischen Urteilen sind wir also nicht für die Sittlichkeit an sich selbst, sondern bloß für die Freiheit interessiert, und jene kann nur insofern unserer Einbildungskraft gefallen, als sie die letzere sichtbar macht"* (*TS*, p. 536).

32 Schiller suggests that freedom is the ability to choose to follow or *refuse* to follow the moral law:

> Now, at the bottom of every moral evaluation there lies a demand by reason that things be done morally, and there is an unconditioned exigency at hand that we intend what is right. But because the will is free, it is (physically) a contingent matter whether we actually do it [*Weil aber der Will frei ist, so ist es (physisch) zufällig, ob wir es wirklich tun*].
>
> ("On the Pathetic," p. 62/*TS*, p. 529)

33   Since, then, the entire essence of the sublime rests upon the consciousness of this rational freedom of ours, and all pleasure afforded by the sublime is grounded precisely in this consciousness alone, it follows of itself (as experience also teaches) that the aesthetic image of what is *frightful* [*Furchtbare*] must stir us more powerfully and more pleasantly than the representation of the *infinite* does, and that the practically-sublime has, accordingly, a very great advantage over the theoretically-sublime, as far as the strength of the feeling is concerned.

("On the Sublime," p. 26/*TS*, p. 492)

34 "On the Pathetic," p. 67/*TS*, p. 535.

35 "The Art of Tragedy" p. 19/*TS*, p. 391.

36 Ibid. p. 391.

37 Ibid. p. 4/*TS*, p. 391; my italics.

> *Auch der schmerzhafte Verlust führt sie nicht über eine Wehmut hinaus, mit der sich noch immer ein merklicher Grad des Vergnügens gatten kann. Sie, die allein fähig sind, sich von sich selbst zu trennen, genießen allein das Vorrecht, an sich selbst telizunehmen und eigenes Leiden in dem milden Widerschein der Sympathie zu empfinden.*
>
> (Ibid. p. 375)

38 *CJ/KU*, p. 250.

39   [What happens is that] our imagination strives to progress towards infinity, while our reasons demands absolute totality as a real idea, and so [the imagination,] our power of estimating the magnitude of things in the world of sense, is inadequate to the idea. Yet this inadequacy itself is the arousal in us of the feeling that we have within us a supersensible power...

(*CJ/KU*, 250)

40   We see from this at once that we express ourselves entirely incorrectly when we call this or that *object of nature* sublime, even though we might quite correctly call a great many natural objects beautiful ... Instead, all

we are entitled to say is that the object is suitable for exhibiting a sublimity that can be found in the mind [*Wir können nicht mehr sagen, als daß der Gegenstand zur Darstellung einer erhabenheit tauglich sei, die im Gemüte angetroffen werden kann*].

(*CJ/KU*, 245)

41 Beiser makes a similar argument, suggesting that Kant identifies *human being* with reason, while Schiller take a more holistic approach:

> It is important to see that Schiller's account of the will does not define its freedom simply in terms of its power to act on the moral law. Unlike Kant in his *Grundlegung* and second *Kritik*, Schiller does not think that the freedom of a human being consists in its acting on the moral law independent of motives and sensibility. Rather, Schiller explains its freedom in terms of its power to act *or* not act on the moral law. He states that the will stands between two domains: that of morality and that of nature. It can choose from which of these domains it receives its law. We use our freedom even when we follow the law of nature contrary to reason.
>
> (*Schiller as Philosopher: A Re-Examination*, p. 112)

Beiser also puts forth a connected claim concerning their views on the highest good:

> While Schiller is indeed correct that Kant does not exclude sensibility as a motive for moral action, he underplays his deeper difference with Kant here: that the highest good consists in an equal cultivation and synthesis of sensibility and reason, individuality and universality.
>
> (p. 145)

42 Hence sublimity is contained not in any thing of nature, but only in our mind, insofar as we can become conscious of our superiority to nature within us, and thereby also to nature outside us (as far as it influences). Whatever arouses this feeling in us, and this includes the *might* [*Macht*] of nature that challenges our forces, is then (although improperly) called sublime. And it is only by presupposing this idea within us, and by referring to it, that we can arrive at the idea of the sublimity of that being who arouses deep respect in us, not just by his might as demonstrated in nature, but even more by the ability, with which we have been endowed, to judge nature without fear and to think of our vocation as being sublimely *above nature* [*über dieselbe*].

(*CJ/KU*, 264; my italics)

43 "Letters on the Aesthetic Education of Man," p. 158.

> *Es ist dem Menschen einmal eigen, das Höchste und das Niedrigste in seiner Natur zu vereinigen, und wenn seine Würde auf einer strengen Unterscheidung des einen von dem andern beruht, so beruht auf einer geschickten Aufhebung dieses Untershieds seine Glückseligkeit. Die Kultur, welche seine Würde mit seiner Glückseligkeit in Übereinstimmung*

bringen soll, wird also für die höchste Reinheit jener beiden Prinzipien
in ihrer innigsten Vermischung zu sorgen haben.

(*TS*, 647)

44   In the case of what is theoretically-sublime, the cognitive instinct is
contradicted by nature as an *object of knowledge*. In the case of what is
practically-sublime, the instinct to preserve ourselves is contradicted by
nature as an *object of feeling*. In the former scenario nature is considered
merely as an object that should have expanded our knowledge; in the
latter case it is represented as a power that can determine *our* own
condition.

("On the Sublime," p. 23/*TS*, p. 490)

45 *CJ/KU*, 259.
46 "Letters on the Aesthetic Education of Man," p. 117.

Solange er bloß empfindet, bloß begehrt, und aus bloßer Begierde wirkt,
ist er noch weiter nichts als Welt, wenn wir unter diesem Namen bloß
den formlosen Inhalt der Zeit verstehen. Seine sinnlichkeit ist zwar
allein, die sein Vermögen zur wirkenden Kraft macht, aber nur seine
Persönlichkeit ist es, die sein Wirken zu dem seinigen macht. Um also
bloß Welt zu sein, muß er der Anlage, die er in sich trägt, Wirklichkeit
geben. Er verwirklichet die Form, wenn er die Zeit erschafft und dem
Beharrlichen die Veränderung, der ewigen Einheit seines Ichs die
Mannigfaltigkeit der Welt gegenüberstellt; er formt die Materie, wenn er
die Zeit wieder aufhebt, Beharrlichkeit im Wechsel behauptet und die
Mannigfaltigkeit der Welt der Einheit seines Ichs unterwürfig macht.

(*TS*, p. 603)

47 "Letters," p. 126/*TS*, pp. 612–613.

48   Both drives, therefore, exert constraint upon the psyche; the former
through the laws of nature, the latter through the laws of reason. The
play drive, in consequence, as the one in which both the others act in
concert, will exert upon the psyche at once a moral and a physical
constraint; it will, therefore, since it annuls all contingency, annul all
constraint too, and set man free both physically and morally.

("Letters," p. 127)

49 Ibid. p. 131.
50 Ibid. p. 147/*TS*, p. 635.
51 See: Sigmund Freud, *Beyond the Pleasure Principle, SE* Vol. XVIII,
pp. 14–17 for a discussion of the *Fort/Da* game Freud's grandson engages in
to deal with his mother's and father's (Freud's daughter's) absence. See also:
pp. 56–60 in Dufresne's translation.
52 "This universally acknowledged and altogether incontestable objectivity of
intellectual intuition is art itself. For the aesthetic intuition is the intellectual

intuition become objective" (*System of Transcendental Idealism*, p. 229/624). Hereafter, cited as *STI.*

53 *STI* p. 18/357–358.
54 Ibid. p. 54/403–404.
55 Ibid. p. 49/397–398.
56 Ibid. p. 49/397–398.
57 Edward Beach develops a useful set of terms to deal with the differences between Schelling's and Hegel's dialectical thinking in *The Potencies of God(s): Schelling's Philosophy of Mythology* in terms of *Erzeugengsdialektik* and *Aufhebungsdialektik*. He writes:

> Hegelian dialectic typically operates by subjecting each concept to a series of "thought experiments" or tests for internal coherency. In the course of these tests, the concept's manifest purport becomes "sublated" (*aufgehoben*)—that is to say, the surface significance, which gives rise to incoherencies, is cancelled, while at the same time the deeper kernel of truth is retained ... Schellingian dialectic, by contrast, seeks to infuse the process of reasoning with a strong volitional component, so as to be capable of recovering the willing that allegedly precedes rational thought itself ... Schelling's treatment of dialectic obtains its successive forms not as though implicitly contained in the foregoing ones, but rather as produced or reproduced (*erzeugt*) by a kind of procreative causality which is supposed to reenact the processes by which the outer universe itself has evolved.
>
> (pp. 84–85)

58 *STI*, p. 12/348–349.
59 Ibid. p. 66/418–419.
60 Ibid. p. 67/419–420.
61 Ibid. p. 27/368–369.
62 Ibid. p. 219/612.
63 Ibid. p. 220/613–614.
64 Ibid. p. 231/626–628.
65 Ibid. pp. 225–226/620–622.
66 Ibid. p. 225/619–620.
67 It is in fact in Schelling's *Lectures on the Philosophy of Mythology* that the definition Freud makes use of first appears.
68 *Philosophy of Art*, p. 38.
69 Ibid. p. 37.
70 Ibid. p. 36.
71 Ibid. p. 45.
72 It is interesting and useful in this context to consider Kant's definition of schematism, and its relation to the imagination, from his *Critique of Pure Reason*:

We will call this formal and pure condition of the sensibility, to which the use of the understanding is restricted, the schema of this concept of the understanding, and we will call the procedure of the understanding with these schemata the schematism of the pure understanding. The schema is in itself always only a product of the imagination; but since the synthesis of the latter has as its aim no individual intuition but rather only the unity in the determination of sensibility, the schema is to be distinguished from an image.

(*CPR*, p. 273/A140/B179)

73 *Philosophy of Art*, p. 46.
74 Ibid. p. 46.
75 "One is almost tempted to say: language itself is only faded mythology; what mythology still preserves in living and concrete differences is preserved in language only in abstract and formal differences" (*Historical-Critical Introduction to the Philosophy of Mythology*, p. 52).
76 *Philosophy of Art*, p. 47.
77 Ibid. p. 49.
78 Ibid. p. 48.
79 Ibid. p. 55.

Chapter 2

Prophetic times

Let all come out,
However vile! However base it be,
I must unlock the secret of my birth.
The woman, with more than woman's pride, is shamed
By my low origin. I am the child of Fortune,
The giver of good, and I shall not be shamed.
She *is my mother; my sisters are the Seasons;*
My rising and my falling march with theirs.
Born thus, I ask to be no other man
*Than that I am, and **will know who I am.***

        —Sophocles, *Oedipus Rex*

Schelling's intuition in *Philosophy of Art*, that tragedy is the convergence of freedom and necessity, needs to be re-examined in light of his *Freiheitsschrift*. Ultimately, I will suggest that the irreducible remainder of the latter, its disruption of both past and future, is the tragic core of freedom itself. Before turning to the *Freiheitsschift* and its account of unconscious guilt and original sin drawn from Kant's *Religion Within the Limits of Reason Alone*, I compare how the Oedipal tragedy grounds the psychoanalytic project and Schelling's philosophy of freedom.[1] It is worth recalling in this regard Sean McGrath's description of Freud as a "tragic" thinker—a characterization that, in the context of that work, serves to minimize Freud's relevance to Schelling's later philosophy of redemption. While McGrath claims that Freud's worldview is tragic because he doesn't grant any ultimate meaning to existence, I would suggest that psychoanalytic therapy is in fact motivated by and reliant upon the same tragic freedom that emerges from Schelling's *Freiheitsschrift*.[2]

The unity of necessity and freedom by which Schelling defines the tragic, exemplified in his reading of *Oedipus*, is a crucial deviation from both Kant's and Schiller's views on the sublimity of tragedy. As we saw in the last chapter, such a departure is already evident in Schelling's insight into the transformation of subject/object relations that characterize the sublime. That is, it is essential to Schelling's conception of the sublime that the limits between subject and object remain porous—that the sublime is, above all, a reawakening to freedom grounded in an irreducible liminality. After a brief recounting of the facts of the plot, Schelling writes of Oedipus:

> That this guilty person, a person who after all only succumbed to the superior power of fate, nevertheless is punished, was necessary precisely *in order* to show the triumph of freedom, and constituted a recognition of freedom and the *honor* due it. The protagonist had to struggle against fate; otherwise there was no struggle at all, no expression of freedom. He had to succumb within that which is subject to necessity. Yet in order not to allow necessity to overcome him without simultaneously overcoming it, the protagonist also had to atone voluntarily for this guilt—guilt imposed by fate itself. This is the most sublime idea and the greatest victory of freedom: voluntarily to bear the punishment for an unavoidable transgression in order to manifest his freedom precisely in the loss of that very same freedom, and to perish amid a declaration of that free will.[3]

It is not that freedom is manifested through the hero's sublime sacrifice, as Kant, and even the early Schelling would have it, but rather that freedom itself is revealed *as* tragic. Freedom is actualized only through relating to its Other—that is, through the force of necessity. Human freedom thus coincides with the act of divine creation, where existence erupts through the perversion of order. In both cases, evil is the indispensable precondition of the individual and of self-consciousness—to be free is to take responsibility for the darkness of that decision, which conditions, and resists the harmony of reason.

As we will see in Schelling's *Freiheitsschrift*, the redemptive possibility of the future depends upon our continued engagement with the past: freedom, the decision for good, or evil, is atemporal in that it presses beyond the limits of consciousness and presence. In just this way, the unfolding of the Oedipal tragedy forces us to experience the uncanny temporality of a prophecy that arrives too early (before the first scene, before Oedipus is born) and too late (after the deeds have been done, after his punishment has begun). The initial prophecy, external to the action that it sets in motion, is not yet an expression of the deeper unity of freedom and necessity: it is treated as an external given, and thus as something to be manipulated, controlled, and avoided—a fact of nature. Only with the return of the prophecy, its (re-)appearance within the narrative as both memory and prediction, do we come to understand the crucial error: to assume that the past can be known and therein overcome.

The fate of freedom

If *Oedipus Rex* were to begin at the beginning, with the prophecy given to Laius and Jocasta before the birth of their son, with the mutilation and banishment of Oedipus, it might still be *a* tragedy but not *the* tragedy. The belated arrival of Tiresias is evocative of the haunting quality of the prophetic as such, displaced, and pervasive, already and yet-to-come, that drives Schelling's system of freedom. We learn that language, whether in the foretelling of Oedipus' fate or in the peculiar discomfort that inhabits even his own name, is both deceptive and revelatory. The prophecy protects neither Oedipus nor his family from evil; indeed, given the inevitability it lays claim to, we might wonder at how the speech act of the prophet assures the very future it proclaims. One is drawn into the kind of questioning usually reserved for sci-fi tales of time travel: If the prophecy were never spoken, would its truth have been secured in another fashion? The deeper impulse behind this question suggests that Oedipus' story concerns a destabilizing form of knowing—of *receiving* truth—that transforms what is known. Prophecy and self-consciousness converge as acts of awareness that inevitably alter the truth they would get hold of. Here, where subjectivity, and interpretability do not exclude truth, Oedipus discovers his freedom. Oedipus recognizes that fate, like freedom, is a mode of illuminating and even disrupting necessity; that his past (the meaning of the prophecy) is no more secured than his future (the nature of its fulfillment); and that certainty and closure are not possible in matters of blood and guilt.[4]

Indeed, it is in regards to the familial—the abyssal beginning from which the prophet derives authority—that Schelling's interpretation of

Oedipus resonates with the aims of psychoanalytic therapy. For psycho-analysis, the particular moments of the Oedipal drama are less important than the manner in which we take up its inexorable repetition. Oedipus, in killing his father and having sex with his mother, does not *know* what he is doing until it is too late. His misrecognition of others, which offers the opportunity for authentic self-discovery, is a consequence of conflat-ing self-knowledge with knowledge of things—that is, of mistaking *self* for *thing*. All of us, according to Freud, are destined to the same fate: we gain self-awareness through trauma, our individuality through acknow-ledging our limitations. One might think that Freud, an atheist, and dis-mantler of superstition, would have no use for an antiquated concept like fate. Yet accepting responsibility for the unconscious—working out how this is possible and indeed beneficial—is the goal of psychoanalytic therapy. Freud as analyst is interested in analyzing and thus interrupting fate through interpretation. The apparent victim of fate, the analysand, is only alienated from his unconscious desires. Or, as Freud puts it in *Beyond the Pleasure Principle:*

> What psychoanalysis reveals in the transference phenomena of neu-rotics appears also in the life of normal persons. With such persons, one has the impression of a persecuting fate or of something demonic in their experience, and from the outset psychoanalysis has con-sidered such a fate to be mainly self-imposed by the individual and determined by early infantile influences.[5]

After briefly recounting the tale of Tancred and Clorinda, where the hero kills his beloved twice, Freud concludes: "Given such observations ... we will be so courageous as to assume that in the mind there really is a repetition compulsion which supersedes the pleasure principle."[6] This is not to say that fate remains unchanged in psychoanalysis, that the neces-sity of unknown, external forces is merely transferred from supernatural powers to the unconscious. It is rather more complicated than that. On the one hand, there is the pleasure principle that would appear to be the heart of Freud's psychic determinism, and which functions as a mechan-ical, quantifiable explanation for all psychical acts; on the other, we have the gradually acknowledged force of the compulsion to repeat, the great exception to yet also the grounding for the pleasure principle, which Freud tends to ally with fate and the "demonic." In their slippery opposition, both the pleasure principle, and the compulsion to repeat are harnessed in therapeutic action—in the continued re-articulation of our constitutive stories. Which is to say: pleasure and death are forms of compulsion that, at the same time, must be acknowledged in order to bring us a measure of freedom.

As I have suggested, the uncanny marks a similar disruption of reality—a possibility for the re-inscription *of* fate that presents itself *as* fate. More than that, the uncanny is a psychoanalytic acknowledgment of Schelling's intuition that freedom is the hidden source of necessity—that order and reason can never entirely sublimate their dark and unruly origins:

> Following the eternal act of self-revelation, the world as we now behold it, is all rule, order and form; but the unruly lies ever in the depths as though it might again break through, and order and form nowhere appear as original, but it seems as though what had initially been unruly had been brought to order. This is the incomprehensible basis of reality in things, the irreducible remainder which cannot be resolved into reason by the greatest exertion but always remains in the depths.[7]

For Oedipus (and Antigone after him), the tragic task of freedom is to actively engage with this "irreducible remainder," to articulate and deconstruct the prophecies we live out with the priority of the "unruly" ever in mind. As Schelling reminds us, and Freud the analyst exhorts us, we have the capacity and the obligation to see that we are blind: only then can we begin to take responsibility for the unconscious structures and wishes that guide and give meaning to our experience and to existence itself. To be free is not just to accept guilt for what we could not or would not know; we must remain available to the empowerment and vulnerability this transformative knowing entails.

All this is to suggest that the dichotomy of fate and freedom—a dichotomy that seems to be sublimated in Schelling's *Philosophy of Art*—itself demands interpretation. Odo Marquard, who has so fruitfully penetrated the interstices of psychoanalysis and transcendental philosophy, opens up such an analysis in "The End of Fate?" Already in the title, Marquard plays with the ambivalence of human ends: bearing finitude (*death*) and meaning (*purpose*), we question, and struggle against fate while freedom is only proved in defeat. Tracing the development of the concept of fate in correlation with that of God, Marquard brings into focus our fixation on the rigid opposition: omnipotent *or* powerless. The death of God, no less than the death of (tragic) fate, signals a failed compromise formation—betraying our resistance to the fundamental ambivalence and unknowability of the unconscious:

> God is the end of fate. If that is the case, what does the end of God mean? ... Is it possible that the official and manifest tendency toward human omnipotence of making is counteracted by a latent and unofficial tendency; an indirect reempowerment of fate ... or, putting it differently, the outcome of the modern disempowerment of divine omnipotence is not only the official triumph of human freedom but also the unofficial return of fate.[8]

At the height of our belief in human freedom, at least insofar as it is understood in terms of powers of production and domination, fate returns. Here the convergence of freedom and necessity is a deception that calls out for a therapeutic self-questioning: What satisfaction is met, what defensive maneuver played out, by reifying the opposition between *omnipotence* and *powerlessness*?

Marquard's analysis of the mutations of fate, from ancient tragedy through divine providence, culminates in what we might call technological man. In Greek tragedy the prophesized fate was inescapable, personal, and inscrutable; freedom was a defiant responsibility and a triumphant failure. In Christianity, necessity is reborn as providence; while fate remains personal and inscrutable, it differs from the tragic conception of freedom through faith in an ultimate judgment beyond this world. After the death of God, fate is given over to science—both in the sense of a psychical/physical determinism that precludes freedom and in the reappearance of divine omnipotence in the guise of human production and technology. Freud's own account of fate, which would prove useful to Marquard here, is peculiar in that it straddles the modern/scientific and ancient/tragic views. Psychoanalysis offers a unique perspective on Marquard's line of questioning: What desires (and defenses) lie hidden, repressed, in the concept(s) of fate? Might our philosophical accounts of freedom be similarly symptomatic?

It is, nota bene, worth pondering the fact that what stood at the beginning of this depletion of God's power was the extreme theology of omnipotence that marked the late Middle Ages. The path from the theology of the *potentia absoluta* (absolute power) by way of the theology of the *Deus absconditus* and the *Deus caché* (hidden God) and the theology of the *Deus emeritus* to theology after the death of God—is a remarkable sequence. *Perhaps even omnipotence was already powerlessness by other means.*[9]

The repeated polarization of fate and freedom, passivity and activity, conceals a horrified ambivalence: such clear oppositions would protect us from the overwhelming anxiety of fearing and desiring both power and vulnerability. The anxiety of the uncanny, marked by a return to the convergence of omnipotence and fate, signals a fault-line in this dualistic structure. Freedom, insofar as it is equated with omnipotence (whether of God or of Man), is only powerlessness—fate—in disguise.

The freedom of fate

For Freud, such a confrontation with fate—whether pathological or uncanny—must be dealt with *therapeutically*. The feeling of being plagued by fate, of victimization, cannot simply be replaced with psychic determinism. Instead, psychoanalysis shares in the cathartic work—the liberation through submission—of tragedy. We are accountable to a history that cannot be settled; escaping a future of unacknowledged repetition requires a reinterpretation of, and acknowledgment of, our role in creating the prophecies constituting our past. This will always also be a question of how to take responsibility for the unconscious without falling into the neurotic polarity of omnipotence or helplessness—the same polarity that, Marquard implies, precipitated the death of God and may well do the same for technological man.

It is telling that in his one description of a personal experience of the uncanny, Freud invokes fate. He writes, "this factor of involuntary repetition which surrounds what would otherwise be innocent enough with an uncanny atmosphere, and forces upon us the idea of something fateful and inescapable when otherwise we should have spoken only of 'chance.'"[10] An aimless stroll through a foreign city leads Freud, again and again, to the neighborhood of "painted ladies."[11] Yet Freud never interprets the particulars of this experience, unwilling to delve into the unconscious motivations that would normally occupy him, that would deconstruct providence, superstition, or chance. Instead, he leaves it as just a feeling of "involuntary repetition"—repetition of a specifically *infantile* helplessness, the belief in which we should have overcome. What Freud leaves out precisely here, however, is the equally powerful sense of omnipotence governing infantile life. His unmasking of fate only goes half-way, failing to see that the feeling of omnipotence has only fled to the unconscious. As Freud teaches us to suspect, it is the narrator's omissions that tell the story: Isn't it peculiar that Freud should end up repeatedly among the prostitutes and seductresses of the red light district? That sexuality would occupy a *foreign* [(*un*)*heimliche*] place? Moreover, Freud's *theoretical* turn away from actual seduction, and toward fantasy, is indeed the founding gesture of psychoanalysis; and the therapeutic process that develops is itself a retracing, a circling back to the unconscious ambiguity between activity and passivity that is so abhorrent to consciousness.

The permeable boundaries between self and world we experience in the uncanny, and the therapeutic demand to recognize these boundaries as our own productions, together suggest that fate cannot be so simply suffered or made: freedom is just this negotiation. The transition from *real* seduction (passivity, victimhood) to our interpretations and fantasies surrounding it (activity, agency) within psychoanalysis is also a movement from deterministic necessity to uncanny freedom. In giving up the seduction theory, there is no longer any absolute separation between what is real and what is desired (the essence of "omnipotent thought"), and yet we are still called to work out the limits of our guilt. It is worth noting that for Freud, no less than for Schelling, it is not the inevitability of Oedipus' actions that makes him a tragic hero but his assumption of an inscrutable guilt. More than the theoretical significance of the Oedipal Complex, psychoanalysis relies on the therapeutic role of Oedipal awareness: on self-discovery that is neither futile nor absolute.

Oedipal knowledge—self-knowledge—turns out to be a form of ignorance: a knowing that negates itself by transforming the past it seeks to take hold of. Oedipus' guilt and punishment, his acquisition of the deeper truth of his defining prophecies, depends upon an understanding of freedom as the capacity to remake our personal narrative. Ancient tragedy, as opposed to its modern iteration, expresses the conflict between who we are and what we can know. Oedipus is *tragic* insofar as he presumes to know himself; he is a *hero* because he makes these limitations his own. This is not only illustrated through his physical appropriation of spiritual blindness, but also in returning to the role of father and guide as he makes his way to the grave in *Oedipus at Colonus*: "Follow, my children/It is my turn now to be your pathfinder,/As you have been to me. Come. Do not touch me/Leave me to find the way to sacred grave/Where this land's soil is to enclose my bones."[12] Oedipus is free only when he becomes a prophet himself—cursing his son and anointing Theseus—and in doing so gathers the power to reshape the future. In the moment that Oedipus recognizes his great sin, and with it the provisional nature and creative potential inherent to memory and self-perception, vulnerability becomes his strength. The events of the past are transformed, indeed shown to be essentially transformable, and he with them. The puzzle at the heart *Oedipus* is, of course, a version of the Sphinx's riddle: of the mystery of time as its inevitable course disrupts, and is disrupted by, the human. Prophecy, we might say, is the past's claim on the future: it is not a denial of freedom, not necessarily, but an insistence on temporal order and continuity. Along with a greater emphasis on self-consciousness or interior life, it is the absence of prophecy that separates modern from ancient tragedy; and, I would argue, these are not unrelated. Schelling's philosophical preference for ancient tragedy, and Freud's as well, hinges on this distinction—the past is not something to be overcome and subjectivity is a great deal more than self-consciousness.

The fundamental claim of psychoanalysis is that the unconscious *is* the ineradicable past and the source of our identity. More importantly, and dangerously, this past is not simply given once and for all; it is not only the ground of the present, but also a creation of it. Freud's term *Nachträglichkeit*, or delayed action, is an articulation of this temporal loop: Freud tells us that the Oedipal trauma, like all trauma, is not an event that has occurred.[13] In fact, it traumatizes us precisely through its temporal disruption, as our identity collapses into the space between memory and fantasy—between the meaning we suffer and the meaning we construct. Jean Laplanche's return to the theory of seduction in *Life and Death in Psychoanalysis* offers a psychoanalytic account of this tragic entanglement of fate, freedom and *Nachträglichkeit* in terms of an essentially traumatized subjectivity:

The "scene"—and we shall soon see how—must necessarily come into contact with the domain of sexuality. Moreover, two scenes, rather than a single one, will be found to be necessary; and it is in their hiatus, and in what one is inclined to call the impressive bit of deceptive trickery they gave rise to, that the objective lie we have translated as "deceit" is generated.[14]

The "objectivity" of the lie needs to be read in two importantly connected ways: first, the lie is itself objective ("inscribed in the facts"), and second, it is precisely the nature and possibility of objectivity (the lie *of* pure objectivity) that is at issue here. On the former interpretation, deceit simply is the very structure of sexuality—inevitably resistant to being known; on the latter, sexuality reveals objectivity *itself* as a fantasy, disturbing our very conception of what truth—even or especially our own truth—is.

Indeed, the realization of our helplessness in making sense of our own and others' unconscious, and simultaneous awareness of the powerful effects of our fantasies and desires on the world and those we share it with, *traumatizes us*. It is not merely that certain desires and events are repressed, but that our very conception of how "desires" and "events" come together *must* be disturbed here. We find ourselves, like Oedipus, too early, and too late; between desire and seduction; helpless, and omnipotent. The expansive role of sexuality in psychoanalysis, particularly in its relation to the time and truth of subjectivity, can be read as an acknowledgment of unsettled and unsettling reality that must remain inextricably bound up with unconscious fantasy—with a ground that both is and is not our own. As we will see, Schelling similarly understands subjectivity—and in fact existence as such—as intrinsically bound to trauma, and particularly to the perversions that are *desire* and *generation*.

Like prophecy, the traumatic is not confined by a beginning and an end, but acts as the atemporal event that would institute such order; the "event" is neither true nor false but rather inaugurates interpretability. Broadly construed, the psychoanalytic method of engaging therapeutically with the past is essentially based on this conception of the traumatic. Therapy depends on a past that remains vulnerable to the present—whether in the deceptive coherence of the dream, or the compromise formations that address us as screen memories and symptoms. While maintaining the "prophetic" power of our earliest experiences,

Freud is equally insistent that the past is only obliquely and incompletely available to us. Insofar as both past and present are pervaded by unconscious desire and the constructions of fantasy, psychoanalysis is a process aimed at taking up the prophetic voice. Oedipus, like all of us, does not inherit his fate (the universal Oedipal Complex)—he inherits a foreign, resistant past: the unconscious.

The "foreignness" of the past, the lineage of transgression that Oedipus is unintentionally born into, is not troubling; the claim that Oedipus' freedom is somehow realized in taking on this guilt, however, is. Implicit in this statement is the notion that who we are—and what we can be held to account for—is not limited to what we do or even to what we intend. Unconscious desire and fantasy, and no doubt Oedipus too is guilty of these, destabilize the past, and our relation to it. In one of Freud's earliest texts, "Screen Memories," he argues that our most intimate connection to the past—memory—is not reliable in the way we imagine it to be;[15] this isn't just to say that our personal narrative is biased, but that insofar as memory is an imaginative production it betrays deeper issues concerning the reality of the past.[16] For Freud, this "productive" memory only becomes apparent in the distortions he deals with in the therapeutic situation: the persistence of infantile modes of experience that are unacceptable to consciousness leads to the disfigured histories—the symptoms and confessions—of the analysand. But it is only in their duplicity that these memories, worked over by defenses, and interwoven with fantasy, can expose the textured reality of the archaic past:

> It may indeed be questioned whether we have any memories at all *from* our childhood: memories *relating to* our childhood may be all that we possess. Our childhood memories show us our earliest years not as they were but as they appeared at the later periods when the memories were aroused. In these periods of arousal, the childhood memories did not, as people are accustomed to say, *emerge*; they were *formed* at that time. And a number of motives, with no concern for historical accuracy, had a part in forming them, as well as in the selection of memories themselves.[17]

The lack of "concern for historical accuracy" on the part of memory is, itself, an opening up of the historical and the objective in and through psychoanalysis. It is due to the nature of the past that its truth is not there to be recovered—to be deemed more or less accurate. Its truth is wrapped up in the same modes of infantile experience that do not tolerate the laws and logic of consciousness—non-contradiction, for example, or linear causality. The ambivalence and malleability that characterize our earliest relationships—activity/passivity, love/hate—also define our most fundamental reality. We can begin to see why the oppositional structures of consciousness, including the distinction between memory and fantasy, are disturbed when confronted with the tragic dialectic of guilt and innocence. To question our responsibility for the past we must enter into its radical alterity—we must return to the disorienting ambivalence from which the dichotomies belonging to agency and desire are first constructed.

Original sin

In his 1809 *Freiheitsschrift*, Schelling begins to define freedom in relation to the problem of evil—to the concrete reality of living, deciding, and historicizing as a creature that is born into and bears the unconscious. And as Schelling only intimated in his account of tragedy, he now explicitly contends that our relationship to the past, to the unconscious ground of our existence, is integral to human freedom. The possibility of radical evil, no less than the possibility of divine love, is also *necessary* to human freedom—to freedom conceived as a potential for self-transformation manifested either in alienation or embrace. As I hope to have shown, such a potential—for vulnerability and potency specifically in relation to the past—is also fundamental to the psychical liberation of Freud's therapeutic approach. Benefiting from Kant's reformulation of freedom in *Religion Within the Limits of Reason Alone*, Schelling's account of evil pries the unconscious from the merely natural, necessary, or animal. As we shall see, it is only in this way that Schelling's early interpretation of Oedipal guilt and freedom comes to fruition.

In the *Groundwork of the Metaphysics of Morals*, in a passage representative of his earlier, Critical period where the unconscious has as yet no space of its own, Kant writes:

> Will is a kind of causality belonging to living beings so far as they are rational. *Freedom* would then be the property this causality has of being able to work independently of *determination* by alien causes;

just as *natural necessity* is a property characterizing the causality of all non-rational beings—the property of being determined to activity by the influence of alien causes ... What else then can freedom of the will be but autonomy—that is, the property which will has of being a law to itself? ... Thus a free will and a will under moral laws are one and the same.[18]

Here Kant clearly maintains that, for rational beings, there are only two options: either we act in a manner that is above the natural order—*freely*, according to self-given, universal law—or we act naturally, which is to say determined by desire, instinct, and inclination. Evil can only be ignorance of the moral law or the inability—a weakness of will—to act in accordance with it. The possibility of acting in such a way that we are *beneath* nature—that is, both freely, *and* in conflict with the moral law—is foreclosed. Freedom is thus equivalent to obeying the moral law, and the reality of evil is reduced to animality that cannot be a free choice and, therefore, that we cannot be held accountable for. It is only with his work in *Religion* that Kant realizes that evil, no less than the good, must be attributable to freedom. As he reflects on the connection between freedom and evil, Kant encounters the unconscious—he considers what it would require to take responsibility for that which we cannot know or experience: the very stuff of tragedy, or of psychoanalysis.

In *Religion Within the Limits of Reason Alone*, Kant revisits the question of freedom with the developments of the *Critique of Judgment* in mind: What kind of cause *is* freedom? This questioning leads Kant to sort out the nature of evil and to acknowledge its atemporal ground. In reformulating freedom as the real possibility of choosing good or evil, and in placing this choice outside of time, Kant leads the way for Schelling's radical assertions about the essence of human freedom. If we are to understand freedom as the essence of the human, we cannot maintain that evil is merely the result of any causally determined series of events—whether physical or psychical. That is to say, the disposition to adopt evil maxims must itself be a free choice—a choice, as we will see, that exceeds the *phenomenal* (spatio-temporal) world. Kant writes:

In order, then, to call a man evil, it would have to be possible *a priori* to infer from several evil acts done with consciousness of their evil, or from one such act, an underlying evil maxim; and further, from this maxim to infer the presence in the agent of an underlying common ground [*allgemein liegenden Grund*], itself a maxim, of all particular morally-evil maxims.[19]

Kant runs up against the notion of a "common ground" in the agent, or a *disposition*; such a disposition, to adopt good or evil maxims, must itself be *freely* chosen. We are not born with a fixed destiny, Kant argues, nor can our moral fate be determined by the contingent facts of our experience. How, then, do we come to *choose* this disposition? What kind of choice—and what kind of chooser—can remain *unexperienced* while still causally effective?

The problem of *nature*—or rather of its duality—arises simultaneously with the problem of evil. This connection between nature and evil takes on another form, as we shall see, in Schelling's text. It is in this vein that Kant deals with the Biblical account of hereditary sin at some length in this work, as he too is concerned with freedom as *opposition* to nature and as integral to *our* nature. This is not merely a question of semantics, but rather speaks to the complications inherent in a being that is simultaneously part of nature and able to stand against nature:

> Lest difficulty at once be encountered in the expression *nature*, which, if it meant (as it usually does) the opposite of *freedom* as a basis of action, would flatly contradict the predicates *morally* good or evil, let it be noted that by "nature of man" we here intend only the subjective ground of the exercise (under objective moral laws) of man's freedom in general; this ground—whatever is its character—is the necessary antecedent of every act apparent to the senses. But this subjective ground, again, must itself always be an expression of freedom [*Dieser subjektive Grund muß aber immer wiederum selbst ein Actus der Freiheit sein*] (for otherwise the use or abuse of man's power of choice in respect of the moral law could not be imputed to him nor could the good or bad in him be called moral).[20]

The "nature of man" is not, Kant argues, equivalent to the nature *in* man. That is, he does not mean to say that man is good or evil in the manner of natural cause, the way one is born a member of a particular race or sex. Despite Kant's reticence in fleshing out this expanded understanding of nature, in reopening the concept of human nature he subtly alters the concept of nature as such. As we can already see in Schelling's early works, for instance, it is precisely the "subjective ground" of nature—the *natura naturans* that is never fully disclosed in its products—that bridges the human and non-human worlds.[21] Kant remains focused on the "subjective ground" of *human* nature that, in its deviation from the laws of nature, "must itself always be an expression of freedom." Although this appears to be a rather familiar claim, that freedom is our *noumenal* essence, it is as if he is suddenly struck by the *weight* of this fact. If we are accustomed to the clarity Kant ascribes to the moral law, here he confronts us with the unfathomable depths of our guilt. *Noumenal* freedom must be the ground of law and *not* the law itself.

If it is by way of duty and the moral law that Kant understood the *phenomenality* of freedom, it seems that only through radical evil can he approach the inexpressible, *noumenal* dimension of freedom:

> We shall say, therefore, of the character (good or evil) distinguishing man from other possible rational beings, that it is *innate* in him. Yet in doing so we shall ever take the position that nature is not to bear the blame (if it is evil) or take the credit (if it is good), but that man himself is its author. But since the ultimate ground of the adoption of our maxims, which must itself lie in free choice, cannot be revealed in experience, it follows that the good or evil in man (as the ultimate subjective ground of the adoption of this or that maxim with reference to the moral law) is termed innate only in *this* sense, that it is posited as the ground antecedent to every use of freedom in experience (in earliest youth as far back as birth) and is thus conceived of as present in man at birth—though birth need not be the cause of it.[22]

The peculiarity of what Kant is saying here is not obvious: it seems a mere recapitulation of his account of the negatively defined, *noumenal* spontaneity of freedom. Yet the paradox of our freedom is laid bare, as we are faced with a grounding that we have no direct access to and yet, somehow, remain ineluctably responsible for at every moment. It is this paradox that Kant's successors try to overcome. His own efforts to move beyond the *phenomenal* expression of freedom are limited because of his equation of consciousness and subjectivity. Before and beyond the *phenomenal* expressions of actions, maxims and disposition, there must be the ungrounded, eternal decision:

To have a good or an evil disposition as an inborn natural constitu-
tion does not here mean that it has not been acquired by the man who
harbors it, that he is not author of it, but rather, that it has not been
acquired in time ... The disposition, *i.e.*, the ultimate subjective
ground of the adoption of maxims, can be one only and applies universally to the whole use of freedom. Yet this disposition itself must
have been adopted by free choice, for otherwise it could not be
imputed [*Sie selbst aber muß auch durch freie Willkür angenommen
worden sein, denn sonst könnte sie nicht zugerechnet werden*]. But
the subjective ground or cause of this adoption cannot further be
known (though it is inevitable that we should inquire into it), since
otherwise still another maxim would have to be adduced in which
this disposition must have been incorporated, a maxim which in itself
must have its ground.[23]

Eventually, we come to a ground that can neither be known nor ignored;
marking the periphery of possible experience, the task of our lives is to
acknowledge this ground as our own. Recognizing that it cannot show
itself, that it cannot be known or experienced, is as essential to this
demand as the effort to claim responsibility for it in and through our
actions. The relevance of the unconscious to this problematic should be
apparent. Freedom is neither the domination nor the refusal of our
unknowable ground, but the possibility of allowing such a ground to be
our own and to remain irreducibly other.

By placing the ground of our disposition outside of time in this way,
while still maintaining our ultimate freedom to determine ourselves, Kant
suggests a relation between the *noumenal* and *phenomenal* realms that
resonates with his work in the *Critique of Judgment*. Pointing to this dialectic of freedom and responsibility, where the unknowable ground is
both the source and effect of our moral bearing, Kant articulates freedom
as creative, organic cause:

However evil a man has been up to the very moment of an impend-
ing free act (so that evil has actually become custom or second
nature) it was not only his duty to have been better [in the past], it is
now his duty to better himself. To do so must be within his power,
and if he does not do so, he is susceptible of, and subjected to, imput-
ability in the very moment of that action, just as much as though,

endowed with a predisposition to good (which is inseparable from freedom) he had stepped out of a state of innocence into evil.[24]

In this passage Kant highlights the ever-present possibility of *redemption*, and indeed of the difficulty involved in conceptualizing how we are always free to recreate the ground of our being even as this ground must be the source of our choice to do so. We are not the agents of one free act that determines our existence; we are, instead, free at every moment to acknowledge and recast who we are through the re-appropriation of what we have done or will do—to be redeemed or damned. Without knowledge of our freedom, Kant suggests, we bear the responsibility for interpreting and creating the meaning of our actions. The decision that grounds our subjectivity is not atemporal in the sense that it is before time, but by virtue of the fact that this decision is the eternal possibility to become who we are. Just at this moment Kant retreats into the Biblical story of original sin, turning away from the chiasmic ground that is both the necessary condition of my subjectivity (that which makes any choice *mine*), and in itself, *my* free choice and responsibility:

> The foregoing agrees well with that manner of presentation which the Scriptures use, whereby the origin of evil in the human race is depicted as having a [temporal] *beginning*, this beginning being presented in a narrative, wherein what in its essence must be considered as primary (without regard to the element of time) appears as coming first in time. According to this account, evil does not start from a propensity thereto as its underlying basis, for otherwise the beginning of evil would not have its source in freedom; rather does it start from *sin* (by which is meant the transgressing of the moral law as a *divine command*). The state of man prior to all propensity to evil is called the state of *innocence*. The moral law became known to mankind, as it must to any being not pure but tempted by desires, in the form of a *prohibition*.[25]

The "radical evil" inherent in human nature is not an inborn propensity or perversion; human freedom, like knowledge in the Critical Philosophy, is only actualized in the living of life. Freedom cannot be abstracted from the conditions through which it is expressed, and so despite its metaphysical priority, depends upon the real possibility of choosing evil. As

Kant points out, the priority of the possibility for evil is *not* a temporal priority, though it has to be expressed this way in the narrative constraints of the Scriptures. The free choice that defines us seems to occur never and always, both cause and effect of our mode of being in the world. Kant goes on to suggest an analogy between the Biblical story of Adam's fall and his own reliance on the concept of obligation in developing his practical philosophy, serving "as it must" to communicate the moral law as a prohibition. Just as the Scriptures use the crutch of a temporal event to explain the origin of evil, Kant seems to admit that his own language of logic and duty similarly conceals the radical consequences of a freedom that we *are* but cannot *know*.

The transition from innocence to guilt is not a matter of preferring evil to the good; it is not an arbitrarily chosen perversion of our nature. Rather, freedom and guilt arrive together: in recognizing that our responsibility exceeds our knowledge, we assume our guilt. Kant, following the myth of original sin, suggests that innocence can only be experienced as having been; in taking up our subjectivity, in the self-consciousness that unifies our experience, the identity of knowing and being—of subject and object—is already lost. Self-knowledge, as the story of Adam and Eve allegorizes, necessarily precludes innocence. In our freedom and our finitude, we could always do otherwise and could not have done otherwise. Original sin, then, is as much the story of the "leap" into self-consciousness as it is into evil:[26]

> From all this it is clear that we daily act in the same way, and that therefore 'in Adam all have sinned' and still sin; except that in us there is presupposed an innate propensity to transgression, whereas in the first man, from the point of view of time, there is presupposed no such propensity but rather innocence; hence transgression on his part is called a *fall into sin*; but with us sin is represented as resulting from an already innate wickedness in our nature. This propensity, however, signifies no more than this, that if we wish to address our-selves to the explanation of evil in terms of its *beginning in time*, we must search for the causes of each deliberate transgression in a previous period of our lives, far back to that period wherein the use of reason had not yet developed, and thus back to a propensity to evil (as a natural ground) which is therefore called innate—the source of evil. But to trace the causes of evil in the instance of the first man, who is depicted as already in full command of the use of his reason,

is neither necessary nor feasible, since otherwise this basis (the evil propensity) would have had to be created in him; therefore his sin is set forth as engendered directly from innocence. We must not, however, look for an origin in time of a moral character for which we are to be held responsible; though to do so is inevitable if we wish to *explain* the contingent existence of this character [*Wir müssen aber von einer moralischen Beschaffenheit, die uns soll zugerechnet werden, keinen Zeitersprung suchen*] (and perhaps it is for this reason that Scripture, in conformity with this weakness of ours, has thus pictured the temporal origin of evil).[27]

It is "neither necessary nor feasible" [*nicht nötig, auch nicht tunlich ist*] to assume that the propensity for evil was created by Adam; yet Adam, like all of us, *is responsible for* his sin. Strangely, it is the reality of sin that seems to create its possibility.[28] We might read this in terms of Kant's own concerns with the temporal confusion that freedom draws us into: How can it be that we freely, and eternally, choose our own ground—the same ground from which choice becomes possible? Kant suggests that, as in the Biblical version, any temporal priority here is a simplification that obscures the truth. In giving precedence to sin, to the action that does not at first seem to belong to Adam essentially but only [does so] retrospectively, the story of the fall fails to think through the self-consciousness that encompasses the alterity of the unconscious.

The logic of longing

In his *Freiheitsschrift* Schelling sketches out the rudiments of an ontological psychoanalysis in his attempt to think through the consequences of a grounding repression—a traumatic union of fate and freedom.[29] In contrast to his earlier works, in this text Schelling presents freedom as the possibility of choosing good *or* evil—innocence *or* guilt. The language of seduction, procreation, and longing is pervasive here: evil, as Schelling tells us, is not a privation but a *perversion*. Freedom must be a certain tendency toward—a possibility for—this perversion. As we will see, this leads Schelling to develop a metaphysical account of the unconscious, as the ground of God and human beings, in terms of drive and desire. Just as Freud develops the temporality of *Nachträglichkeit* in order to make sense of our essentially neurotic subjectivity, so does Schelling articulate a new form of causation in his efforts to redefine human nature: an ontology grounded in will and desire, where objectivity and self-presence can no longer be equated with truth, inevitably disrupts the temporal order. I will suggest that Schelling takes an even more radical approach than Freud, developing a theory of an originary, *erotic* temporality that extends beyond the human to being as such.[30]

Schelling's essay, which can almost be read as a series of digressions on the limitations of reason, is a performance of the radically incomplete and disruptive freedom he encounters. That is, he initially attempts to develop a system *of* freedom in the weaker sense, a system that does not contradict freedom; through the course of the text, however, he constructs (and deconstructs) a system of freedom in the strongest sense, where freedom is the unifying and foundational principle. Partially in response to the "pantheism controversy," Schelling points out that the equation of system with pantheism, and of pantheism with fatalism, stem from fundamental misunderstandings of the terms involved: if pantheism is understood as the culmination of reason, and furthermore as the identity of God and His creation, this need not inevitably lead to determinism or nihilism. Rather, such a claim calls for an investigation into the structure of identity.[31] Schelling is quite clear that Kant's critical account of freedom—or "mere mastery of intelligence over senses and passions"—will not suffice. Indeed, Schelling sees that Kant can only approach freedom in its *phenomenal* expression—and thus *as* determined. The question of how we might reconcile system and freedom, then, is fundamentally the question of how to bring together what Kant emphatically tore apart. The *essence* of freedom is at issue, though not as an object or thing accessible to knowledge, and for Schelling this remains the singular task of philosophy:

> For the true conception of freedom was lacking in all modern systems ... until the discovery of Idealism. And the sort of freedom which many among us have conceived, even those boasting of the liveliest sense thereof, a freedom, namely, consisting of the mere mastery of intelligence over senses and passions [*in der bloßen Herrschaft des intelligenten Prinzips über das sinnliche und die Begierden besteht*], could be deduced from Spinoza himself without difficulty, indeed quite easily with superior decisiveness.[32]

Schelling's criticism of dogmatic and Kantian freedom, already prefig-
ured in his emphasis on the priority of organism and generation over
mechanism and production in the *Naturphilosophie*, is finally made
explicit: "God is not a god of the dead but of the living. It is incomprehensible that an all-perfect being could rejoice in even the most perfect
mechanism possible."[33] It is in this sense that Idealism alone offers the
tools to develop a positive account of freedom, as every coming-into-
being presupposes, and remains tied to a structure of inexhaustible, active
subjectivity—here understood as a vital exchange between consciousness
and the unconscious.

In a system of freedom the principle of sufficient reason cannot be
primary, and Schelling recognizes that he has to make room for causation
that is neither reducible to nor entirely disconnected from determinism: the
fact of creation (the existential consequent) is neither logically implied by,
nor undifferentiated from, the act of creation (its antecedent)—both
accounts of pantheism fail to grasp the space of the human, between finitude and eternity. The bond of identity that simultaneously individuates and
unites Creator and creation still needs to be articulated: "The principle does
not express a unity which, revolving in the indifferent circle of sameness,
would get us nowhere and remain meaningless and lifeless. The unity of
the law is of an intrinsically creative kind [*ist eine unmittelbar schöpfer-
ische*]."[34] If God and creation were identical in the sense of an inert sameness, there could be no relationship at all; there can be no terms connected
as identical without these terms remaining in some sense discrete—without
there being a way to distinguish antecedent from consequence. In order to
avoid such undifferentiated confusion, which could never account for a
being that is both created and free, Schelling aligns freedom with the differentiation proper to *birth* and the *familial*. In order to reconcile finitude with
freedom, we need to understand this (re-)productive identity as *creaturely*
dependence—as a form of generation that must be ontologically prior to
mechanistic production:

> Every organic individual, insofar as it has come into being, is
> dependent upon another organism with respect to its genesis but not
> at all with regard to its essential being ... on the contrary, it would
> indeed be contradictory if that which is dependent or consequent
> were not autonomous. There would be dependence without some-
> thing being dependent.[35]

The investigation that Schelling takes up here is an attempt to flesh out the form of causation that a system of freedom requires. It is a question of what kind of identity-in-difference, an inherently *active* identity, grounds the possibility of being both *created* and *free*—or the convergence of the temporal and eternal. As it turns out, this requires an account of the relationship that God and the human being bear to themselves as well as to each other—that is, that each bears to their own dark ground or the otherness at the root of selfhood. These free unions relate that which is irreducibly concealed/concealing to that which is essentially revealed/revealing—a language, both rule-bound, and creative. The active identity that holds together the individual human being is also the active identity *of* God and *with* God, precisely insofar as they are all expressions of the bond of *personality*—of the belonging-together of the unconscious and consciousness, ground and existence: the originary disruption that is life, the condition of possibility for love and hate, psychosis and neurosis.[36]

The *Freiheitsschrift* is a meditation on the unconscious as it pertains to the *personal* and *divine*: here it is no longer merely the condition for consciousness, but a force of its own, structured by drives toward appropriating and excluding otherness. Paradoxically, in narrowing the unconscious to the personal Schelling simultaneously extends freedom beyond the human; the strange development of the essay (with its ceaseless regressions and digressions) suggests that an investigation of human freedom inevitably leads beyond itself, to something that exceeds even the Absolute: the *Ungrund*. In making freedom and the unconscious personal, Schelling actually designates personality as the original and definitive *system*. In this way Schelling defies Kant's hypothetical approach to organic cause, asserting instead that organism is systematic in a more primordial sense than reason or mechanism. God and human beings are *personalities*—self-conscious organisms— insofar as they are always already engaged with otherness, with what they could be or could have been. A personality *is* insofar as it must be entangled in what it *is not*, capable of inhabiting its own possibilities— its self-development and self-concealment—*as* freedom.[37] Schelling argues that it is only in personality, which draws the human near to God, that the possibility of evil arises—and, therein, human freedom. Personality and freedom are thus inextricably linked for Schelling, descriptions of a systematicity that can encompass the self-potentiating interplay between ground and existence: that is, between the unconscious and consciousness in becoming an individual, between concealment and revelation in coming-to-expression.

The arc of Schelling's argument is itself an enactment of the strange temporality at work in personality—and it is the very emergence of time, of course, that is at stake in the system of freedom. Beginning with the dual aspects of God—His ground and existence—Schelling progresses to the human. But it is only toward the end of the essay that the ultimate ground, the *Ungrund*, makes its appearance as absolute freedom or indifference. It seems that Schelling performs a freedom that is the beginning and the end of philosophy, both in the content and the form of the *Freiheitsschrift*:[38]

> In the cycle whence all things come, it is no contradiction to say that that which gives birth to the one is, in its turn, produced by it. There is here no first and last, since everything mutually implies everything else, nothing being the "other" and yet no being without the other.[39]

If it is not quite clear why an investigation into human freedom opens immediately onto the relation between ground and existence, it is worth keeping in view the difficulty in approaching freedom by way of evil. Schelling's tendency to circle back to the beginning might be more fruitfully understood as a method for drawing us into the reciprocal activity of personality. Existence is the infinite capacity to return to, and to reinterpret, its inexhaustible ground. As we have already seen, the question of freedom concerns the unconscious as primordial cause. The relationship between ground and existence, then, is Schelling's explanation of individuality—of simultaneously being created and creating oneself—as neither capricious nor determined. Freedom *requires* a certain kind of distance, a vital grounding that needs to be thought through to its most originary form.

Although Schelling finds the rationalized, sanitized freedom of the *Critiques* insufficient, he takes up in earnest the Kantian equation of independence from time with freedom. While this connection is first presented in the Critical Philosophy, Schelling's inquiry into the role of the unconscious here is more indebted to Kant's confrontation with radical evil in *Religion Within the Bounds of Reason Alone*. While recognizing these resonances, Schelling maintains that Kant does not see his insights through to their natural—if disturbing—conclusion:

But it will always remain strange that Kant, after first distinguishing the things-in-themselves from appearances only negatively, as being independent of time, and later, in the metaphysical explications of his *Critique of Practical Reason*, treated independence of time and freedom as correlative concepts, did not proceed to the thought of transferring this only possible positive conception of *per-se-ity* to things.[40]

Freedom is not just one *noumenal* property among others, nor is it attributable only to the human being. Indeed, we might even say that Schelling's main contention in the *Freiheitsschrift* is that freedom is the essence of the *noumenal as such*. That is, "[i]n the final and highest instance there is no other Being than Will. Will is primordial Being and all predicates apply to it alone—groundlessness, eternity, independence of time, self-affirmation!"[41] Pressing beyond Kant and expanding the unconscious to include the ground of God, Schelling claims that not only human beings but being as such belong to freedom. Only through approaching all existence as expressions of living personality, and attending to the structure of such expression, can his philosophy of freedom find any traction. These concepts of personality and life can be too easily dismissed as an anthropomorphizing of God, of the Absolute, or of being. However, such language ought instead to call attention to the distinction Schelling makes between freedom as the mere property of a creature or a being, and as the very principle of *creating* or *coming-to-be*. Schelling's quite human terms actually belie a *de*-anthropomorphizing and reopening of freedom, as he seeks to reclaim its primordial essence.[42]

Having provisionally worked out why Schelling approaches human freedom through ground and existence, we can now consider the ways in which this relationship functions in God, human being, and finally in the *Ungrund*. Following Schelling, we begin neither with that which is nearest (human experience) nor most distant (*Ungrund*), but with the grounding relationship shared by God and human beings:

But since there can be nothing outside God, this contradiction can only be solved by things having their basis in that within God which is not *God himself* [*daß die Dinge ihren Grund in dem haben, was in Gott selbst nicht Er Selbst ist*] i.e. in that which is the basis of his existence. If we wish to bring this Being nearer to us from a human standpoint, we may say: it is the longing which the eternal One feels to give birth to itself [*es sei die Sensucht, die das ewige Eine empfindent, sich selbst zu gebären*]. This is not the One itself, but is co-eternal with it. This longing seeks to give birth to God, i.e. the unfathomable unity, but to this extent it has not yet the unity in its own self.[43]

The human is called to re-gather itself through the first stirrings of creation, appropriating itself anew as a reverberation of freedom, rather than deforming the Absolute in the effort to make it accessible, conceivable—knowable. Our melancholy, as Schelling puts it in his *Stuttgart Seminars*, is just such a call from this shared ground:

> The most obscure and thus the deepest aspect of human nature is that of nostalgia [*Sensucht*], which is the inner gravity of the temperament, so to speak; in its most profound manifestation it appears a *melancholy* [*Schwermuth*]. It is by means of the latter that man feels a sympathetic relation to nature. What is most profound in nature is also melancholy; for it, too, mourns a lost good, and likewise such an indestructible melancholy inheres in all forms of life because all life is *founded* upon something independent from itself.[44]

Schelling's use of melancholy is not an allegory, but a way of making manifest the necessity and difficulty of a *living* Absolute. That is, the deepest structures of human experience are not cognitive, but *emotional*—it is life that we share with God and with each other, and for Schelling life is expressed in and as feeling. More specifically, as Schelling notes, our attunement to life is an attunement to *loss*, to finitude, limit and otherness ("mourns a lost good"; "founded upon something independent"). This is by no means an escape into irrational speculation or mysticism, but a nuanced articulation of Schelling's central concern with the emergence of reason—of thought and language—from *its* other:

> We are speaking of the essence of longing regarded in and for itself, which we must view clearly although it was long ago submerged by the higher principle which had risen from it, and although we cannot grasp it perceptively but only spiritually ... Following the eternal act of self-revelation, the world as we now behold it, is all rule, order and form; but the unruly lies ever in the depths as though it might

again break through, and order and form nowhere appear to have been original, but it seems as though what had initially been unruly had been brought to order. This is the incomprehensible basis of reality in things [*Dieses ist an den Dingen die unergreifliche Basis der Realität*], the irreducible remainder [*der nie aufgehende Rest*] which cannot be resolved [*auflösen*] into reason by the greatest exertion but always remains in the depths.[45]

Schelling understands that within a system of freedom, the characteristic distinctions, or analyses of reason are not given but rather in need of explanation. Any investigation into the structure of grounding depends upon an acknowledgment of "the irreducible remainder" that is "the incomprehensible basis of reality." Insofar as we are to understand freedom here in its most primordial sense, as the source of reason and the confines of its system, so too are we to consider longing as the ground of intelligibility.

Part of what Schelling is doing here is emphasizing the *darkness* that human beings share with the act of creation—appealing to the ground that resists reason even as and because it allows it to come forth. We need to look at Schelling's entire essay as a meditation on the nature of identity, as a sustained effort to show that existence is a manifestation of the deepest structures of personality—of the longing and anxiety from which a subject might emerge. The fundamental structure that Schelling will propose, an unconscious differentiation and gathering in personality, must be prior to any mere analogy between the divine and the human. Heidegger calls attention to Schelling's privileging of the differentiating-gathering *activity* over any stabilized *being*, suggesting that in longing we touch upon that which allows for and resists the paradigm of subject-object opposition.[46]

The nature of the ground in God is longing? Here the objection can hardly be held back any longer that a human state is transferred to God in this statement. Yes! But it could also be otherwise. Who has ever shown that longing is something merely human? Who has ever completely dismissed the possibility with adequate reasons that what we call "longing" and live within might ultimately be something other than we ourselves? Is there not contained in longing something which we have *no* reason to limit to man, something which rather gives us occasion to understand it as that in which we humans are freed *beyond* ourselves?[47]

Longing, like the freedom it "gives us occasion to understand," is a mode of reaching out toward that within us that is not us—toward that within God which is not God: the Absolute ground, or the *Ungrund*. It is a consequence of Schelling's method of investigation that we are called upon to recognize *otherness* even, or especially, at the heart of self-absorption and evil.

Before we can even enter into the functioning of this ground in God, we already find ourselves caught up in the dialectic of identity and difference. In the very language through which Schelling binds God and human being, the strange forms of resonance and reflection that lead from the one to the other, it becomes clear that *grounding* must be intrinsically connected to *expressing*. Schelling explicitly unites ground and expression in his description of God's self-constituting, imaginative act:

> This primal longing moves in anticipation like a surging, billowing sea, similar to the "matter" of Plato, following some dark, uncertain law, incapable in itself of forming anything that can endure. But there is born in God himself an inward, imaginative response, corresponding to this longing, which is the first stirring of the divine Being in its still dark depths. Through this response, God sees himself in his own image, since his imagination can have no other object than himself. This image is the first in which God, viewed absolutely, is realized, though only in himself; it is in the beginning in God, and is the God-begotten God himself.[48]

The "imaginative response" [*eine inner relflexive Vorstellung*] to this primal longing is the gathering of an "image" [*Ebenbilde*]—God's own image, as there is as yet no other possible object.[49] The dark order of longing is given shape through the work of the imagination—the subject/object distinction, the very possibility of reason, is a product of fantasy.

Schelling's use of imagination in the *Freiheitsschrift* both resonates with and challenges his earlier preoccupations with intellectual intuition, human freedom, and creation. In this context, Schelling equates divine fantasy with the temporal dislocation of an origin that *is* only in the revelatory process that would also depend upon it. God does not imagine creation and so it appears: rather, more miraculously, and yet more humanly, the movement of letting-be must be prior to God and His (self-)generation.

We are left with the problem of how to articulate this primordial letting-be, this grounding that is the image of imagination itself. How is it
that the essential darkness of inchoate longing is always already an imagining? And why should this imagining longing call forth its own reflection in and as reason? The image, Schelling continues, is the first
emergence of reason as "the logic of that longing" [*das Wort jener
Sensucht*],[50] which in itself, follows only "some dark, uncertain law"
[*nach dunkelm ungewissem Gesetz*]:

> This image is at one and the same time, reason—the logic of that
> longing, and the eternal Spirit which feels within it the Logos and the
> everlasting longing ... The first effect of reason in nature is the separa-
> tion of forces, which is the only way in which reason can unfold and
> develop the unity which had necessarily but unconsciously existed
> within nature, as in a seed. Just as in man there comes to light, when in
> the dark longing to create something, thoughts separate out of the
> chaotic confusion of thinking in which all are connected but each pre-
> vents the other from coming forth—so the unity appears which con-
> tains all within it and which had lain hidden in the depths.[51]

We will need to approach the "logic" [*Wort*] of the primordial longing,
which Schelling calls reason, in its essential contradiction: indifference is
drawn out of itself by self-need. Reason is the exposure and attempted reso-
lution of difference—of a doubling—at the very root of identity. My suggestion is that the primordial imagining that is reason, *as* an imagining,
betrays a duplicity already—albeit unconsciously—at work in longing itself.
As Kyriaki Goudeli points out in her text, *Challenges to German Idealism:*

> *Logogrif*, as the reflection of longing upon itself, is not only the *word*
> of longing but also its *act*. As such, *logogrif* contains not only the
> thoughtful reflection on experience but is a form of experience itself.
> The *image* which longing sees in its reflection is not its *representa-
> tion*, but what is *caught in the net* of its bending movement, for *grifos*
> originally meant plait, and *logogrif*, the plaited *image* of longing
> which sees and utters itself.[52]

It is not as if reason somehow "adds" an order to longing that was not
there before. Rather, as an image of an even more fundamental

giving-forth, reason is a reflection in the most uncanny sense. Its arrival evokes what should have been, but cannot be, overcome: the disordering disclosure at the basis of all order and limitation. Or, as Goudeli goes on to say:

> *Logos*, rather than being frustrated by its inability to conquer the absolute, rediscovers meaning in its activities, precisely by virtue of its finitude; not by a self-heroising resolution to perform the extraordinary, but by means of its ability to be perennially fascinated, intrigued, provoked by a puzzling cosmos.[53]

Heidegger's reading of the longing that is the ground [*die Sensucht*] is useful here, as he suggests that reason emerges as both a (re-)shaping and (re-)presentation of primal imagination conceived of as an ontological self-addiction:

> "Addiction" (*Die "Sucht"*)—which has nothing to do with searching (*Suchen*) etymologically—primordially means sickness which strives to spread itself; sickly, disease. Addiction is a striving and desiring, indeed, the addiction of longing, of being concerned with oneself. A double, *contrary* movement is contained in longing: the striving away from itself to spread itself, and yet precisely back to itself. As the essential determination of the ground (of being a ground) in God, longing characterizes this Being as urging away from itself into the most indeterminate breadth of absolute essential fullness, and at the same time as the overpowering of joining itself to itself. In that the general nature of the will lies in desiring, longing is a will in which what is striving wills itself in the indeterminate, that is, wills to find itself in itself and wills to present itself in the expanded breadth of itself … Eternal longing is a striving which itself, however, never admits of a stable formation because it always wants to remain longing … it does not know any name; it is unable to name what it is striving for. It is lacking the *possibility of words*.[54]

Longing is thus a process of differentiation without which there could be no identity—and no *being*—at all. Insofar as we are seeking a way to understand the co-primordiality of longing and imagining in Schelling, we would do well to consider the connection Heidegger makes here between repetition and difference. Existence is the repetition of self-concern, but the eruption of self-concern is always already infected by the intimation of difference. Thus, longing is the imaginative act par excellence to the extent that creation, as the letting-be of existence as such, is an act of dissociation *and* reiteration. Through Heidegger we can begin to see the error in attributing a subject and object—or an anthropomorphic frame—to the longing Schelling names "ground." It is the very structure of a subject that wills an object that is in need of *grounding*. Thus, it is not that the ground *longs*, but rather that *longing grounds*; through the imaginings of reason there emerges the "*possibility of words*." And only through the opposition between being and doing that such a possibility announces can the seeker and what is sought begin to take shape.

Although primordial reason here might look like an external ordering, a distinguishing capacity external to the chaotic ground it organizes, we ought to pay close attention to Schelling's claim that "the first effect of reason in nature is the separation of forces." He does not say reason *is* the separation of forces. We can equally say that the first effect of the image, insofar as the image of the logic of longing *is* reason, is the separation of forces. By forces, Schelling means the fundamental oppositions of concealment and revelation, contraction and expansion; yet the separation of these forces, the unity of which already but only "unconsciously" existed, is not somehow *in* the image, but emerges *through* imaginative productivity. Reason, then, is this response—dependent upon and distinct from the structural *responsiveness* already at work in longing itself.

It is clear that for Schelling longing is not overcome or negated by reason; nor can it be that order follows necessarily from the unruly. Rather, the activity of grounding is both a withdrawing from existence and also that which is expressed in existence. And this duplicity, where self-differentiation sustains identity, is precisely the structure of freedom that Schelling wants us to open up to: the splitting within the ground that is only made manifest as existence, or the doubled identity of longing that can only be manifested in the image of reason, *are both subject-less, and free*. That is, ground and existence are bound together *unconsciously* and, through a still unconscious longing, the subject and object of this longing take shape—that is, they separate out of their unconscious unity and are gathered together again.

Insofar as the ground *is* longing, there is already within it the presentiment of the responsiveness or relating that prefigures separation. *As* longing, the ground unconsciously belongs to something other than itself and its implicit self-division is made explicit through its expression into existence. It is only later in his essay that Schelling takes on the division within ground itself, when he posits that the being of the ground is itself grounded—in the *Ungrund*, the indifferent, unconscious unity. And this *Ungrund* is itself pure freedom. If the ground is itself already involved in a grounding relationship, its very mode of existence depends upon yet deeper roots. For now, I only want to keep in mind that it is not longing and its logic that, so to speak, come first: rather, the ground *as* longing is itself only the first expression, the first "existence," of the *Ungrund*—of the Absolute freedom to be or not to be. In looking closely at the duplicity concealed within the term "ground," we are also retracing the active identity of longing and reason, of the unconscious and consciousness. Only in having begun to work out the ground in relation to existence—a relation that hinges on concealment or negation as *that which* appears and affirms—can Schelling reach back toward the unfathomable *Ungrund*, or that of which the ground itself is an expression.

Longing is thus *not* the being of grounding as such, but the being of that which holds together the grounded and the grounding. In this way, bringing us quite close to its ordinary meaning, longing becomes a mode of existing *between* or remaining in transition. Schelling's refusal to let identity collapse into sameness breaks down the viability of his language: it is not only the being of existence, but also the *being of the ground*, that must be divided between ground and existence. The expression of the *Ungrund* is *longing*, while that which is withdrawn from or grounding this expression can only be *indifference*.[55] As the most primordial grounding, the non-existence of the *Ungrund* is disrupted by a longing to return to itself. Because the *Ungrund* itself cannot be the expression of some further ground, the fullness of its being can only be grasped as an abyssal loss, in the nostalgia for what must have been but never was.

The *Ungrund* is a testament to the depth of unruliness that Schelling contends with in his investigations into the essence of human freedom. Because creation *is*, it is necessary that the *Ungrund* has in fact eternally fractured and re-gathered itself. However, the free decision to express its indifference *imaginatively*, insofar as it is always already decided, is necessarily effected through the reflection of the image: the dialectic of concealment and revelation. At first, Schelling's professed interest in human freedom—the real possibility of good or evil—seems far removed from such unthinkable metaphysical positions as absolute indifference or ontological desire. However, the way in which even the absolute freedom of the *Ungrund* is bound by necessity to a particular expression—as withdrawing/revealing, as longing/imagining—is essentially a reformulation of real and radical evil. The temporal disruption that Kant approached through original sin, albeit obliquely, is taken up by Schelling in a more rigorous and philosophical manner. Freedom, whether we are referring to the indifference and infinite determinability of the *Ungrund* or to the concrete possibility of choosing between good and evil, is inevitably an engagement with *being* always already permeated by *desire*.

It is in this way that I understand the *Freiheitsschrift* as a presentation of *uncanny* freedom. Schelling realizes that freedom is not the capacity to separate ourselves from our actions and to judge them, as it were, objectively, or sublimely; as in the Freudian experience of the uncanny, freedom is a confrontation with the depth of our responsibility and the limitations of our knowledge—a disturbing recognition of our inability to either escape from or to fully inhabit our subjectivity. Because freedom and life are inextricably joined for Schelling, objective truth is a contradiction in terms: the culmination of freedom, as laid out in the *Freiheitsschrift*, is not the exhibition of some ultimate truth but the imaginative possibilities of personality and love. In other words, the truth of creation is not *something* revealed, it is not the sublimation of all darkness into light; it is the infinite capacity to orient ourselves to otherness—to the unknowable, to the unconscious, to the liminal as such—in a way that creates rather than closes off possibilities for meaningful engagement. We have seen that freedom is not the mastery of the intellect over the senses and passions; it is not a denial of the creaturely. In fact, to be free is to acknowledge our dependency—to claim responsibility for, to identify with, the deepest foundation of our being that is expressed and developed through our choices and yet exceeds all choice.

Notes

1 Immanuel Kant, *Religion Within the Limits of Reason Alone*. Trans. Theodore M. Greene and Hoyt H. Hudson (New York: HarperOne, 2008).
2 Heinz Politzer, *Freud & Tragedy*. Trans. Michael Mitchell (Riverside: Ariadne Press, 2006). Here, Politzer discusses several strains of Freud's thought that converge with tragedy, including the idea of the tragedy endemic to the therapeutic process.

3 *The Philosophy of Art*, p. 253. See also Schmidt's discussion of this point in reference to Schelling's tenth letter in *Letters on Dogmatism and Criticism*, cited in *On Germans and Other Greeks*:

> In order not to transgress the bounds of art, tragedy was obliged to have the mortal *succumb*; yet, in order to compensate for this humiliation of human freedom imposed by art, it also had to allow him to undergo punishment—even for a crime committed on account of *fate* ... It was a *great* idea to have man willingly accept punishment even for an *inevitable* crime; in this way he was able to demonstrate his freedom precisely through the loss of this freedom.
>
> (p. 77)

4 Schelling's emphasis on prophecy and the role of the prophet is particularly notable in *Ages of the World*; prophecy is there presented both as the power belonging to the writer of the would-be "heroic poem" (to whom, perhaps, the work is dedicated) and our mode of relating to the future (p. 119). In contrast to narrating the past and knowing the present—we "prophesize" the future (p. 113).

5 *BPP*, p. 63/*SE* XVIII p. 21.

6 Ibid. p. 64/p. 22.

7 *FS*, p. 34/*SW* VII, 360.

8 Odo Marquard. "The End of Fate?" in *Farewell to Matters of Principle* (Oxford, 1989), p. 72.

9 Ibid. p. 72; my emphasis.

10 *SE* Vol. XVII, p. 237.

11 Freud writes:

> As I was walking, one hot summer afternoon, through the deserted streets of a provincial town in Italy which was unknown to me, I found myself in a quarter of whose character I could not long remain in doubt. Nothing but painted women were to be seen at the windows of the small houses, and I hastened to leave the narrow street at the next turning. But after having wandered about for a time without enquiring my way, I suddenly found myself back in the same street, where my presence was now beginning to excite attention. I hurried away once more, only to arrive by another *detour* at the same place yet a third time. Now, however, a feeling overcame me which I can only describe as uncanny...
>
> (p. 237)

However, this is not, in fact, the *singular* personal experience of the uncanny Freud mentions—but the only one that is in the body of the essay. In a footnote that follows some pages later, Freud relates another "adventure," this time relating to the "double":

> Since the uncanny effect of a 'double' also belongs to this same group it is interesting to observe what the effect is of meeting one's own image

unbidden and unexpected. Ernst Mach has related two such observations ... I can report a similar adventure. I was sitting alone in my *wagon-lit* compartment when a more than usually violent jolt of the train swung back the door of the adjoining washing-cabinet, and an elderly gentleman in a dressing gown and a travelling cap came in. I assumed that in leaving the washing-cabinet, which lay between the two compartments, he had taken the wrong direction and come into my compartment by mistake. Jumping up with the intention of putting him right, I at once realized to my dismay that the intruder was nothing but my own reflection in the looking-glass on the open door. I can still recollect that I thoroughly disliked his appearance. Instead, therefore, of being *frightened* by our "doubles," both Mach and I simply failed to recognize them as such. Is it not possible, though, that our dislike of them was a vestigial trace of the archaic reaction which feels the 'double' to be something uncanny?

(p. 248)

Here, it is the *literal* projection of one's *physical* image, rather than the realization of unconscious, *psychic* structures, and desires, that provokes the feeling of the uncanny.

12 Sophocles, *The Theban Plays*. Middlesex: Penguin Books, 1970. p. 118/1529–1595.
13 In Laplanche and Pontalis' seminal *The Language of Psychoanalysis*, they write that *Nachträglichkeit* is a:

Term frequently used by Freud in connection with his view of psychical temporality and causality: experiences, impressions and memory-traces may be revised at a later date to fit in with fresh experiences or with the attainment of a new stage of development. They may un!!! that event be endowed not only with a new meaning but also with psychical effectiveness.

(p. 111)

14 Jean Laplanche, *Life and Death in Psychoanalysis*, trans. Jeffrey Mehlman (Baltimore: The Johns Hopkins University Press, 1993), p. 38.
15 *SE* Vol. III, pp. 303–322.
16 Gail S Reed and Howard B. Levine, Eds., *On Freud's "Screen Memories"* (London: Karnac, 2015).
17 Ibid. p. 24/*SE* Vol. III, 322.
18 Immanuel Kant, *Groundwork of the Metaphysics of Morals*, trans., H.J. Patton (New York: Harper Torchbooks, 1964) p. 446.
19 Immanuel Kant, *Die Religion innerhalb der Grenzen der bloßen Vernunft* (Berliner Ausgabe, 2013, 2. Auflage, p. 16). Hereafter *DR*.
20 Ibid. pp. 16–17/*DR*, 16.

21   For although only transcendental philosophy raises itself to the Absolute Unconditioned [*Unbedingt*] in human knowledge, it must nevertheless

demonstrate that every science that is *science* at all has its unconditioned. The above principle thus obtains for the philosophy of nature: "the unconditioned of Nature *as such* cannot be sought in any individual natural object;" rather a *principle* of being, that itself "is" not, manifests itself in each natural object ... Now, what is this *being itself* for transcendental philosophy, of which every individual being is only a particular form? If, according to these very principles, everything that exists is a construction of the spirit, then *being itself* is nothing other than *the constructing itself*, or since construction is thinkable at all only as activity, *being itself* is nothing other than the *highest constructing activity*, which, although never itself an object, is the principle of everything objective.

> (*First Outline of a System of the Philosophy of Nature*, I,
> p. 13/SW III, pp. 11–12)

22 *Religion*, p. 17/*DR*, 17.
23 Ibid. pp. 20–21/*DR*, 20.
24 Ibid. p. 36/*DR*, 34.
25 Ibid. pp. 36–37/*DR*, 34–35.
26 See also: Soren Kierkegaard, *The Concept of Anxiety: A Simple Psychologically Orienting Deliberation on the Dogmatic Issue of Hereditary Sin*, trans. Reidar Thomte (Princeton: Princeton University Press, 1980). Kierkegaard writes, as if in communication with Kant:

> Thus sin comes into the world as the sudden, i.e., by a leap; but the leap also posits the quality, and since the quality is posited, the leap in the very moment is turned into the quality and is presupposed by the quality, and the quality by the leap.
>
> (p. 32)

27 *Religion*, pp. 37–38/*DR*, pp. 35–36.
28 This peculiar temporality of original sin, of mutual production of innocence and guilt, is the focus of Kierkegaard's *The Concept of Anxiety*, a work heavily influenced by Schelling:

> Through the first sin, sin came into the world. Precisely in the same way it is true of every subsequent man's first sin, that through it sin comes into the world ... Just as Adam lost innocence by guilt, so every man loses it in the same way. If it was not by guilt that he lost it, then it was not innocence that he lost; and if he was not innocent before becoming guilty, he never became guilty.
>
> (p. 31/*DR*, 35)

He continues,

> Innocence, unlike immediacy, is not something that must be annulled, something whose quality is to be annulled, something that properly does

not exist, but rather, when it is annulled, and as a result of being annulled, it for the first time comes into existence as that which it was before being annulled and which now is annulled ... Innocence is not a perfection that one should wish to regain, for as soon as one wishes for it, it is lost...

(pp. 36–37)

29 Maurice Merleau-Ponty, *The Visible and the Invisible* (Evanston: Northwestern University Press, 1968). In this text, Merleau-Ponty introduces the concept of a "psychoanalysis of Nature," and this alongside a discussion of his "barbaric Principle," in his notes from November, 1960:

"Nature is at the first day": it is there today. This does not mean: myth of the original indivision and coincidence as *return*.

The *Urtümlich*, the *Ursprünglich* is not of long ago.
It is a question of finding in the present, the flesh of the world (and not in the past) an "ever new" and "always the same"—A sort of time of sleep (which is Bergson's nascent duration, ever new and always the same). The sensible, Nature, transcend the past present distinction, realize from within· a passage from one into the other Existential eternity. The indestructible, the barbaric Principle.
Do a psychoanalysis of Nature: it is the flesh, the mother.
A philosophy of the flesh is the condition without which psychoanalysis remains anthropology.
In what sense the visible landscape under my eyes is not exterior to, and bound synthetically to ... other moments of time and the past, but has them really *behind itself* in simultaneity, inside itself and not it they side by side "in" time.
Time and chiasm.

(p. 267)

30 In Robert Vallier's essay "*Être Sauvage* and the Barbarian Principle," in the collection *The Barbarian Principle*, where he discusses the relationship between Merleau-Ponty's concept of a psychoanalysis of Nature in reference to Schelling's work, he makes use of Freud's *Nachträglichkeit* in order to account for God's auto-production. However, Vallier does not consider the Freudian roots of this temporality, which I will go on to consider here. Yet he does imply that, as with the coming-to-be of God, the relationship between ground and existence that characterizes human freedom must also take part in this disruption of linear time:

Like light, God comes to His existence, He becomes Himself. Yet He also belongs to the ground, and so when God comes to His existence, the ground flees. Once again we see this structure of *Nachträglichkeit* ... When God represses Nature, when He masters Himself, He properly exists; but Nature can be His ground only if He already exists. But He is never independent of this ground, which remains in Him as repressed.

(p. 140)

31 See: Frederick C. Beiser, *The Fate of Reason: German Philosophy from Kant to Fichte* (Cambridge: Harvard University Press, 1987). Beiser offers an illuminating and in-depth discussion of the pantheism controversy and its importance in the development of post-Kantian German philosophy (pp. 44–108). He writes,

> It is difficult to imagine a controversy whose cause was so incidental—Jacobi's disclosure of Lessing's Spinozism—and whose effects were so great. The pantheism controversy completely changed the intellectual map of eighteenth-century Germany; and it continued to preoccupy thinkers well into the nineteenth century. The main problem raised by the controversy—the dilemma of a rational nihilism or an irrational fideism—became a central issue for Fichte, Schelling, Hegel, Kierkegaard, and Nietzsche. It is indeed no exaggeration to say that the pantheism controversy had as great an impact upon nineteenth-century philosophy as Kant's first *Kritik*.

(p. 44)

32 *Philosophical Inquiries into the Essence of Human Freedom*, p. 17/*SW* VII, p. 345.

33 Ibid. p. 346.

34 Ibid. p. 345.

35 Ibid. p. 346.

36 See: Sigmund Freud, "The Loss of Reality in Neurosis and Psychosis" *SE* Vol. XIX, pp. 183–190. Freud contrasts neurosis and psychosis in the following manner:

> Accordingly, the initial difference is expressed thus in the final outcome: in neurosis a piece of reality is avoided by a sort of flight, whereas in psychosis it is remodeled. Or we might say: in psychosis, the initial flight is succeeded by an active phase of remodeling; in neurosis, the initial obedience is succeeded by a deferred attempt at flight. Or again, expressed in yet another way: neurosis does not disavow reality, it only ignores it; psychosis disavows it and tries to replace it.

(p. 185)

37 It goes without saying that this principle [for judging nature teleologically] holds only for reflective but not for determinative judgment, that it is regulative and not constitutive. It only serves us as a guide that allows us to consider natural things in terms of a new law-governed order by referring them to an already given basis [a purpose] as that which determines them. Thus we expand natural science in terms of a different

principle, that of final causes, yet without detracting from the principle of mechanism in the causality of nature.

(*CJ/KU* 379)

38 "The alpha and omega of all philosophy is freedom" (*Schelling's Organic Form of Philosophy*, p. 5).

39 *FS*, p. 358.

40 Ibid. pp. 351–352.

41 Ibid. p. 350.

42 This is Heidegger's claim as well, as cited on the following page.

43 *FS*, p. 359.

44 *Stuttgart Seminars*, p. 7/*SW*, 466.

45 *SW* VII, pp. 359–360.

46 Martin Heidegger, *Schelling's Treatise on the Essence of Human Freedom*, trans. Joan Stambaugh (Athens: Ohio University Press, 1985).

47 Ibid. p. 124.

48 *FS*, pp. 360–361.

49 See: John Sallis, *Logic of Imagination: The Expanse of the Elemental* (Bloomington: Indiana University Press, 2012).

50 In a footnote to this phrase, Schelling adds "*in dem Sinne, wie man sagt: Das Wort des Rätsels,*" or "in the sense in which one finds Logos in Logogriphs." In other words, Logos, or the Word is here understood as something like a key to a puzzle—that which shows the order within the apparently unordered.

51 *FS*, p. 361.

52 Kyriaki Goudeli. *Challenges to German Idealism*, p. 11.

53 Ibid. p. 11.

54 *Schelling's Treatise*, p. 125.

55   Reality and Ideality, darkness and light, or however else we wish to designate the two principles, can never be predicated of the groundless *as antitheses*. But nothing prevents their being predicated as non-antitheses, that is, in disjunction and each *for itself*; wherein, however, this duality (the real two-foldness of the principles) is established. There is in the groundless itself nothing to prevent this. For just because its relation towards both is a relation of total indifference, it is neutral towards both.

Chapter 3

The absolute past

Verily at the first Chaos came to be.

—Hesiod, Theogony

Nothing less than the origin of differentiation, the transition from the timeless to the temporal, is at stake in the development—and frustration—of Schelling's and Freud's drive theories. Continuing last chapter's investigation of the obscure convergences of freedom and prophesy in tragedy, the focus in this chapter is on Schelling's and Freud's formulations of the chaotic unconscious drives as they exist "before" their organization into and generation of life. Schelling's efforts to reclaim or narrate the Absolute Past in his *Weltalter*, and Freud's attempts to uncover the drives at the origin of life in *Beyond the Pleasure Principle*, represent the simultaneous culmination, and dissolution of their drive theories. In these similarly fragmentary texts, the logic of identity within and division among distinct drives is disturbed—undone by a very different logic of unconscious temporalization and the transformations of pleasure. Taken together, the vanishing difference between the drives bring Freud and Schelling to the limit of their systems and, ultimately, toward unveiling liminality in all its uncanniness.

Whereas *Trieb* is a fundamental concept for psychoanalysis from the start, the term is absent from Schelling's early *Naturphilosophie*, where he instead relies on the language of *potency* and *force*. By the time of the *Freiheitsschrift* (1809) and the *Weltalter* (1811–1815), *Trieb* has become the fundamental, dynamic unit for Schelling. This seems to occur simultaneously with his turn to the language of *desire*, suggesting that this departure from the *Naturphilosophie* correlates with a rethinking of the psychical/physical divide. Notably, Schelling develops his first truly drive-based theory in his *System of Transcendental Idealism* (1800). As argued in Chapter 2, it is in the latter text that the unconscious becomes more nuanced than the blind productivity of *natura naturans* and is first connected with the repressed. For their part, the potencies no longer act as a quantitative differentiation and integration of "forces" as they do in the *Naturphilosophie* and *Identitätphilosophie*, signaling in this context an apparent separation of the Real from the Ideal, but they do remain essential to Schelling's later philosophy of freedom and positive philosophy. As a non-deterministic, creative process of development, the potencies continue to serve an explanatory function for the activities and productions of drive activity in these later texts.[1] Indeed, the connection between the retroactive temporality of organism in Schelling's early texts, and of the unconscious (both the human and the Absolute) in the *Weltalter*, depends upon the potencies' adaptability to a philosophy of drive. As Edward Beach writes, contrasting Schelling's dialectic with Hegel's, "Because the truth, for Schelling, emerges in this process of (re)production, subsequent phases in the dialectic can supplement and perhaps subordinate, but by no means cancel or reconstitute (as for Hegel), what the previous phases have revealed."[2] In other words, setting the stage for his later philosophy of drive, Schelling's potencies help create a space for a past that is neither completely overcome in, nor entirely resistant to, the present.

With this in mind, I begin with a brief discussion of organism in Schelling's *Naturphilosophie*, highlighting the connection between life as such and a certain temporal "backwardness." I then suggest that it is a similar conception of retroactive existence that leads both Freud and Schelling to theorize a beginning that, eternally becoming, and eternally dying, is never fully present. Through a reading of Schelling's *Weltalter*, I focus more explicitly on the ways in which Schelling's theory of drives evolves into a temporalization of eternity—the Absolute Past—inherent in desire itself; finally, I go on to consider Schelling's disruption of the dyad drive/satisfaction within the primal will, and the consequent slippage from pleasure-in-nothingness to pleasure-in-difference. My hope is that detailing this progression in Schelling can help untangle Freud's late drive theory, and in particular the collapsing distinctions between and within Eros/Thanatos that we find there. With the help of Jean Laplanche's reading of Freud's primary masochism, I then suggest a way forward in reconciling this failed dualism with the early, "polymorphous" pleasures of *Three Essays on Sexuality*. Just as Schelling's efforts in the *Weltalter* lead him away from the conceptual underpinnings of his negative philosophy, so Freud's struggle to understand the development of life and consciousness leads to a rejection of the foundational pleasure principle. This apparent fissure in the Freudian project, where pleasure loses its former scientific and psyche-orienting status, might in turn offer a way to better understand Schelling's claim that to know the past is to take part in the genealogy of desire.[3]

Backwards progress

Schelling's approach to organism as the fundamental form of causation and existence extends from his *Naturphilosophie* all the way through to his positive philosophy. Focusing on the potentiation of opposed drives (toward development and inhibition, for example, or attraction and repulsion), Schelling reformulates Kant's work in the *Critique of Judgment* on organism as a hypothetical instantiation of freedom in nature into a foundational, metaphysical truth. Specifically, the *Naturphilosophie* suggests the primacy of organic temporality.

Schelling's treatment of organism brings together several problematic lines of thought stemming from Kant's aesthetic-teleological approach to cause and temporality in the *Critique of Judgment*. Through the dynamic structure of the organism, Schelling responds to the temporal disruption we have already noted in Kant's account of the sublime in Chapter 2. He thus rejects a linear, mechanistic understanding of causation to highlight an ongoing, infinite conflict and attempted reconciliation between the forces of expansion and contraction, freedom and determination, and the universal and the particular. Whereas Kant implies that organism and the sublime can only symbolize human freedom, Schelling insists that they are real manifestations of a freedom that extends beyond and grounds the human. As Bruce Matthews writes in *Schelling's Organic Form of Philosophy: Life as the Schema of Freedom*:

> The common epistemological requirement of these elements—apprehending a reciprocal causal system, organism, and the sublime—is their common need to effect what Kant calls "a comprehension of the manifold in unity" (*KU*, 107). Only if we can comprehend the reciprocal establishment of whole and part—*simultaneously* with the

interaction among the parts themselves—only then can we understand the dynamic whole that is organic nature ... What this requires however, is that Kant must *shatter the static form of our pure a priori intuition of time ... he must qualify intuition's sequential processing of time and permit an experience in which the time-condition is removed.*[4]

Matthews points to the analogous structure between our comprehension of the organic and that of the sublime in terms of Schelling's overarching claim that the philosopher/scientist's task—no less than the artist's—is to strive to unite the infinite and the finite, the eternal and the temporal.[5] Contrary to Kant's claims in the *Critique of Pure Reason*, experiences of the sublime and the organic require that the "static" (and thus measurable) "form of our a priori intuition of time" be "removed." The subject must be implicated in this synthesis of finite and infinite rather than merely receptive to it. Insofar as organic cause—irreducible to the mechanism of the phenomenal realm—is *primary* for Schelling, this static form must be derivative; whatever the altered temporality of organism (and of sublimity) entails, as the structure of *life* and *freedom* it must ground static, deathly, linear temporality and its necessity:

> Every organic product exists *for itself*; its being is dependent on no other being. But now the cause is never the *same as* the effect; only between quite *different* things is a relation of cause and effect possible. The organic, however, produces *itself*, arises *out of itself*; every single plant is the product only of an individual *of its own kind*, and so every single organism endlessly produces and reproduces only *its own species*. Hence no organization progresses *forward*, but is forever turning back always into *itself*.[6]

The independence or self-sufficiency of organism already implies a kind of retroactive causation, a circular movement that is simultaneously self-transformative (change) and self-sustaining (continuity). Here, Schelling introduces a notion of generative repetition that allows him to defend identity that is an *activity*, rather than a *state*. The temporal repercussions of this organic union of unifying and differentiating forces, however, are only really cashed out through Schelling's turn to drive theory; the transition from force to drive is also a transition from organism to personality.[7] Thus, organism is not only the great achievement of Nature's non-conscious polarities. Sharing the temporal structure of Schellingian personality, organism is also the site where the distinction between force and drive becomes relevant. Schelling writes in the opening pages of the *Weltalter*:

> Every physical and moral whole requires for its maintenance a reduction, from time to time, to its innermost beginning.... Every thing runs through certain moments in order to attain completion: a set of processes coming one after the other *where the later always intrudes on the earlier*, bringing it to fruition.[8]

In view of this later text, then, Schelling's insistence that no organization can "progress forward" becomes a critique of a certain understanding of scientific knowledge and, even more so, a refusal to reduce self-knowledge to such a model. The incessant and mutual intrusion of past and future is a rejection of truth as presence, at least insofar as this sense of objectivity would lay claim to a totalizing neutrality. Progress forward is equated with the mechanistic trope of effects as implicit in, and pouring forth from, similarly circumscribed causes—science conceived as an inert accumulation of discrete and homogeneous events.

Schelling's account of organic backwardness—characterized by the mutual activity of uniting identity (the whole/persistence) and difference (the unfolding of parts/development)—is not only a claim about how to know a particular type of being; it is a claim about the most fundamental and philosophical form of knowing. As Schelling writes in the *Outline*, "[n]o subsistence of a product [of Nature] is thinkable without a continual process of being reproduced. The product must be thought of as annihilated at every step, and at every step reproduced anew."[9] And, when Schelling later locates organism at the root of creation in his *Weltalter*, he is quite explicit that this (re)generative activity is the essence and origin of temporality as such: "We have a presentiment that one organism lies hidden deep in time and encompasses even the smallest of things."[10] Thus to temporalize—to begin—is to reach back; the eternal and unconscious past will always already have been intruded upon by the longing for the origin that it *was* and cannot *be*, and philosophical knowing must structure itself accordingly. Linearity is but a defense against the shifting temporality of desire. In this way, Schelling poses a serious challenge to the equation of knowledge with presence. To know is not to intuit the eternally present within the temporal, but to trace the desiring, temporalizing activity already at work in eternity.

In Schelling's *Naturphilosophie*, the seeming independence and priority of thing-like stability (and, by extension, the deterministic paradigm that presents us with a thing-like world) is unmasked as a product of inhibitive and creative forces alike: A deceptive stagnancy conceals the conflict between infinite productivity and infinite constraint.[11] Equally, our ordinary conception of time as a series of discrete, causally connected now-points, would be the illusory result of an infinite *becoming* and that which resists it—an equally eternal *returning*. Indeed, Schelling's struggle to articulate this conflict as the source of both the ontological and the temporal is evident in the various and unfinished drafts of the *Weltalter*:

> Whoever takes time only as it presents itself feels a conflict of two principles in it; one strives forward, driving towards development, and one holds back, inhibiting [*hemmend*] and striving against development. If this other principle were to provide no resistance, then there would be no time, because development would occur in an uninterrupted flash rather than successively; yet if the other principle were not constantly overcome by the first, there would be absolute rest, death, standstill and hence there would again be no time ... Thus, the principles we perceive in time are the authentic inner principles of all life, and contradiction is not only possible but necessary.[12]

The strangeness of this claim cannot be overstated: for Schelling, the eternal is not unmoving in contrast to the dynamism of the temporal, but rather the other way round. The eternity or timelessness of Schelling's Absolute Past, which he often equates with the unconscious, is not immobility—neither the absence of temporalization nor of differentiation. Time as we perceive it is a "compromise formation," brought about through the same potentiation of contradictory drives toward inhibition and development presented in his *Naturphilosophie*. The timelessness belonging to the Absolute Past is a more fundamental form of relating these eternal tendencies of will. It is no mere illusion: if anything, it is our experience of mechanistic cause (time as a series of now-points) that is akin to the illusory, static appearance of natural objects (existence as a concatenation of things).

This dialectical engagement between apparent stability and eternally united and opposed potencies is revisited in the *Weltalter*; here it is through contradictory *drives* toward expression and concealment, along with the bond [*das Band*] that unites them, that the Absolute reveals itself. By way of the identity-activity of organisms, the infinite forces that Schelling first posits in his *Naturphilosophie* are temporalized into drives; the implicit presence of these forces already begins to erode in the *Ungrund* of the *Freiheitsschrift*, as Schelling senses the need to historicize the emergence and development of temporality in terms of desire and repetition—as a function of an eternally withdrawing beginning. In the *Weltalter* Schelling returns to the essential backwardness of the organism, to the temporalizing attraction and withdrawal of the Absolute Past: he suggests that it is the *being-as-craving* of the drives that ultimately draws non-being into being, indifference into decision. Through the course of the *Weltalter*, Schelling suggests that it is the diffusion/integration of drive as such that unites the developmental logic of the potencies (necessity) and the eternal decision (freedom) of the beginning.[13]

Schelling can only approach the cyclical, self-devouring drives *before* their contraction into existence—the potencies of A_1/the contracting drive, A_2/the expansive drive, and A_3/the bond that unites them; that is, in relation to A_0/the *Ungrund*, which constitutes the disintegrative possibility threatening and supporting the coherence of presence:

> With this there is nothing left over except an alternating positing, where alternately now one is that which has being and other is that which does not have being and then, in turn, it is the other of these which has being and the one which does not have being. Yet, so that it thereby also comes exclusively to this alternating positing in the primordial urge for Being, it is necessary that one of them be the beginning or that which first has being and after this, one of them is the second and one of them is the third. From this, the movement again goes back to the first and, as such, is an eternally expiring and eternally recommencing life.[14]

His description of a beginning before the beginning already includes what can only come after—difference and life—just as he goes on to depict the primal will as already divided between self-absorption (indifference) and self-seeking (tension).[15] It is not that Schelling is limited to a narration of the past distorted by the biases of the present; rather, it is only through this retroactive structure that he can enact and come to know the contradiction of eternal beginning. The Absolute Past *is not*—until, of course, it *was*.

In the language of the book's 1815 draft that which will have become the Absolute Past—the pulsation of potencies that withdraw from and contract being—are already differentiated; but it is a differentiation that itself can only want existence, that must remain in the mode of craving and non-presence: A_1. The transition to the Absolute Present, to expression, revelation and development, is thus both a re-organization of the relation between the potencies (where A_1 *lets be* A_2 as that which ought to have being) and an actualization of the potency of expression or differentiation: A_2. But the lingering mystery of the differentiation and unity of these potencies *in and as creation*, in and as the cision separating Absolute Past from Absolute Present, is ultimately ascribed to free decision (albeit through a *necessary* union of God's nature and spirit): A_3. This eternal decision for self-revelation is itself a desire for the beginning—a desire that cannot *have* a beginning. Existence erupts as an orientation toward, and delimitation of, what no-longer-is:

> But precisely *that* one commences and one of them is first, must result from a decision that certainly has not been made consciously or through deliberation but can happen rather only when a violent power blindly breaks the unity in the jostling between the necessity and the impossibility to be. But the only place in which a ground of determination can be sought for the precedence of one of them and the succession of the other is the particular nature of each of the principles, which is different from their general nature which consists in being equally originary and equally independent and each having the same claim to be that which has being ... It is now clear that what is posited at the beginning is precisely that which is subordinated in the successor. The beginning is only the beginning insofar as it is not that which should actually be, that which truthfully and in itself has being. If there is therefore a decision, then that which can only be posited at the beginning inclines, for the most part and in its particular way, to the nature of that which does not have being.[16]

We should note that the necessity belonging to this eternal beginning, as Schelling tells us, only comes *after*. It is only characterizable as a decision retroactively—thus its *Nachträglichkeit*. The rupture of the beginning that occupies Schelling in the *Weltalter*, as he traces the absent moment of transition from the logic of potency to its (re)productive realization, is thus tied to an uncanny temporality. That is, it depends upon an originary, eternal act of repression—upon a "decision that inclines ... to the nature of that which does not have being"[17]—which conditions and always threatens to dissolve existence as such.

We can see that Schelling views this *other* temporality that grounds creation in terms of the dynamics of drive and repression. The unconscious, as the timeless past, is repressed as blind craving [*vorweltliche*]; gives way to vital contradiction [*weltliche*]; and intimates the possibility of renewed integration [*nachweltliche*].[18] Schelling implies that consciousness and presence, no less than sublimation, and futurity, depend upon the dual identity of drive—upon the structural confusion involved in separating what the drive *is* (which can only be what it *wants*) from its *aim* (which must also be its defining characteristic). The drive occupies a virtual space because it is split between returning to, and differentiating itself from, non-existence. As we shall see, this collapse of the antagonism between the drives—and specifically the connection such collapse bears to temporality—is quite close to Freud's work in *Beyond the Pleasure Principle*.[19] Often read as an affirmation of Freud's dualism, this latter text actually makes manifest the extent to which even the most basic contrast between life and death drives conceals an oscillation within or resistance to oppositional frameworks. Freud's clinging to this oppositional paradigm for the drives in fact serves to elicit their bizarre and productive transformations. Indeed, his difficulty in maintaining a dualism between the drives in this work brings him quite close to the Schellingian drive that must bear both possibilities: to progression that always conceals repetition/regression, and to presence that is disrupted by the destabilized and destabilizing existence of the past:

> It would not be without a kind of horror that spirit would finally recognize that even in the primordial essence itself something had to be posited as past before the present time became possible, and that it is precisely this past that is borne by the present creation, and that still remains fundamentally concealed.[20]

Schelling's language of "horror" and "concealment" is of course pervasive in Freud. The ground is not as firm as we like to imagine, but volatile and frightening, in that existence depends upon a past that *fundamentally resists (self-)presence.* Moreover, Freud's accounts of both the phylogenetic and individual inheritance of the unconscious echo Schelling's claim that the Absolute Past—the true, and truly horrific, past—is *producing* and *eroding* itself in every moment and in us:

> Indeed, we will hazard the assertion that every act of generation occurring in nature marks a return to a moment of the past, a moment that is allowed for an instant to enter the present time as an alienated (re)appearance. For, since time commences absolutely in each living thing, and since at the beginning of each life time is connected to eternity anew, then an eternity must precede each life.[21]

Each moment is tied to an unfathomable past, scarring the clarity of presence with its abyssal origins, and thus disrupting any linear sense of an unqualified individual agency. At the same time, the repressed past must be a function of what comes after. Already, "before" the beginning, there is difference: there is drive divided within itself. The Absolute Past, like the *Ungrund* hovering at the periphery of the *Freiheitsschrift*, remains in the depths of the individual and of existence as such. We *are* as a frustrated striving, as an insatiable need to recuperate the past into presence—into a presence that is, impossibly, grounded in a past that *is no longer*. This existential longing to return—to know the past—would be wrongly conceived as a desire for some *thing*.[22] Rather, this self-defining and self-dissolving desire *is* the cision: a repetition grounding every act of existence.[23] Disturbing the equation of reality and presence, bringing to awareness the precarious denial holding together all appearance, the Absolute Past is not there once and for all to give a name to and protect us from the meaningless transformations within non-existence. Indeed, if its withdrawal were complete, this would constitute Schellingian evil—an absolute self-absorption that excludes the otherness of expression. It is only as a continued claim on the present and future, as the primordially repressed ambivalence of the desire to become (other) and to return (to itself), that the Absolute Past provides the space for love and freedom.

Two beginnings

What becomes evident in reading Schelling's *Weltalter* alongside Freud's *Beyond the Pleasure Principle* is that these texts are disrupted by two seemingly irreconcilable versions of the beginning. On the one hand, there is the undifferentiated, tranquil immobility of indifference or primal narcissism; on the other, there is the originary perversion and repetition of the drives. With this in mind, I have separated this section into two subsections, although I hope that the mutual dependency of these two accounts becomes clear through the course of the chapter. The two sections that follow, "Primal Fantasy" and "Primary Masochism," can be read as elaborations of "The Oceanic Feeling" and "Fort/Da," respectively. While this leads to a certain lack of clarity in the presentation, it seems to me that this is the only way to do justice to the complications at work in Freud's and Schelling's own texts dealing with the problem of origins.

The oceanic feeling

Already in the opening lines of Schelling's *Weltalter*, we find the condensed, structural irony that motivates the therapeutic project of the text: to develop an account of the ages of the world, Schelling is—like all neurotics—engulfed by the past. In each of his drafts Schelling begins with the decisive assertion: "The past is known, the present is recognized, the future is divined."[24] The simplicity of these claims obscures what it is that keeps demanding to be re-written: a sense of (self-)knowledge that could be adequate to the ongoing transition between the timeless and the temporal:

> Man must be granted an essence outside and above the world; for how could he alone, of all creatures, retrace the long path of developments from the present back into the deepest night of the past, how could he alone rise up to the beginning of things unless there were in him an essence from the beginning of times? Drawn from the source of things and akin to it, what is eternal of the soul has a co-science/con-sciousness of creation ... Accordingly, the unfathomable, prehistoric age rests in this essence; although it faithfully protects the treasures of the holy past, this essence is in itself mute and cannot express what is enclosed within it.[25]

The past Schelling is concerned with is pre-historical in that it both resists language—"the authentic past, the past as such, is what came before the world [*vorweltliche*]"—and must be *narrated*.[26] The past here imagined is importantly connected to the unconscious, or rather to that condition from which the division between consciousness and the unconscious arises: "This separation, this doubling of ourselves, this secret intercourse between two essences, one questioning and one answering, one ignorant though seeking to know and one knowledgeable without knowing its knowledge ... is the authentic secret of the philosopher."[27] The Absolute Past—and man's knowing/unknowing essence that participates in it—is a mutual desiring: a vital difference within a primal drive(s) that always, already disturbs indifference; that has always, already duplicated itself. As Schelling goes on to say:

> Put most succinctly, the Highest can be what-is, and it can be being ... A thing that is free, not either to be *something* or not to be it, but rather to exist or not to exist—such a thing, by itself and with respect to its essence, can only be *will* ... It alone is allowed to stand in the middle as it were, between being and nonbeing.[28]

If we *ought* to narrate the beginning, as Schelling suggests here, we shall name it will; but a peculiarly desireless will ("the will that wills nothing, that *desires* no object") out of which opposing wills emerge.[29] It is a will that remains, essentially and eternally, in transition.

It remains to be seen whether or how such an originary, transitional space may already contain the present and future. Time is redefined and transformed through Schelling's various attempts at going back to the beginning. As David Krell points out in *The Tragic Absolute*, that Schelling does in fact offer more than the past in the *Weltalter* is already suggested in his notes for the first draft: from the very first line, "1. Ich beginne," Krell reminds us that "the simple past ... is *not* among the tenses into which we can translate *Ich beginne*."[30] At the outset, the past shows itself as heterogeneous, ambiguous, and already entangled in present and future tenses. The eternal beginning, an act that is both paradigmatically past and the condition for there being a past at all, *is* only insofar as it makes itself past—it *is* insofar as it *is not*.

The tranquil immobility of the past already carries within it the seeds of contradiction—and most essentially, the self-contradiction constitutive of desire. The will to remain as it was silently, *freely* unfolds, giving rise to the founding question of philosophy:

> Now the great riddle of all times originates precisely here, the riddle of how anything could have come from what is neither externally active nor is anything in itself. And yet life did not remain in the state of immobility, and time is just as certain as eternity.[31]

Schelling goes on to offer the following solution, grasping for language that can express the very possibility of expression in tracing the potentiating movement from the First to the Second, from the eternal One to the temporalizing Two:[32]

> Everything that is something without actually being it must by nature seek itself; but this is not to say that it will find itself, and still less that a movement or a going out from itself takes place. This is a seeking that remains silent and completely unconscious, in which the essence remains alone with itself, and is all the more profound, deep, and unconscious, the greater the fullness it contains in itself. If we could say that the resting will is the First, then we can also say that an unconscious, tranquil, self-seeking will is the Second ... This will *produces itself* and is therefore unconditioned and *in itself* omnipotent; it produces itself absolutely—that is, out of itself and from itself. Unconscious longing is its mother, but she only conceived it and it has *produced* itself.[33]

As unconscious seeking, the will simultaneously negates itself (as what-*is*) and posits itself as lack (as what *is not*). Self-seeking is the enactment of a cut indistinguishable from the longing to be healed. That is to say, the will to *be itself* is indistinguishable from the will to *be Other*: self-production is self-mutilation. The longing Schelling wants to account for appears—or rather, is neither present, nor absent—already in the resting First will ("everything that is something without actually being it must by nature seek itself"); the self-sufficiency of the First is simultaneously affirmed and refused. At the same time, the Second will, which would disturb the First, is characterized as tranquil. What Schelling glimpses here is a beginning that is always, eternally, too late. The will that wills *nothing* is already congealed into self-seeking desire, into the will that *wills* nothing. And such a beginning can only appear as "having been," as a grounding that resists presence—a grounding that cannot just *be*—and thus as an *un*grounding.

There is a tendency in readings of Schelling and Freud to conflate the unconscious that fundamentally resists consciousness (the Absolute Past) with the unconscious that is only potentially or problematically conscious (the past). However, such a reading obscures the reality of an unconscious that is not merely the shadow of consciousness, and protects us from an Absolute Past that is more than just faded presence. Indeed, it seems to me that Schelling's own vacillation on this point is one of the reasons he can never be finished with the *Weltalter*; and why, in the *Freiheitsschrift*, the loving sublimation of ground into existence—the filtering or molding of the darkness of desire into the light of reason—is complicated by an eternal "remainder."[34] Finishing the *Weltalter* would require a final victory of presence—a beginning and an ending, which have been, and will be. As we shall see, there is a similar hesitancy pervading Freud's reflections on time, as the above competing senses of the unconscious rise to the surface. It is worth noting that when Freud most self-consciously indulges in this sort of temporal "speculation," he compares his work with Kant's: in *Beyond the Pleasure Principle*, the timelessness of the unconscious is notably presented alongside and supported by the philosopher's equation of the noumenal and the atemporal.[35] And so we need to ask: Why is the Kantian tradition evoked here? Why does pleasure lead Freud to develop the rudiments of a psychoanalytic theory of temporality?[36]

> Today, due to certain psychoanalytic discoveries, Kant's pronouncement that time and space are necessary categories of the mind can be brought to discussion. We have discovered that the unconscious mental processes are in themselves timeless. That is to say, first of all, that they are not ordered chronologically, that time changes nothing in them, and that one cannot really apply to them the concept of time. These are negative characteristics that can only be clarified through comparison with the conscious mental processes. Our abstract concept of time, by contrast, seems to be completely derived from the modus operandi of the system P-C [Perception-Consciousness] and to correspond to a self-perception by that modus operandi. This mode of function in the system might

possibly be another way of providing a shield against stimuli. These comments will surely sound very obscure, but I must restrict myself to such hints.[37]

Freud's suggestion that conscious time is a defense can be seen as a gesture toward the silent, traumatic transitionality that haunts the text—the emergence of consciousness from the unconscious, life from death, pleasure from pain. Indeed, *Beyond the Pleasure Principle* is a text defined by repeated and failed beginnings—one that is always in transition, unable to truly and decisively begin. Before considering that work in some detail, I would briefly point to the opening pages of its later companion text, where (in this writer's estimation) *Beyond the Pleasure Principle* (finally) begins. In *Civilization and Its Discontents*, citing a letter from a friend, Freud implies that although timelessness threatens consciousness, it is not excluded from reality or even inherently traumatic:

> I had sent him my small book that treats religion as an illusion, and he answered that he entirely agreed with my judgment upon religion, but that he was sorry I had not properly appreciated the true source of religious sentiments. This, he says, consists in a peculiar feeling, which he himself is never without, which he finds confirmed by many others ... It is a feeling which he would like to call a sensation of "eternity," a feeling as of something limitless, unbounded—as it were, "oceanic."[38]

It is in this belated introduction to pleasure in excess of its "principle" that Freud first posits the oceanic feeling; by presenting this feeling through a personal letter, he draws our attention to the particular quality or *specificity* of pleasure. To include this private account so prominently is to demand from psychoanalysis a reevaluation of the tension between the individual and the universal that so disrupted *Beyond the Pleasure Principle*—hovering, as that text does, between biology and myth, between organic immortality and individual death.[39] From the opening pages of *Civilization and Its Discontents* it is clear that Freud's move *beyond* the pleasure principle only leads him more deeply *into* pleasure, no longer comfortably identified with "diminution of tension." He goes on, as we saw in his accounts of the uncanny and telepathy, to remind us that while he personally lacks these feelings he can nonetheless use them to illustrate psychoanalytic discoveries:

> From my own experiences I could not convince myself of the *primary* nature of such a feeling ... Further reflection tells us that the adult's ego-feeling cannot have been the same from the beginning. It must have gone through a process of development, which cannot, of course, be demonstrated but which admits of being constructed with a fair degree of probability. An infant at the breast does not as yet distinguish his ego from the external world as the source of the sensations flowing in upon him. He gradually learns to do so, in response to various promptings ... A tendency arises to separate from the ego everything that can become a source of unpleasure ... One comes to learn a procedure by which ... one can differentiate between what is internal—what belongs to the ego—and what is external—what emanates from the outer world. In this way one makes the first step towards the introduction of the reality principle which is to dominate future development ... In this way, then, the ego detaches itself from the external world. Or, to put it more correctly, originally the ego is everything, later it separates off an external world from itself. Our present ego-feeling is, therefore, only a shrunken residue of a much more inclusive—indeed an all-embracing—feeling which corresponded to a more intimate bond between the ego and the world about it.[40]

Freud re-appropriates his friend's religious language in order to explain that the boundaries between ego and world remain permeable. These are not given from the start but produced through, and ever vulnerable to, our modes of experiencing pleasure and pain. The dichotomies of internal and external, and active and passive, seem to derive from an "oceanic" engulfment that remains the ambivalent source of pleasure (repetition) and anxiety (dissolution).

Fort/Da

Freud and Schelling both repeatedly compare their work to archaeology and its ruins—to the unearthing of an inconceivably distant past preserved in the unconscious.[41] But there is a deeper similarity in their revitalization of the past, as they problematize the continuity and homogeneity that holds together the very *being* of past, present, and future. As Schelling writes in his *Weltalter:*

> For different times (a concept that, like many others, has gotten lost in modern philosophy) can certainly be, as different, at the same time, nay, to speak more accurately, they are necessarily at the same time. Past time is not sublimated time. What has past certainly cannot be as something present, but it must be as something past at the same time with the present. What is future is certainly not something that has being now, but it is a future being at the same time with the present. And it is equally inconsistent to think of past being, as well as future being, as utterly without being.[42]

This passage recalls the opening lines, retained from both the 1811 and 1813 drafts, in which Schelling tells us with a deceptive simplicity that "The known is narrated, the discerned is presented, the intimated is prophesied." I say "deceptive" because we must take care not to confuse (past or future) *times* with *things*—with objects that can be put at a distance and dissected. Since Schelling himself never explicitly reaches beyond the past, what are we to make of his claim that the "past is known … the known is narrated"? This cannot imply that there is nothing left unknown or unexpressed. We, at least, have no such privileged relationship with the past. Perhaps it is better to think of this knowing not as a structure that is external or applied to the past, but one that is instead constitutive of it.

In disclosing the great (de-)cision [(*Ent-)scheidung*] of the *Weltalter*, the crisis through which God takes up His nature (the drives) by separating the Absolute Past from the Absolute Present of creation, Schelling again focuses on an abyssal site of transition: from succession to simultaneity and back again.[43] The chaotic, annular pulsation of negating, and affirming drives, though not yet actualized, or brought to presence, is described as a *succession*. Before the beginning, each drive, and that which unites them—which is to say the expressible (being and what-is) and the expressing—excludes the others in its singular craving for being.[44] It is only in the contraction of being that this unruly succession is realized in the simultaneity of the beginning. Thus simultaneity returns to succession (past, present, future) in the

Absolute Present, and the drives regain their lost unity through historical revelation:

> [T]he talk here is of the highest self of the Godhead, which can never
> become Being with respect to something else. This self can only have
> being and be active in each of its forms (if one is to permit this
> expression), as the Yes and as the No and as the unity of both. Given
> the decisive contradiction between the Yes and the No, this self is
> thinkable only because of the concept of different times. Hence, here
> it depends much more on the simultaneity among the different forms
> being sublimated and transformed into a succession.[45]

In other words, Schelling's insistence on distinct *times* does not imply a
disorder that *precedes* the beginning. Times, as we experience them, are
rather the return of the primordially repressed transition, an actualization
of what already actively belongs together in the Absolute Past. Schelling
also refers to this "transition" as a "perversion." Like Freud, he understands the primordiality of perversion; he will claim that existence itself
depends upon it. The interplay of negating, affirming, and unifying potencies contracts being—both in the sense of withdrawal and disease—
through a perverse act. A_1, the indeterminate subject that desires being,
becomes B: the impermeable object that will no longer submit to A_2.[46] As
Edward Beach writes:

> Not just randomly unordered, the actualized first Potency transforms
> into a positive force for disorder, disruptive and tumultuous in the
> extreme. This new substrate, Schelling continues, would in effect be
> an "inversion" [*Umkehrung*]—or, more forcefully still, a "perver-
> sion" [*Verkehrung*]—of the first Potency as it was in its original state
> of rest. In its capacity as the material ground of a concrete, but dis-
> ordered and (in this sense) "blind" existence, this principle would
> ceaselessly work against all that is systematically ordered and
> rational in the world.[47]

In this manner, the harmonious unity of the potencies is inverted, marking
the "second beginning" in Schelling as an actualization of the purely
logical first potency as a "positive force for disorder." For now, I would
just note that perversion in some sense lies at the origin—that while the

radical move from A_1 to B remains logically inexplicable, its truth is ensured by the fact of creation. If this seems like a *deus ex machina*, we need to remember that the movement of perversion coincides with freedom for Schelling—that, as we have already seen in the *Freiheitsschrift*, freedom requires the originary possibility of evil, of the ground erupting out of its *proper* place.[48] The *thatness* [*Daß*] of being cannot be derived from the merely logical order of the potencies, but requires a force that is in fact positively opposed to such order and, consequently, repressed by the increasingly rational reality it both works against and makes possible.

What strikes me most in bringing Schelling together with Freud is the extent to which their projects rely on a past that does not—that *cannot*—come to presence, yet despite this existential uncertainty, remains at the center of their work. For Schelling, this insight penetrates the deepest logic of existence. So that beings can *be*, the positively irrational and chaotic past must ground rational, ordered existence. In Freud, this is much less an ontological claim than it is a therapeutic discovery: whether verbal or bodily, narration is inherently symptomatic—it is not a re-presentation of the past but a trace of its resistance. Such a past is never finished but remains eternally in transition, its traumatizing opacity a challenge to the familiar order of presence. Freud's unconscious, in its absorption in the past, suggests a great deal more than psychic determinism. It is evocative of Schelling's eternal beginning and the originary decision that represses the Absolute Past. If this self-limitation were to be made present, it could no longer act as the beginning, and presence itself would collapse. Similarly, the Absolute Past that is reconstructed in psychoanalysis is not some content or event. What *is* revealed, or glimpsed through repeated dissimulation, is a mode of being that remains utterly foreign to and yet harbored within presence. To posit a way of existing that is neither potential nor actual coming-to-expression—an existing that nevertheless defines who we are and what we will become—such is the strangeness of the true unconscious and the Absolute Past.

And so it is that before the beginning, before the oceanic feeling, Freud opens *Beyond the Pleasure Principle* with a discussion of constancy (the pleasure principle's urge for stasis) that is almost immediately overcome by trauma and anxiety.[49] Acting out the process he describes, tranquility is already disturbed from within. Freud goes on to interrupt his account of war neuroses and its nightmares, the first disruption in the text, with a discussion of the repetition in a child's play (his own grandson, i.e., Freud's own repetition).[50] The seamless functioning of the pleasure principle, which ultimately aims at the tensionless state of primary narcissism, is doubly disturbed—first by repetition (the inability to escape the past and the consequent attempt to *have no past*) and then, again, by repetition (the ability to attribute meaning to the past and thus to *make past*). It is within this strange [*unheimlich*] scene that the authenticity of the personal converges with the detachment of the theoretical: the convergence that forces psychoanalysis toward a *Weltanschauung* all its own.[51]

The psychoanalytic challenge to science depends on a singular method for translating the individual into the universal. Freud's interpretation of his grandson's game is particularly useful as an illustration, insofar as it brings into relief the therapeutic position of intimacy/objectivity. It is perhaps due to the difficulty of navigating this peculiar neutrality that Freud cannot see the fundamental structure of the game—an exploration, creation, and dissolution of boundaries: "[H]e very skillfully threw the spool, attached to the string, over the edge of his little curtained bed ... then, using the string, he pulled the spool out of the bed again."[52] More than an attempt at mastery, Ernst is engaged in a playful recognition of the intersection between vulnerability and control, self and other.

As Freud understands him, Ernst repeats the disappearance of his parents in order to cope with the traumatic experience of passive loss and separation; but it is also the case that in doing so, Ernst opens himself to the equally traumatic possibilities of responsibility and guilt. After all, his violent and sexual desires—now that they are becoming *his*—cannot be without consequence. It is from this latter perspective that we might interpret Ernst's preference for the first half of the game—"Fort"—which Freud the grandfather refuses to take seriously. Despite the fact that Ernst for the most part only plays "Fort" ["gone"], Freud still proclaims that he derives the greatest pleasure from its proper completion, "Da" ["here"].[53] This merely begs the question: Why would Ernst generally play "Fort" if he prefers the complete game—if the pleasure is in return? One way to approach an answer would be through the transformation of pleasure at work within the game itself: Ernst's absorption in the world (his union with his mother) is no longer merely pleasurable but also a source of anxiety (loss of self/fear of castration). At the same time, the pain of separation offers Ernst a new model of desire and satisfaction altogether.

While Freud seems to explain away his grandson's game in terms of a putative instinct for mastery, he too remains unsure about its finality. Freud thus shows a sensitivity to the problem of "inheritance"—to the viability of analytic metapsychology—in immediately going on to question the most fundamental axiom of psychoanalysis as science:

> But if a compulsion to repeat *does* operate in the mind, we should be glad to know something about it, to learn what function it corresponds to, under what conditions it can emerge and what its relation is to the pleasure principle—to which, after all, we have hitherto ascribed dominance over the course of the processes of excitation in mental life.[54]

A beginning that operates beyond and independently of the physiology of pleasure suggests that psychoanalysis is no longer beholden to determinism. The repetition of the drives, whether paralyzing, or productive, is now *primary*.

Freud develops his final theory of drives, the inseparability and opposition of Eros and Thanatos, in response to the threat this original repetition poses to the scientific *Weltanschauung*. Like Ernst, Freud is caught up in the dual anxiety—the two beginnings—of union and differentiation. While it has generally been assumed that it is the death drive that first makes its appearance here, it is really Eros that marks a decisive shift in Freud's thought.[55] Or more specifically, the essential insight of the text concerns the relation that holds Eros and Thanatos—conflict and tranquility, union and dissolution—together. Freud opens up the realm beyond opposition; first and foremost, beyond the opposition of pleasure and pain. The primacy of the transitional, evidenced in the *Nachträglichkeit* origin of subject and pleasure alike, disrupts the deathly mechanism of constancy and establishes the temporality of psychoanalysis. Repetition, Freud suggests, is what makes drives *drives*—"all instincts [*Trieb*] tend towards the restoration of an earlier state of things."[56]

What precisely this is to mean, given the ambiguous sense of "repetition" which emerges in *Beyond the Pleasure Principle*, is to the point. This repetitive structure of the drive is neither an escape from the past nor an unqualified immersion in it. It delimits the space between the objective and the intimate, between a vanquished past, and a static present. Freud's pleasure principle failed to do justice to precisely this understanding of the drive.

In Chapter 6 of *Beyond the Pleasure Principle*, Freud ponders at length the emergence of life from the inanimate, depicting the death drive as a demand to return to the tensionless state of non-existence. Life entails increased tension and complication, and the aim of the drive is to be rid of tension. We settle into a restatement of the Nirvana principle and a re-justification of Freud's understanding of the instinctual need to decrease or eliminate tension. It is less obvious how Eros or the life drive aims at an "earlier state of things," or how it might be reconciled with the general aim of pleasure as a decrease in tension.[57] From his earliest texts, Freud argues that we have a tendency to retain attachments to our first sexual aims and satisfactions. In expanding Eros beyond the sexual to a class of drives toward greater and more complex unities—and in further breaking down and distributing the sexual drives between Eros and the death drive—the connection between pleasure and repetition-qua-stasis is weakened. Indeed, if Eros is not merely a mutation of the death drive, and thus truly opposed to it, pleasure in tension must be equiprimordial with pleasure in the reduction or absence of tension. This double aspect of pleasure also shows up in Freud's efforts to distinguish the reality principle from the pleasure principle. In exploring the origin of limits, Freud runs up against the liminality of origins:

> The attributes of life were at some time evoked in inanimate matter *by the action of a force of whose nature we can form no conception. It may perhaps have been a process similar in type to that which later caused the development of consciousness in a particular stratum of living matter.* The tension which then arose in what had hitherto been an inanimate substance endeavored to cancel itself out. In this way the first instinct [*Trieb*] came into being: the instinct to return to the inanimate state.[58]

The drive, we might say, is not inherently responsive but—as a longing (differentiation) to be what it is not (undifferentiated)—self-productive. Without yet delving into the complications of Eros, Freud suggests that drives are by nature split: both tension, and the desire to be rid of tension.

The death drive, which Freud here refers to as the "first," is more obviously self-negating. While its existence *is* a disruption, it is only through the drive that release becomes an aim—a satisfaction lost and a source to return to. In more human terms, as Schelling argues in "On the Nature of

Philosophy as Science," the longing to restore the past is precisely what separates us from it: "Here, then, emerges the contradiction of man destroying what he wants *by* wanting it. From this contradiction arises that drifting movement, because that which the searcher searches for escapes him, so to speak, in constant flight."[59] This self-defeating longing—this "drifting movement" between the searcher and what is sought—defines Eros and Thanatos insofar as they are drives. And it is this beginning-in-transition that Freud's final theory of the drives hits upon, but cannot resolve: the essential mutability and mutual formation of the drives (as emphasized in *Three Essays on Sexuality*), seemingly forgotten amidst the theoretical dyads and triads of his metapsychology, returns in repetition.[60]

The central contradiction of Freud's metapsychology is thus made explicit in *Beyond the Pleasure Principle*. Ultimately, Freud will equate Thanatos and Eros with unbinding and binding, respectively.[61] The work of Eros is to prepare the way for restoration, return, and satisfaction. It is only because psychic energy is bound—brought to unity—that an organism is able to unbind or release it. Freud makes the case that erotic *repetition* is essentially *conservation;* although Eros seems to be a force of differentiation and development, at its most fundamental level it is the retroactive gathering that grounds identity.[62] Freud's juxtaposition of the useless nightmares of war neuroses and the all-too-serious play of Fort/Da implies that to repeat is to prepare, however inconceivably, for our past.

The subtle shift here between conservation and pathological repetition echoes the move from the First will to the Second in Schelling: what begins as a restful, proto-satisfaction turns into an active desire to be what it already is—to *preserve*, though not yet to desirously *repeat*. It is as if the longing to maintain its current state necessitates a doubling—an unconscious splitting that is the opening up of desire. What Freud senses in *Beyond the Pleasure Principle* is that the beginning cannot be reduced to either opposition or identity. Through Eros, Freud is forced to move not only beyond the pleasure principle, but also beyond his own fantasies of dualistic/monistic paradigms. He is better able to express the insufficiency of such views by the time of *Civilization and Its Discontents* where, once again, it is the connection between pleasure and time that is at issue:

> *It is in sadism, where the death instinct twists the erotic aim in its own sense and yet at the same time fully satisfies the erotic urge, that we*

succeed in gaining the clearest insight into its nature and its relation to Eros. But even where it emerges without any sexual purpose, in the blindest fury of destructiveness, we cannot fail to recognize that the satisfaction of the instinct is accompanied by an extraordinarily high degree of narcissistic enjoyment, owing to its presenting the ego with a fulfillment of the latter's old wishes for omnipotence.[63]

The bond that holds Eros and Thanatos together *as* drives—neither identical nor opposed—hinges on Freud's eventual acceptance of primary masochism: a primal transitionality where pain coincides with pleasure, object with subject, repetition with temporalization.

Primal fantasy

In "On Narcissism," Freud traces the development of a more stable boundary between ego and world. He proposes that this relatively undifferentiated state is repeated or returned to in what he terms secondary narcissism. My hope here is to unpack his account of just what narcissism is; how it relates to auto-erotism as a mode of subject/object unity; and how, if at all, the fantasy that is characteristic of the narcissistic level of psychic integration parallels the freedom and auto-production of Schelling's imagining, self-reflective Absolute considered in the previous chapter.

Starting out with a discussion of the schizophrenic turning away from the world, Freud continues with an explanation of narcissism and its derivative status:

> The libido that has been withdrawn from the external world has been directed to the ego and thus gives rise to an attitude which may be called narcissism. But the megalomania itself is no new creation; on the contrary, it is, as we know, a magnification and plainer manifestation of a condition which had already existed previously. This leads us to look upon the narcissism which arises through the drawing in of object-cathexes as a secondary one, superimposed upon a primary narcissism that is obscured by a number of different influences ... This extension of the libido theory—in my opinion a legitimate one—receives reinforcement from a third quarter, namely, from our observations of the mental life of children and primitive peoples.

In the latter we find characteristics which, if they occurred singly, might be put down to megalomania: an overestimation of the power of their wishes and mental acts, the "omnipotence of thoughts," a belief in the thaumaturgic force of words, and a technique for dealing with the external world—"*magic*"—which appears to be a logical application of these grandiose premises.[64]

Freud posits primary narcissism and connects it to the "primitive" belief in the "omnipotence of thought," a term familiar to us from "The Uncanny." The pathological narcissism occurring in adults is a repetition of a more primal experience in which the limit between ego and world is first being worked out, a repetition that nonetheless complicates that undifferentiated "oceanic feeling."

Freud's claim that the boundary between ego and reality is an accomplishment, a development generated from the permutations of pleasure and satisfaction, is first made explicit in *Three Essays on the Theory of Sexuality*. In this text Freud claims sexual drives and fantasy are *the* distinguishing characteristics of human subjectivity. Freud shows that adult sexuality (both normal and neurotic) has its roots in the polymorphous perversions of infantile life rather than in any physiological instinct developing during puberty; he further claims that it is infantile sexuality, and its inevitable repression, that determine the varieties of adult sexuality and pathologies. These observations lead Freud to ask the question that will define his life's work: How is it that the limit between ego and world—*reality*—develops out of infantile sexual life? Part of my claim here is that such development depends, paradoxically, on a repeated return to and reclaiming/reintegrating of earlier states in the process of creating just such a limit.

Whether limitation reveals itself as our own activity in the anxiety-provoking uncanny, or in the therapeutic scene of transference, the regression that propels psychic development can be traced to auto-erotism—to the site where subject and object converge in fantasy:

... [W]e are bound to suppose that unity comparable to the ego cannot exist in the individual from the start; the ego has to be developed. The auto-erotic instincts [*Trieb*], however, are there from the very first; so there must be something added to auto-erotism—a new psychical action—in order to bring about narcissism.[65]

A more nuanced account of narcissism can help explain Schelling's self-desiring, self-generating Absolute in the *Weltalter*, but we first need to consider what it means that these auto-erotic drives are there "from the very first."[66] Laplanche's approach to this question in *Life and Death in Psychoanalysis* hinges on a close reading of *Three Essays* and, more specifically, on a more narrowly defined understanding of drive. Laplanche contends that the drives are perversions of the instincts—"propping" themselves upon vital needs; this reading in turn grounds Laplanche's claim that the translation of *Trieb* into *instinct* rather than *drive* in the *Standard Edition* is faulty. Indeed, Laplanche argues that much of the confusion surrounding the drive centers on Freud's failure to flesh out the consequences of his theory of "propping":

> Our study of thumb-sucking or sensual sucking [taken as a model of oral sexuality] has already given us three essential characteristics of an infantile sexual manifestation. At its origin it *attaches itself to* [or *props itself upon; ensteht en Anlehnung an*] one of the vital somatic functions; it has as yet no sexual object, and is thus *auto-erotic*; and its sexual aim is dominated by an *erotogenic zone*.[67]

The essence of the drive is its dependence upon and subsequent separation from the vital instinct. We might also say, though this will require some working out, that the perversion of the drives is "beyond" the pleasure principle: insofar as desire is no longer connected to need, fantasy is already a perversion of the mechanics of pleasure.

What remains unclear is the kind of proto-object (and proto-subject) that belongs to auto-erotic drives. Laplanche gives us the following explanation, in response to Freud's proposal in the just-cited work that "the finding of an object is in fact the re-finding of it":

> The text cited has an entirely different ring to it from that vast fable of autoerotism as a state of the primary and total absence of an object: a state which one leaves in order to *find* an object; autoerotism is, on the contrary, the stage of the loss of the object ... But above all, if such a text is to be taken seriously, it means that *on the one hand there is from the beginning an object, but that on the other hand sexuality does not, from the beginning, have a real object*. It should be understood that the real object, milk, was the object of the

function, which is virtually preordained to the world of satisfaction. Such is the real object which has been lost, but the object linked to the autoerotic turn, the breast—become a fantasmatic breast—is, for its part, the object of the sexual drive ... From this, of course, arises the impossibility of ultimately ever rediscovering the object, since the object which has been lost *is not the same* as that which is to be rediscovered. Therein lies the key to the essential "duplicity" situated at the very beginning of the sexual quest.[68]

We are again faced with the beginning that is not the beginning. The first object of the instinct, on which the fantasized object of the drive models itself, is not an object in the proper sense. As Laplanche says, the initial "real" object is "the object *of* the function," which is precisely to say that it is not an object *for* any subjectivity. Subject/object opposition is not a creation at all, but a *re*-creation: in the displacement that occurs between the needed "milk" and the fantasied "breast," Laplanche reminds us that a certain kind of linguistic magic—a productive symbolism—must already be in play before a unified subject can arise. He maintains that the beginning *is* loss (of undifferentiated unity) and also the fantasy of its restoration (wish-fulfillment). For Laplanche, auto-erotism is the Freudian term for this grounding duplicity—a *proton pseudos*—from which the subject and objects for it emerge.

The psychoanalytic obsession with the past reflects and distorts this more fundamental relationship to the Absolute Past, and to the beginning that destabilizes all opposition:

> Because this essence holds time enveloped, it serves as a link that enables man to make an immediate connection with the most ancient past as well as with the most distant future. Man often sees himself transported into such wonderful relations and inner connections through precisely this innermost essence, such as when he encounters a moment in the present as one long past, or a distant event as if he himself were witness to it.[69]

The very assumption of a compulsion to repeat, where an origin to be repeated is taken for granted, belies the alterity of such a past. It is this relationship— the creative gesture that is no longer tranquility and not yet opposition—that Schelling struggles to speak to in his *Weltalter*. He marks the beginning as an unconscious longing between the First and the Second, between the resting will and the tranquil, self-seeking will:

> The eternal will alone provides the initial point that starts up the great process of the whole. It posits itself as the mere *willing* of eternity, and to that extent as negated. But in positing itself as negated, it is at the same time the self-negated will. Yet it cannot negate itself by positing itself as not being at all; rather, it can only posit itself as not being the *essence*, or what affirms, or what— (genuinely and by nature) is. Moreover, the will cannot negate itself as being the essence without positing itself as lack and—to the extent that it is also active—as hunger, as yearning, as desire for essence. Returning into itself, it necessarily finds itself to be empty and in need but is for that reason all the more eager to fill itself, to satiate itself with essence. But it finds essence neither inside itself nor outside itself; for it does not recognize eternity, and by returning into itself it is turned much more away from eternity than toward it. Thus, nothing is left but for the will to posit essence or affirmation absolutely outside of itself through an unconditioned and totally generative force.[70]

From this dense passage, I would like for the moment merely to pull out two ideas: the will posits itself as "desire for essence," and the will posits essence as "absolutely outside of itself through an unconditioned and totally generative force." In other words, the seeking subject, and the object it seeks are aspects of the *same will*—as if viewed from the inside and outside, respectively. Through what Schelling elsewhere calls a "dark presentiment and longing," the will is driven out of its complacency by way of searching for and creating its own limits— producing selfhood from otherness and otherness from selfhood. The "dark presentiment" that urges the will out of itself is of course no event within time or consciousness—but then how are we to approach this longing, which is simultaneously world-constructing, and self-revealing?

The problem of beginning is not merely pushed back to the inexplicable awakening of unconscious discomfort. Although we cannot yet speak of a "before," in order for there to be a beginning there must be an unconscious inscription of desire. The satisfied will *longs*—but what could it long for if not for satisfaction? And what could provide satisfaction when there is as yet no Other? This would be a self-defeating desire indeed. But what if *satisfaction* were not the inchoate aim of this dark presentiment, what if *longing* erupted as an end (and as a beginning) in itself? What if the opposition between being and what-is did not come from frustrated desire but from the primordial play of fantasy? In "On the Nature of Philosophy as Science" Schelling makes an important distinction between desire *for* and desire *as such*:

> The concepts of ability and will are united in the word "to desire..." Eternal freedom is eternal desire, not the desire for something but desire in itself or, as it can also be expressed, eternal magic. I am using this expression because it expresses my concept; true, it is a strange word, but when we use it for ourselves it is in our possession again. Saying eternal ability or eternal magic is one and the same. This expression, however, suggests itself because it expresses the capacity both to adopt any form and not remain in any given one ... The *original* magic contains more than mere knowledge, that is, objective production.[71]

Freud's primal fantasy—and its reappearance in dreams and symptoms—is nothing other than the (hallucinatory) production of its object: a wish that provides its own satisfaction.[72] Desire extends beyond its common usage in connection with an object to its *original* form as a ceaseless productivity of *its own object*—of itself as well as its Other. Schelling goes on to claim:

> That which is the absolute beginning cannot know itself. In its transition to knowledge it ceases to be the beginning and it therefore has to proceed until it rediscovers itself as the beginning. The beginning, restored as a beginning that knows itself, is the end of all knowledge.[73]

The task, for Schelling and for Freud, is to explain the movement from primal fantasy—a fantasy that "cannot know itself" because there is as yet no subject distinct from its object—to self-knowledge and freedom. In Schelling's words, the task is to discover how to "break through to the bliss of ignorance again (which at this point is a knowing ignorance)."[74]

Primary masochism

We have seen that beginnings in general, and the drives in particular, are essentially duplicitous. The repetition proper to the life and death drives is a perversion and dislocation of *instinctual* or *mechanical* repetition. And while Freud sees that there is something disturbing in the kind of repetition that Eros demands, he fails to recognize that Thanatos—*as drive*—must disturb us in the same manner. Perhaps here one might note that both primary masochism, and the aggression which is the fruit of the death drive in *Civilization and Its Discontents*, are worlds away from the Nirvana principle: destruction is no mere return home. In "The Economic Problem of Masochism" Freud suggests that primary masochism is the site where Eros and Thanatos "coalesce":

> If one is prepared to overlook a little inexactitude, it may be said that the death instinct which is operative in the organism—primal sadism—is identical with masochism. After the main portion of it has been transposed outwards on to objects, there remains inside, as a residuum of it, the erotogenic masochism proper, which on the one hand has become a component of the libido and, on the other, still has the self as its object. This masochism would thus be evidence of, and a remainder from, the phase of development in which the coalescence, which is so important for life, between the death instinct and Eros took place.[75]

Life, as Freud suggests, requires *difference*—but this difference is not mere antagonism. The interpenetration of Eros and Thanatos depends upon their grounding in something that is common to, but distinct from, both. In order to show that primary masochism can serve such a function for psychoanalysis, we would do well to return briefly to where Freud initially deals with sadism and masochism in Part 1 of *Three Essays*: "Sexual Aberrations." It is part of Freud's larger aim in this work to show that heterosexual intercourse aimed at procreation is an achievement, not the result of an instinct [*Instinkt*]: what we take to be perversions of the sexual instinct are in fact evidence that human sexuality is itself *perverse*—which is to say, *driven* rather than *instinctual*. By beginning with the aberrations, Freud forces us to see that perversion is originary. Any stable opposition between ego and world derives from, and remains dependent upon, the disruptive, the chaotic, and the perverse.

Freud writes that sadism/masochism is "the most common and the most significant of all the perversions—the desire to inflict pain upon the sexual object, and its reverse." His reasons for giving such weight to sadism and masochism are twofold: First, "sadism and masochism occupy a special position among the perversions, since the contrast between activity and passivity which lies behind them is among the universal characteristics of sexual life"; second, "the most remarkable feature of this perversion is that its active and passive forms are habitually found to occur in the same individual."[76] It is not just that sadism and masochism embody activity and passivity, two primitive drive fates, but also that activity and passivity are so often entangled there.[77] The union of pleasure and pain in masochism reflects Freud's emphasis on the sexual as the site of ambivalence and the source of subjectivity. According to Laplanche, Freud's fascination with sadism-masochism is a consequence of its connection with the *fantasy* that distinguishes drive from instinct:

> Finally, we have situated, in the position of what we called reflexive masochism, or the middle voice, a fantasy which, however, has a properly masochistic content in the "passive" sense: I am being beaten by my father. But that is because, as we have emphasized, the process of turning round is not to be thought of only at the level of the content of the fantasy, but *in the very movement of fantasmatization*. To shift to the reflexive is not only or even necessarily to give a reflexive content to the "sentence" of the fantasy; it is also and above all to reflect the action, internalize it, make it enter into oneself as fantasy. To fantasize aggression is to turn it round upon oneself, to aggress oneself: such is the moment of autoerotism, in which the indissoluble bond between fantasy as such, sexuality, and the unconscious is confirmed.[78]

In effect, Laplanche rejects the *originality* of primary narcissism and the viability of a completely undifferentiated state, and offers *trauma* and perversion instead. There is no "before" the intrusion of adult sexuality, nothing that precedes relating to the Other, because primary masochism is the traumatic beginning of time and memory. The primal fantasy, the movement from instinct to drive, essentially turns round upon oneself the inscrutability of sexuality. Because adult fantasy—the unconscious of the Other—is *already there, already addressing*, the subject emerges in frustrated, fantasied attempts to receive and make sense of this address. The priority of masochism is a function of its disturbing location *between* the structured drives of a more coherent subjectivity that addresses/ aggresses on the one hand, and the instinctual incoherence, or disorgani- zation of infantile life on the other. Put differently, the simultaneous emergence of fantasy and drive is a response to the intrusion and inscrip- tion of something *other* than instinct.

Auto-erotism, and its traumatic origin in and as primary masochism, takes the place of Freud's underdeveloped, theoretical construct of primary narcissism. In Laplanche, this undifferentiated state is compli- cated by the "vital differences" of the Other that is always already there. The "propping" of the drive upon vital instincts, the gap that appears between them, is the emergence of a pleasure that resonates with the desires and fantasies of the Other but cannot yet be perceived as such. Perversion is a movement away from that negative or pleasure-less pleasure that merely satisfies an instinct—the release or absence of tension. Perverse pleasure is detached from such a mechanistic paradigm, to the extent that it can even account for pleasure *in* pain, in the excessive tension of suffering and desire, and in the differentiation of Eros. Primary masochism is not only a way for Freud to "prove" the death drive, or to distinguish drive from instinct, but also a vehicle for temporality and sub- jectivity to become fundamental issues for psychoanalysis. The imagined tranquility of primal narcissism is not upset by something other than itself, but rather by the propping or slippage from the pleasure of non- existence (instinctual life) to the pleasure of longing (the life of the drives). It would seem that there is something about this self-enclosed pleasure—pleasure that is initially satisfaction *belonging to no subject*— that already seeks subjectivity. In fantasy, pleasure attracts/contracts sub- jectivity and otherness.

Pleasure *as* preservation becomes pleasure *as* repetition, as we have already seen in "Fort/Da," where little Ernst's sense of the unity of self and world is threatened by the perversion of desire. In order to preserve this felt unity, Ernst puts himself in the place of another who, as he is in the process of discovering, is not merely an extension of himself. He repeats the process of separation and integration, of boundary-making, that initially traumatized him from without.[79] For Laplanche, of course, such play is pos- sible only through the intrusion of adult sexuality—through the suggestion of another form of pleasure. But even for Laplanche, this is not an intrusion that occurs in time, but one that is already a condition for temporal existence. Human beings do not simply arrive: we are born. It seems at least viable, then, to approach Schelling's account of the movement from the resting will to the self-seeking will—with unconscious longing as the Mother of the latter and born of the former—in terms of such transformations of pleasure. Although Laplanche suggests that the *other* pleasure of drive and sexuality is proper only to human being, dependent upon the adult unconscious that impinges upon us, we might instead consider existence itself to be generated by—*birthed* by—the internal dynamics of pleasure. When Freud pushes against the limits of psychoanalysis, as he does in *Beyond the Pleasure Principle*, he moves toward biology, myth, and philosophy. With great reticence, he suggests that the beginnings of human being inherently lead us toward the origins of being as such.

Freud recognizes that the primacy of repetition/preservation he argues for would threaten conscious temporality. He quite explicitly ties together pleasure/unpleasure and temporality, albeit without claiming any final solution. Conscious time is put forward as a form of *defense* against traumatic, unconscious time—"this mode of functioning [the self-perception of the system *Pcpt.-Cs.*] may perhaps constitute another way of providing a shield against stimuli ... but I must limit myself to these hints."[80] Freud is quite clear that *external* traumas are "any excitations from outside which are powerful enough to break through the protective shield."[81] But if conscious time is a defense against the unconscious—and thus the drives—how do we understand *this* trauma? Schelling's project in the *Weltalter* can be of use here: in this text, the perversion that precipitates the differentiation of times is also the origin of the internal and the external, subject and object. Internal trauma, the trauma *of* the drives, simultaneously creates and is created by a more primordial, unbearable excess. Such an originary trauma, where there are as yet no boundaries to be overwhelmed, forces Freud closer to Schelling's ontological account of pleasure/pain:

> We have decided to relate pleasure and unpleasure to the quantity of excitation that is present in the mind but is not in any way "bound"; and to relate them in such a manner that unpleasure corresponds to an *increase* in the quantity of excitation and pleasure to a *dimunition* ... the factor that determines the feeling is probably the amount of increase

or dimunition in the quantity of excitation *in a given period of time* …
it is not advisable for us analysts to go into the problem further so long
as our way is not pointed by quite definite observations.

(*BPP*, p. 4)[82]

In both passages where Freud brings up the problem of time in relation to
pleasure, he pointedly refuses to go *beyond*. Freud's unwillingness to
engage with the kind of temporality that psychoanalysis opens up,
however, belies his contributions in the form of his theory of *Nachträglichkeit*. Although in the "speculative" *Beyond the Pleasure Principle*
Freud circles around the tangled relationship between trauma, repetition,
and time, the practice of psychoanalysis quite clearly depends upon a
temporality that defies consciousness. After all, the founding discovery
of psychoanalysis may well boil down to the joint claims that "hysterics
suffer mainly from reminiscences," and that in the unconscious reality
and fantasy are indistinguishable. The ways in which the past disrupts
our present, and the present redefines, and recreates the past, already
invokes a troubling, and profound attack on any notion of linear time or
the stasis of history.[83]

Notes

1 Edward Allen Beach, *The Potencies of God(s): Schelling's Philosophy of
Mythology* (Albany: State University of New York Press, 1994).

> Schellingian dialectic, by contrast [with Hegel's *Aufhebung*], seeks to
> infuse the process of reasoning with a strong volitional component, so
> as to be capable of recovering the willing that allegedly precedes
> rational thought itself. Proceeding from this perspective in structured
> stages [the potencies], the thinker must then elucidate how this willing
> guides the development of determinate being. The emphasis on volition
> is directly coupled with a call for experience; for willing and experi-
> encing alone can *produce* a truth that goes beyond the abstract demon-
> strations of logic.
>
> (p. 85)

Beach goes on,

> Schelling's treatment of dialectic obtains its successive forms not as
> though implicitly contained in the foregoing ones, but rather as produced
> or reproduced (*erzeugt*) by a kind of procreative causality which is sup-
> posed to reenact the processes by which the outer universe itself has

evolved. The proper aim of philosophy is to find a path of conative (re)production (*Erzeugung*) by which the universal forms of volition sequentially emerge in poses of mutual reinforcement or conflict. Furthermore, inasmuch as this "reenactment" depends upon causal influences as well as logical inferences, any conclusions that it yields must remain incomplete until they can be exemplified in direct historical experience.

(p. 85)

2 Ibid. p. 85.

3 In *Time Driven: Metapsychology and the Splitting of the Drive*, Adrian Johnston's arguments concerning the two versions of cause/temporality in Freud are indebted to Cutrofello's work and, at times, converge with my own claims:

In identifying *Trieb* as the place of intersection for Freud's two temporal models, these models no longer need to be thought of as mutually exclusive. In fact, the hypothesis of *Trieb* as split between two temporal organizations avoids favoring one portrayal of the drive at the expense of the others—for example, stressing the conservative, "deathly" side of the drive to the detriment of the drive's potential for constant modification. The problem is that Freud himself, in part due to his neglect of the role of time in psychoanalysis, doesn't attempt any sort of reconciliation between his two unharmonized schemas.

(p. 22)

Using Lacan, Johnston connects the Kantian "transcendental" with the Freudian unconscious, and particularly with certain aspects of the drives themselves—suggesting that drives are split into mutable (aim/object) and eternal (source/pressure) components. His overarching concern in this text is with what it might mean for the unconscious to be "timeless"—why it is that Freud tends to shy away from a psychoanalytic account of temporality and how the drives are central to this project. I will be in conversation with Johnston's work at various points throughout the chapter.

4 Bruce Matthews. *Schelling's Organic Form of Philosophy* (SUNY, 2011), p. 146; my italics.

5 In Chapter 2, I have already suggested the ways in which the Kantian sublime is transformed in Schelling; it should be clear that the latter's insistence on the renegotiation of the boundaries between subject and object, self and other, in the sublime are also relevant in terms of the reciprocity belonging to organism.

6 F. W. J. Schelling, *Ideas for a Philosophy of Nature*, trans., Errol E. Harris and Peter Heath (Cambridge: Cambridge University Press, 1988). p. 30. *SW* Vol. II, pp. 1–344.

7 Joseph L. Esposito, *Schelling's Idealism and Philosophy of Nature* (Lewisburg: Bucknell University Press, 1977). Esposito writes: "Our very concept

of a *thing* cannot be separated from the notion of interaction and reciprocal determination ... A *thing* is actually a locus of activity, resulting from the interaction of several or all parts of the community" (p. 61).

8 *AW* 1813, p. 117; my italics.

9 F. W. J Schelling, *First Outline of a System of the Philosophy of Nature*, Trans., Keith R. Peterson (Albany: State University of New York Press, 2004).

> Evidently every (finite) product is only a *seeming* product, *if again infinity lies in it*, i.e., if it is itself again capable of an infinite development. If it engages in this development, then it would have no permanent existence at all; every product that now appears *fixed* in Nature would exist only for a moment, gripped in continuous evolution, always changeable, appearing only to fade away again.
>
> (p. 18, cited in Esposito, p. 86)

10 *AW* 1813, p. 123.

11 In his *Ideas for a Philosophy of Nature* (1797), which is considered Schelling's first complete *Naturphilosophie* text, he is already making use of the language of conflict between *forces* to account for the apparent stability of products of nature and to illustrate the identity (and apparent distinction) between the Real and Ideal in terms of potencies. This language continues in the work that follows, *First Outline of a System of the Philosophy of Nature*. It is in fact not until his *System of Transcendental Idealism* (1800) that he first makes use of the term *Trieb* [drive] in reference to these generative forces of opposition (*SW* Vol. III, pp. 545–547).

12 *AW* 1813, p. 123.

13 Part of the reason I focus on Schelling's 1813 draft is due to his increasing minimization of spontaneity and his consequent return to the language of potencies in the 1815 draft. I find his movement away from the language of desire and drive to be indicative of his wanting to distance himself from the human that is so much at the heart of his *Freiheitsschrift*. That is, I find more compelling Schelling's willingness to make the philosophical essentially human, while remaining able to avoid an anthropomorphism of being and time. Furthermore, in the 1815 version Schelling emphasizes the *necessity* of decision, of the cision of the Absolute Past, whereas the 1813 draft focuses almost entirely on its *freedom*.

14 *AW*, 1815, pp. 12–13/*SW*, p. 220.

15   Therefore, two principles are already in what is necessary of God: the outpouring, outstretching, self-giving being, and an equivalently eternal force of self-hood, of retreat into itself, of Being in itself. That being and this force are both already God itself, without God's assistance.

                                                 (1815, p. 6/*SW*, p. 211)

16 *AW*, 1815, p. 13/*SW*, p. 221.

17 Ibid. p. 13/221.

18 Schelling makes it clear in the 1813 draft that the Absolute Past, Present, and Future refer to what comes before, during, and after creation, respectively. Immediately after suggesting that one must put the past behind him in order to have a present, "only the man with the strength to rise above himself is able to create a true past; he alone can savor a true present, just as he alone looks forward to a genuine future," Schelling posits that:

> the world has in itself no past and no future. [This would entail] that everything that has happened in it from the beginning and everything that will happen up to the end belongs to a single overarching time; that the authentic past, the past as such, is what came before the world [*vorweltliche*]; that the authentic future, the future as such, is what will come after the world [*nachweltliche*]. And so a system of times would unfold for us, of which the human system would be just a copy, a repetition within a narrower sphere.
>
> (1813, p. 121)

19 Sigmund Freud, *Beyond the Pleasure Principle*. Trans., Gregory C. Richter (Toronto: Broadview Press, 2011). *SE* XVIII, pp. 7–66.
20 *AW*, 1813, p. 122.
21 Ibid. p. 162.
22 See Sean McGrath's *Dark Ground of Spirit* for a discussion of Freud's nihilism/relativism, most notably pp. 179–190.
23 Unfortunately, Schelling's own language can often lead to this kind of reading. His suggestion, for instance, that we must put the past behind us to truly have a present implies that such an exclusion of the past is both possible and desirable. I think, however, that the spirit of Schelling's texts calls for another interpretation, one perhaps exemplified in the following:

> The beginning that a being has outside of itself and the beginning that a being has within itself are different. A beginning from which it can be alienated and from which it can distance itself is different than a beginning in which it eternally remains because it itself is the beginning.
>
> (1815, p. 17/*SW*, p. 226)

24 *AW*, 1813, p. 113.
25 Ibid. p. 114.
26 Ibid. p. 121.
27 Ibid. p. 115. See also "On the Nature of Philosophy as Science" in Bubner, Rüdiger, ed. *German Idealist Philosophy* (London: Penguin Books, 1997):

> There is a contradiction in the idea of knowing eternal freedom. It is absolute subject = primordial state. How, then, can it become object? It is impossible for it to become object *as* absolute subject, for, as such, it has no object-like relation to anything … Instead of absolute subject, it can also be called pure knowledge, and as such it cannot be that which is known.
>
> (p. 224)

28 *AW*, 1813, p. 132.

29 Ibid. p. 133.

30 David Farrell Krell, *The Tragic Absolute: German Idealism and the Languishing God* (Bloomington: Indiana University Press, 2005), p. 109.

31 *AW*, 1813, p. 135.

32 Krell writes in *The Tragic Absolute*, quite beautifully, and with great and original insight, of the movement from One to Two in Schelling—its relevance to his project as a whole:

> The tragic absolute is in multiple senses the stroke of one—the stroke *of* one *by* one. That stroke instigates critique, judgment, crisis, separation, severance and divorce; it also initiates the more languid moments of love and desire that we call *languor* and *languishment*. The stroke severs one not into two, that is not into two clearly definable units, but into a manifold that resists synthesis. The stroke of one severs "that loved clasp" of Una and Dua, severs all singular identities and all binary oppositions ... The stroke of one marks the end of all philosophies of eternity and the instauration of a new understanding of time and temporality. It sounds a knell, initiating a period of progressive paralysis and ultimate decrepitude for all absolutes; yet it also rings the bell, at least to Schelling's ear, at the birth of a finite human freedom.
>
> (p. 70)

This sense of the stroke both *of* and *by* one, a unity in self-division, is in part what leads me to consider Freud (and Laplanche) on primary masochism in connection with Schelling's *Die Weltalter* in this chapter. Indeed, I was inspired by Krell's work and, in a sense, consider my efforts in this dissertation (and specifically in this chapter) to be one way of heeding his call to:

> problematize (or at least leave open) the very meaning of "inheritance" and historical succession. One would thereby show greater respect for both psychoanalysis and Schelling, precisely by setting out in quest of the undiscovered source of primal repression. That source lies hidden in a time so remote that it appears—to both Schelling and Freud—as timeless.
>
> (p. 117)

33 *AW*, 1813, p. 137.

34 See Sean McGrath's *The Dark Ground of Spirit* for a reading that emphasizes this conception of the teleological interpretation, where darkness is made light, where the unconscious is translated into consciousness. See also: *FS*, pp. 399–407.

35 In *Imagining Otherwise: Metapsychology and the Analytic A Posteriori* Andrew Cutrofello brings together Kant, Freud, and Lacan, making the case that metapsychology brings out the possibility of the analytic a posteriori concealed within transcendental philosophy; in particular, he argues that

Lacan's *objet a*, and the Freudian conception of the subject's relation to his unconscious more generally, are instantiations of this elusive form of judgment. Making use of Kripke's claim that an analytic judgment is one that the subject will not give up under any circumstances, Cutrrtofello claims that the repressed desires of the hysteric, and the manifest beliefs of the psychotic, offer cases of judgments that are both analytic (necessary) and a priori (deriving from experience). I will return to these claims later in the chapter.

36 Freud's relevance to the trajectory of transcendental philosophy is noted and expounded upon by a great variety of philosophers, from all areas of the field. As Stanley Cavell writes in "Freud and Philosophy: A Fragment":

> In these paths of inheritance, Freud's distinction is to have broken through to a practice in which the Idealist philosophy, the reigning philosophy of German culture, becomes concrete (which is roughly what Marx said socialism was to accomplish). In Freud's practice, one human being represents to another all that that other has conceived of humanity in his or her life, and moves with that other toward an expression of the conditions which condition that utterly specific life. It is a vision and an achievement quite worthy of the most heroic attributes Freud assigned himself. But psychoanalysis has not surmounted the obscurities of the philosophical problematic of representation and reality it inherits. Until it stops shrinking from philosophy (from its own past), it will continue to shrink before the derivative question, for example, whether the stories of its patients are fantasy merely or (also?) reality; it will continue to waver between regarding the question as irrelevant to its work and as the essence of it.
>
> (*Critical Inquiry*, Winter 1987, 393)

37 *BPP*, p. 68./*SE* Vol. XVIII, p. 27.

38 *Civilization and Its Discontents* (1933), p. 11/*SE* Vol. XXI, pp. 64–65.

39 It is strange, to say the least, that in a text that claims to introduce the death drive, Freud should also concern himself with the possibility of immortality:

> But maybe this belief in the internal necessity of dying is only one of the illusions we have created for ourselves *um die Schwere des Daseins zu ertragen* [to bear the weight of existence] (Schiller, *Die Braut von Messina* [*The Bride of Messina*], I, 8) ... The greatest interest for us is connected with the treatment of the duration of life and the death of organisms in the works of August Weismann (Weismann 1882, 1884, 1892). It was he who proposed a distinction in living substance between mortal and immortal halves. The mortal half is the body in the narrower sense, the soma, which alone is subject to natural death. The gametes, by contrast, are potentially immortal: under certain favorable conditions they can develop into a new individual, or, in other words, surround themselves with a new soma (Weismann 1884).
>
> (*BPP*, pp. 82–83)

Freud's quick transitions from war neuroses to play, from biology to myth, are particularly astounding here: the convergence of immortality and finitude is also a point of contact between the delusions of religion and the axioms of science.

40 *Civilization and Its Discontents*, pp. 13–15; my italics/*SE* Vol. XXI, pp. 66–67.

41 Schelling writes in the *Weltalter*:

> Everything that surrounds us points back to a past of incredible grandeur. The oldest formations of the earth bear such a foreign aspect that we are hardly in a position to form a concept of their time of origin or the forces that were then at work ... In a series of time immemorial, each era has always obscured its predecessor, so that it hardly betrays any sign of its origin; an abundance of strata—the work of thousands of years—must be stripped away to come at last to the foundation, to the ground.
>
> (1813, p. 121)

42 *AW*, 1815, p. 76/*SW*, p. 302.

43
> Hence, the contradiction only breaks with eternity when it is in its highest intensity and, instead of a single eternity, posits a succession of eternities (eons) or times. But this succession of eternities is precisely what we, by and large, call time. Hence, eternity opens up into time in this decision.
>
> (1815, p. 76)

Schelling continues, comparing the free necessity of *human* decisiveness—a return to Kant's work in *Religion Within the Bounds of Reason Alone* and his own *Freiheitsschrift*—to this eternal beginning:

> We say that the person who doubts whether they should be utterly one thing or the other is without character. We say that a decisive person, in whom something definitely expressive of the entire being is revealed, has character. And yet it is recognized that no one has chosen the character following reasoning or reflection. One did not consult oneself. Likewise, everyone assesses this character as a work of freedom, as, so to speak, an eternal (incessant, constant) deed. Consequently, the universal ethical judgment discerns a freedom in each person that is in itself ground, in itself destiny and necessity. But most people are frightened precisely by this abyssal freedom in the same way that they are frightened by the necessity to be utterly one thing or another. And where they see a flash of freedom, they turn away from it as if from an utterly injurious flash of lightening and they feel prostrated by freedom as an appearance that comes from the ineffable, from eternal freedom, from where there is no ground whatsoever.
>
> (p. 78)

44 *AW* 1813, p. 145.

45 *AW*, 1815, p. 77.

46   This progressive generation can be represented as an increase. If one posits
        the affirming principle as such = A, and the negating principle as such = B,
        then the first active will is indeed in itself what-is, but it also negates itself
        as such. It is thus an A that acts as such = B; that is = (A = B). This is the
        beginning, and hence the first potency.

        (*AW* 1813, p. 144)

47 Beach (1994), p. 133.

48 Beach also obliquely points out the connection between the perversion of the
    first Potency and Schelling's radical account of evil in his *Freiheitsschrift*:

        Assuming that there is a God, therefore, B would be a principle funda-
        mentally opposed to the divine Providence. It would assume the aspect
        of "that-which-ought-not-to-be" (*das nicht-sein-Sollende*). In this capa-
        city, then, B would take on the role of the cosmic Antagonist, the dark
        Other which needs to be subdued ... Yet although B would in this way
        become the counterweight poised against the good, it would not for that
        reason be an absolute evil, but only a relative one. For without it, without
        a firm foundation for self-assertiveness that would be capable of resist-
        ing, at least for a time, the grand designs of the Deity, neither inde-
        pendent selfhood nor real freedom would be possible

        (pp. 133–134)

49 Schelling makes an almost identical claim in his introduction to *Die Weltalter*,
    writing:

        But movement never occurs for its own sake; all movement is only for
        the sake of rest ... all movement seeks only rest, and rest is its nourish-
        ment or that from which alone it takes its power and sustains itself.

        (1813, p. 133)

50 Though I will not pursue this here, Freud's *interpretation* of his grandson's
    game of *Fort/Da* is by no means irrelevant to this discussion. Indeed, Freud
    does not finally explain *how* it is that the frustrations the child experiences
    can be relieved by repeating them; Freud variously attributes this to a natural
    pleasure in imitation, to the compulsion to repeat and to the narcissistic
    pleasure of mastery/omnipotence. The relationship between *interpretation*
    and Eros, indeed of interpretation *as* Eros, will also be relevant to under-
    standing the possibility of pleasure in tension that periodically disturbs the
    text of *Beyond the Pleasure Principle*.

51 Stanley Cavell. "Freud and Philosophy: A Fragment." *Critical Inquiry*, Vol.
    13, No. 2, *The Trial(s) of Psychoanalysis* (Winter, 1987), pp. 386–393:

        This is the question enacted by the scenes of Freud the father and grand-
        father circling the Fort/Da game of repetition and domination, looking so

much like the inheritance of language itself, of selfhood itself. What is at stake is whether psychoanalysis is inheritable—you may say repeatable—as science is inheritable, our modern paradigm for the teachable. If psychoanalysis is not thus inheritable, it follows that it is not exactly (what we mean by) a science, then its intellectual achievement may be lost to humankind. But now if this expresses Freud's preoccupation in *Beyond the Pleasure Principle* and elsewhere, then this preoccupation links his work with philosophy, for it is in philosophy that the question of the loss of itself is internal to its faithfulness to itself.

(389)

52 *BPP*, p. 57/*SE* Vol. XVIII, p. 14.
53 See Section II of *BPP* for the description of the *Fort/Da* game.
54 *BPP*, p. 25/*SE* Vol. XVIII, p. 23.
55 In Peter Gay's seminal *Freud: A Life For Our Time*, it is clear from Freud's own correspondence and the mixed responses of the psychoanalytic circle that the death drive was considered the major innovation of *Beyond the Pleasure Principle*, with Eros rather just an expansion and reformulation of the sexual drives of his earlier works:

> This slim volume [*Beyond the Pleasure Principle*], and its two successors, demonstrated why he could not publish that much-announced, much-postponed book on metapsychology. He had complicated and modified his ideas too much. Not least of all, they had not had enough about death in them—or, more precisely, he had not integrated what they had to say about death into his theory.
>
> (394)

Gay also points out how the death drive—unlike Eros—divided psychoanalysts:

> As they debated Freud's new theory of instinctual dualism, psychoanalysts were assisted by the distinction Freud drew between the silent death drive, working to reduce living matter to an inorganic condition, and showy aggressiveness, which one encountered, and could daily substantiate, in clinical experience ... But for most analysts Freud's idea of a hidden primitive urge toward death, of a primary masochism, was something else again ... In distinguishing the death drive from sheer aggression, Freud enabled his followers to uncouple the two, reject his epic vision of Thanatos confronting Eros, and yet retain the concept of the two warring drives.
>
> (p. 402)

56 *BPP*, p. 44/*SE* Vol. XVIII, pp. 37–38.
57 Freud himself initially seems confused about whether Eros is a radical addition to psychoanalytic theory or a long-familiar concept—indeed, this may be the motivating question of the whole text: "As for the sex drives ... it is obvious that they reproduce primitive states of the organism, but the goal for

which they strive with all their means is a merging of two gametes differentiated in a specific manner" (*BPP*, pp. 81–82). However, Freud begins *Beyond
the Pleasure Principle* with the opposition between "ego" and "sex" drives,
only to complicate this paradigm by suggesting that the sex drives themselves can be further broken down between Eros and death drives. As we
will see, however, this opposition cannot fare much better—the relationship
between differentiation and dissolution cannot be simply oppositional or
dualistic.

58 *BPP*, p. 48/*SE* Vol. XVIII, p. 38.
59 *German Idealist Philosophy*, p. 233.
60 Freud's paper "Drives and their Fates," however, is a remarkable instance
within the metapsychological papers of paying heed to a possible primacy of
ambivalence—a reflective, or transitional, beginning. Though Freud does not
quite see this through, his attention to the intermediate phase is essential to
understanding the problems he faces in *Beyond the Pleasure Principle* and
his eventual acceptance of a primary masochism. Dealing with the fates of
the drives that are prior to and less sophisticated than repression or sublimation, reversal into its opposite and turning round upon the subject, Freud
approaches their peculiar union in sadism/masochism:

> With the pair of opposites sadism-masochism, the process may be repres-
> ented as follows:
>
> (a) Sadism consists in the exercise of violence or power upon some
>   other person as its object.
> (b) This object is abandoned and replaced by the subject's self.
>   Together with the turning round upon the self the change from
>   active to a passive aim in the instinct is also brought about.
> (c) Again another person is sought as object; this person, in con-
>   sequence of the alteration which has taken place in the aim of the
>   instinct, has to take over the original role of the subject.
>
> (*SE* 1915, p. 81)

Freud goes on to define (b) in the following terms: "The active voice is
changed, not into the passive, but into the reflexive middle voice" (p. 81). As
we will see in what follows, this stage (b) not only begins to take on a more
primary place in Freud's thinking, but already did so in his *Three Essays on the
Theory of Sexuality*, where auto-erotism is the initial phase of drive activity.

61 See: Section IV of *BPP*.
62 This sense of Eros as repetition and development resonates with Schelling's
claim in the *Outline* (already cited) that "[n]o subsistence of a product [of
Nature] is thinkable without a continual process of being reproduced."
63 *Civilization and Its Discontents*, pp. 80–81/*SE* Vol. XXI, p. 121. Freud's fear
of falling into a monistic account is in no small part a reaction against Jung's
theory:

Our views have from the very first been *dualistic*, and to-day they are even more definitely dualistic than before—now that we describe the opposition as being, not between ego-instincts and sexual instincts but between life instincts and death instincts. Jung's libido theory is on the contrary *monistic*.

(*BPP*, p. 64)

Of course, Freud's insistence belies his discomfort, writing in *Beyond the Pleasure Principle*:

Wherever the original sadism has undergone no mitigation or intermixture, we find the familiar ambivalence of love and hate in erotic life. If such an assumption as this is permissible, then we have met the demand that we should produce an example of a death instinct—though, it is true, a displaced one. But this way of looking at things is very far from being easy to grasp and creates a positively *mystical* impression.

(p. 65; my emphasis)

64 "On Narcissism," *SE* Vol. XIV, p. 75; my emphasis.
65 Ibid. p. 77.
66 Jean Laplanche, *Life and Death in Psychoanalysis*. Trans. Jeffrey Mehlman (Baltimore: Johns Hopkins University Press, 1970).
67 Cited in Laplanche, ibid. p. 15; his emphasis.
68 Ibid. pp. 19–20.
69 *AW*, 1813, p. 114.
70 Ibid. pp. 138–139.
71 *German Idealist Philosophy*, p. 222.
72 Sigmund Freud, *Three Essays on the Theory of Sexuality*. SE VII, pp. 136–243. See Part II, Infantile Sexuality, for Freud's first elaboration of auto-erotism and the object-less sexual drives of infantile life.
73 *German Idealist Philosophy*, p. 222.
74 Ibid. p. 222.
75 *SE* Vol. XIX, p. 164.
76 *Three Essays on Sexuality* (1905), p. 25.
77 As Freud also writes 10 years later in "Instincts and their Vicissitudes," (sometimes and better translated as "Drives and their Fates"),

it is not only the *object* of the drive that gets reversed in sadism-masochism, but also its *aim*. In other words, a transitional, auto-erotic space opens up between subject and object (I am both the one that inflicts pain and the one that receives it) and between pain and pleasure (I derive pleasure from the pain of the other and I am the other that experiences pain).

(*SE* XIV, p. 81)

78 Laplanche (1970), p. 102. Laplanche continues:

If we press the idea to its necessary conclusion, we are led to emphasize the privileged character of masochism in human sexuality. The analysis, in its very content, of an essential fantasy—the "primal scene"—would illustrate it as well: the child, impotent in his crib, is Ulysses tied to the mast or Tantalus, on whom is imposed the spectacle of parental intercourse ... the passive position of the child in relation to the adult is not simply a passivity in relation to adult activity, but passivity in relation to the adult fantasy intruding within him.

(Ibid.)

79   The child had a wooden spool with a piece of string tied around it. It never occurred to him to drag it along on the floor behind him and pretend it was a carriage, for example. Instead, he very skillfully threw the spool, attached to the string, over the edge of his little curtained bed so that it disappeared therein, all the while uttering his meaningful "o-o-o-o." Then, using the string, he pulled the spool out of the bed again and greeted its appearance with a joyful *da* [there]. So this was the whole game—disappearance and return—of which it was usually possible to see only the first act, tirelessly repeated as a game in its own right, though the greater pleasure was no doubt associated with the second act. The interpretation of the game was then clear. It was connected with the child's great cultural achievement: by renouncing his drives (renunciation of drive gratification) he allowed his mother to leave without protest. He compensated for this, so to speak, by enacting the same sort of disappearance and return of the objects in his reach.

(pp. 57–58/*SE* Vol. XVIII, p. 15)

80 *BPP*, p. 31/*SE* Vol. XVIII, p. 28.
81 Ibid. p. 33/*SE* Vol. XVIIII, p. 29.
82 Ibid. p. 4.
83 See: *Studies on Hysteria, SE* Vol. II, pp. 1–306 and *"Screen Memories," SE* Vol. III, pp. 303–322.

Chapter 4

The mythical symptom

More memories, mine, than from a thousand years.
—*Baudelaire, Spleen*

The approach to the Absolute Past we have considered in Schelling and Freud is *therapeutic*: in order to know such a past we must allow ourselves to be altered by it, to become intimate with the methods and depths of our own concealment. The therapeutic is here conceived as an active engagement with our own repressed beginnings that, remaining vulnerable to the reconstructions of the present, challenge our assumptions about the past as such. Therapeutic engagement would constitute a holding together of the past both as irretrievable origin, and as a continuous possibility for (re-)creation. The Absolute Past is thus not only the *object* of philosophical and psychoanalytic desire but also, in its eternal becoming, the very *form* of therapeutic desire—a desire that can sustain and stabilize itself in its own provisional nature.

I begin with a discussion of the role of primal repression in both Freud and Schelling in order to better understand the privileged place of mythology in their respective systems. Having offered an argument for the centrality of primal repression to their methods of interpretation, I look to *Historical-Critical Introduction to the Philosophy of Mythology*, where Schelling attempts to locate the origins of differentiation—and of meaning—within a primary and recurrent transitionality: to radicalize the notion of origin and, in turn, the therapeutic connection between its explanatory and transformative possibilities. Schelling's account of unconscious desire giving way to creation and history, which in turn shape unconscious desire, lends narration a *metaphysical* weight.

Schelling's insistence on our paradoxical intimacy with, and alienation from, the Absolute Past suggests that its truth must be both familiar and disorienting. In other words, we come to know the Absolute Past in, and as, the uncanny.

Unpacking Schelling's lectures will entail dealing with some fundamental questions about the relationship between trauma, language, and the emergence of a people. These questions fall out of Schelling's initial inquiry into the meaning of mythology—and, in particular, its relation to philosophy, and to poetry.[1] As an introduction to his positive philosophy, Schelling's lectures on mythology bring the conclusions and insights of the freedom essay and his *Weltalter* into contact with actual historical development and revelation. In line with the earlier texts' account of freedom, particularly its relationship to the unconscious, Schelling argues that mythology is neither a capricious invention nor a mechanical necessity. Indeed, he writes:

> Mythology would not in general be only a *natural* product, but rather an organic one; this is certainly a meaningful step in comparison to the merely mechanistic type of explanation. But it would also be an organic product in the following respect. Poetry and philosophy each for itself, is for us a principle of free, intentional invention, but because they are bound to one another neither, properly speaking, can freely be active; mythology would thus be a product of in themselves free activities, but here, however, of unfreely causally effective activities, just as the organic is a birth of freely necessary emergence; and to the extent that the word invention is still applicable, mythology is here a product of an unintentional-intentional, instinctive invention, which on the one hand would hold at a distance from itself everything merely fabricated and artificial, but on the other hand would at the same time allow that the deepest meaning and the soundest relations inherent in mythology be seen as not merely contingent.[2]

At first glance, this appears to be a recapitulation of Schelling's description of the conscious-unconscious production in his much earlier lectures on *The Philosophy of Art*. Here, however, the model of artistic creation is brought to bear on the *historical* differentiation of languages, world-views, and peoples. Schelling writes of Genesis:

Also, it is not at all a mere fabrication; on the contrary, this story is created from actual memory, which is in part also preserved by other peoples, a *reminiscence*—out of mythical time to be sure, but from a real event of the same.[3]

As we shall see, this will lead Schelling to view mythology as a response to and retroactive framing of a traumatic, originary cision or, "as *we* have called it, a crisis."[4]

Despite his professed distaste for metaphysics, Freud's account of the traumatic development of ego and reality out of a state of non-differentiation offers a parallel vision of this "beginning before the beginning"; for Freud, of course, the therapeutic bond between trauma, mythology, and language is the founding discovery of psychoanalysis. Narration neither corresponds to nor falsifies some historical event but, through its emphases and caesurae, gestures toward both personal and universal mythologies, as well as the bond that holds these together. Through the process of free association—the breaks of memory, slips of the tongue, and transferences that analyst and analysand take as their starting point—psychoanalysis focuses on the fractures that signal a forced coherence and an opening to (re)interpretation.[5] This does not suggest a failure to accurately remember past events, but rather redirects us to the way narrative can expose the *unrepresentable, unspeakable* Absolute Past.

While the place of mythology in psychoanalysis is not always entirely clear, it is certainly a quite prominent one. Far from merely a tool to aid in interpretation, or a text to be psychoanalyzed, mythology unites the unique experience of the individual with the broader realities of the culture and species he is born into. That is to say, part of what Freud discovers in therapeutic practice is that each of us creates a mythology—a language—that constitutes the specific pathology that we ourselves are. It is our capacity as unique myth-makers that undergirds Freud's refusal, in *Interpretation of Dreams* for example, to rely on any universal symbolism.[6] Of course, Freud is equally insistent on the inheritance of common desires and frustrations—most notably, the Oedipal Complex—that are in some sense universal. Thus, psychoanalysis might be described as the process by which an analyst becomes "fluent" in the mythological expressions of the analysand. At the same time, by bringing the analysand's symptom-language into a broader, communicable mythology, therapy can effectively provide relief. It is the task of this chapter to show that Schelling's insistence on (mythological) narrative as the philosophical approach to the Absolute Past can be re-framed around this Freudian therapeutic model, with a focus on the development of the latter as it is presented in *Interpretation of Dreams* and other texts that deal with the process of cure.

Primal repression

How do I separate from myself a world? This is both Freud's question about individual human beings, and Schelling's concerning the origin of peoples and the emergence of consciousness. I believe that in order to address either dimension of the issue, we need to look at just what it is that repression represses. Primal repression, like the primary masochism we encountered in the last chapter, seems to lead back to the inherently fantasized site of an identity that can never be settled and yet must be decided: to an abyssal freedom, an eternal beginning, that we need only engage with in order to feel for ourselves its traumatic effect on the conceptual order.

Freud first uses the term "primal repression" as a way of differentiating between an idea that is repressed on its own account, and the derivatives, or associated ideas that are repressed as a consequence of their connection to it. At the economic level, Freud argues that primal repression, as opposed to "actual repression," is maintained by the counterinvestment of the preconscious (*pcs*) system:

> What is required here, then, is another process, which in the first case maintains the repression and in the second is responsible both for establishing and continuing it. For this we need to postulate a counterinvestment, by means of which the pcs system protects itself against the pressure of the unconscious idea ... It is the counterinvestment that represents the ongoing expenditure in primal repression and which also guarantees the durability of the repression. In primal repression it is the sole mechanism, whereas in actual (follow-up) repression it is accompanied by the withdrawal of pcs investment. It may very well be that it is precisely this energy withdrawn from the idea that is used to create the counterinvestment.[7]

Freud seems merely to say that there is as yet no energy invested that could be revoked—that there must instead be an active warding off, energetically, on the part of the *pcs*. But this merely begs the question: Why is this increase in tension on the part of the *pcs* called for in the first place? Why, indeed, does Freud want to distinguish between primal and actual repression at all? Further along in the same essay, there is another account of the nature of and need for primal repression:

> If human beings do inherit psychic formations, something analogous to animal instincts, then these are what form the core of the ucs. Everything that is discarded over the course of infantile development—material not necessarily different in nature from that which is inherited—is then subsequently added to this core.[8]

The "core of the ucs" is inherited in the form of something akin to animal instincts. Once the psychic structure is sufficiently organized and capable of repression, one would assume that ideas bearing some resemblance to this "core" would be the best candidates. Strangely, Freud says only that the subsequently "discarded" (not "repressed") material is "not necessarily different in nature from that which is inherited." Wouldn't he want to say something much stronger—that this discarded material is likely similar in nature to what is inherited? Instead, he seems to go in the opposite direction. Why does Freud do this?

Here, it is not so much an economic account of primal repression as it is a developmental one. Freud sees repression as a defense against the overwhelming force of the drives, but by no means as the first or most basic of such mechanisms. In "Repression," he argues that:

> [R]epression is not one of the original defense mechanisms, that it cannot occur until a sharp division has been established between conscious and unconscious psychic activity ... prior to this stage of psychic organization, the task of defense against drive impulses was dealt with by the other drive fates, such as reversal into the opposite and turning back on the self.[9]

It is at this point that Freud introduces primal repression, having just explained that repression itself is precisely not primal. Repression, he tells us, develops from more primitive mechanisms of "reversal into the opposite" and "turning back on the self." Indeed, Freud suggests that in one and the same moment—sadism-masochism—both of these mechanisms appear simultaneously: "These two drive fates—turning back on the self and reversal of activity into passivity—are dependent on the narcissistic organization of the ego and bear the imprint of this phase."[10] These earlier methods of coping with the demands of the drives "bear the imprint" of a time before any stable boundary between ucs/pcs or ego/world has been developed; they are the primary modes of working out and constructing such a limit to defend against, or indeed even recognize, the intolerable force of the drives.

The real need for primal repression, it seems, should come here: Freud has to differentiate between the boundary-making and dissolving process through which the unconscious develops on the one hand, and the defense mechanism that depends upon there already being such a boundary on the other. Primal repression would represent the making unconscious of those originary moments where the boundary between ego/world has not yet stabilized. In support of this claim, I turn briefly to Julia Kristeva's discussion of the abject as an objectification (an *abject*ification) of the transitional as such, which she too relates to primal repression and the sublime:

> If, on account of that Other, a space becomes demarcated, separating the abject from what will be a subject and its objects, it is because a repression that one might call "primal" has been effected prior to the springing forth of the ego, of its objects and representations. The latter, in turn, as they depend on another repression, the "secondary" one, arrive only a posteriori on an enigmatic foundation that has already been marked off; its return, in a phobic, obsessional, psychotic guise, or more generally and in more imaginary fashion in the shape of *abjection*, notifies us of the limits of the human universe.[11]

In the same text, Kristeva writes that in the abject "[t]he border has become an object."[12] I am proposing that we understand the uncanny as the potentially creative, rather than merely paralyzing, dimension of this experience. In other words, while I agree with Kristeva that the border is the material of primal repression, I would suggest that our access to this primal repression comes by way of the uncanny: in the experience of the liminal not *as* object, but precisely *in its liminality*.

I am borrowing and remaking Freud's term, "primal repression," as a way to approach the processes that must form the core of the unconscious. This is to say that the inheritance Freud refers to hinges on the fundamental movement of auto-erotism—on the self-differentiation of desire. So just what is repressed here, originally, so to speak? The perversion of instinct into drive; the trauma that grounds our subjectivity. Primal repression is inseparable from *Nachträglichkeit*: only after limitation, once actual repression begins to function and to fail, can primal repression manifest itself as having been. Freud only sketches out what the temporality of unconscious processes are not—"processes in the ucs system are timeless, i.e., are not chronologically ordered, are not altered by the passage of time, indeed bear no relation to time whatsoever." When Freud warns us "we should not think of the process of repression as a single event with permanent results, as when, say, a living thing is killed and from then on remains dead," we must take this further. Primal repression must be approached as a challenge to and foundation for the deterministic structure of event/result, cause/effect, and desire/satisfaction.[13]

If the unconscious is the timeless origin where fantasy and reality cannot be differentiated, then its truth must be radically reconceived. Insofar as the unconscious is the ground of consciousness, to begin is to find ourselves already divided. And yet it is only because we are divided that the beginning can speak to us—can belong to us—at all:

> The man who cannot separate himself from himself, who cannot break loose from everything that happens to him and actively oppose it—such a man has no past, or more likely he never emerges from it, but lives in it continually.[14]

Paradoxically, it is the very act of repression—of foreclosing the past and claiming ourselves in so doing—that allows us to be historical, to have a past at all.

Schelling's claim that "philosophy is thus a history of self-consciousness" suggests that this kind of re-appropriation is in fact the demand of philosophy—that this creative remembrance of the past is freedom itself.[15] Schelling claims that repression is an unavoidable and continuous condition of this freedom. In order for there to be an objective world outside of us, or a world within, the productivity of the self—the originary subject/object, self-itself, thing-in-itself—must successively "disappear" from consciousness:

> The thing–in-itself arises for it (the self) through an action; the outcome remains behind, but not the action that gave rise to it. Thus the self is originally ignorant of the fact that this opposite is its own production, and must remain in the same ignorance so long as it remains enclosed in the magic circle which self-consciousness describes about the self; only the philosopher, in breaking out of this circle, can penetrate behind the illusion.[16]

Schelling's philosopher bears a close similarity to the Freudian analyst: at an engaged remove, the philosopher and the therapist each interpret the return of the repressed—whether in bearing witness to the deeper ground of the transcendental conditions of knowledge, or the symptoms of a neurotic. Taking this comparison seriously, I believe that we can find support for Schelling's historical metaphysics in Freud's therapeutic method. If it is indeed the case that the transitional space of the beginning is primordially repressed, that it cannot be fully translated into or overcome by consciousness, how can it be acknowledged? The question of how one interprets or recognizes the traces of the past in the present—of how our history is profoundly lost and yet inescapably alive—is one that both Schelling and Freud force us to consider.[17] Moreover, we have to ask: What kind of truth necessitates such a method? What kind of truth does such a method make visible?

Archaic truth

What Schelling sees as a misconceived search for the real meaning of mythology, achieved by removing the distortions of fantasy, sounds quite like one way of understanding Freud's therapeutic technique. Allying psychoanalysis with the scientific worldview, Freud often claims to be seeking bare reality salvaged from the fantasies we project upon it, as he does quite explicitly in "The Question of a *Weltanschauung*":

> In summary, therefore, the judgment of science on the religious *Weltanschauung* is this. While the different religions wrangle with one another as to which of them is in possession of the truth, our view is

that the question of the truth of religious beliefs may be left altogether on one side. Religion is an attempt to master the sensory world
in which we are situated by means of the wishful world which we
have developed within us as a result of biological and psychological
necessities. But religion cannot achieve this. Its doctrines bear the
imprint of the times in which they arose, the ignorant times of the
childhood of humanity.[18]

However, it is also the case that in denying the truth of the religious *Weltanschauung*, Freud unwittingly exposes a similar wish—for an undis-
torted, recoverable reality—reflected in scientific constructions.[19] If
psychoanalysis does have a *Weltanschauung* of its own, it would center
on a capacity for self-analysis—for recognizing its own fundamental and
motivating fantasies. In this sense, we should keep in mind that while
Schelling dismisses a poetic reading of mythology, he admits that this is
integral to his own work and, in fact, the only place to begin:

> The poetic view is also one such first interpretation. It undoubtedly
> contains what is correct, to the extent that it excludes no meaning and
> indeed permits mythology to be taken properly. And so we will be
> careful not to say that it is false; on the contrary, it shows what is to
> be reached.[20]

The question of whether and how the "truth" of mythology might be presented is also an invitation to rethink the correspondence between science
and the reality it knows.

As the experience of the uncanny illustrates, the subjective processes
through which we (re)negotiate the boundaries of reality are never really
overcome: the unconscious, indelibly marked by the trauma of separating
"off an external world from itself," is timeless and indestructible.[21] Moreover, it is through these varied modes of relating to the world and to ourselves that mythology, as a dynamic process of identification with and
differentiation from reality, remains meaningful.[22] In his insistence that a
true philosophy of mythology must seek out the source of its religious
power—what he calls the "dark and uncanny power of the belief in
gods"—Schelling comes quite close to the psychoanalytic unconscious
and to Freudian interpretation.[23] As Freud points out, the uncanny is a
return to the original horror and to the horror of origins: consciousness,

including scientific consciousness, is born from unconscious desire. It is born like we ourselves are, like the gods are; generated not from bloodless logic, but from dark, familiar longing.

For Freud and Schelling, unconscious fantasies and dynamics do not disappear with the advent of the higher levels of organization that they give rise to. The unconscious can never be entirely reducible to consciousness, insofar as only the former can hold together the contradictory attitudes and relationships that constitute our earliest and most fundamental grasp on reality.[24] In psychoanalysis, this means that the goal of therapy could never be the complete destruction or sublimation of the unconscious, but only the development and practice of a language that can resonate with the inchoate communications of our deepest selves.[25] In the process of psychoanalytic therapy, then, it is not a matter of *translation* but of *transformation*: becoming who we are requires a return to more primitive forms of relating to ourselves and to the world—which is to say, to the various methods of "making sense" that continue to operate unconsciously. The goal of psychoanalytic therapy is not the destruction of the unconscious, but the increased capacity to remain open to the unconscious as the impetus of such transformative power.

As I have suggested, this "return" to modes of experience that we thought had been overcome is integral both to therapeutic success and to the anxiety of the uncanny. In the psychoanalytic uncanny, we experience a haunting realization of our primitive modes of relating to the world *in reality*. Our sense that we have overcome infantile fears, wishes, theories of knowledge, and desire—that now we *really* understand—is radically disturbed by their continuing to "come true." Part of what I take from Freud's investigation of the uncanny is that we are disturbed precisely *because* the distinctions that define our conscious experience and the scientific *Weltanschauung* do not extend to the unconscious—that there are other kinds of truth. Although Freud can sometimes claim that psychoanalysis is a science in that it rids reality of all traces of wish-fulfillment, his insistence on the indestructibility of the unconscious threatens any such model. The unconscious is the site where the contradiction between fantasy and reality is undone, or rather has not yet arisen, even while it remains the ineradicable and dynamic grounding of consciousness and the reality it confronts. This is not to say merely that fantasy is one kind of experience among others that make up human being, but rather that the non-contradiction of truth and fantasy remains the vital *source* of conscious, rational life, and all the distinctions this entails. Reality cannot be finally and completely disentangled from fantasy because, in the beginning that continues to *act* as beginning, they are bound together.

By insisting upon the connection between the uncanny and the force of religion, I hope to show that Schelling, too, senses the therapeutic possibilities of mythology. Because reality includes the unconscious, truth cannot merely be correlated with a heightened level of objectivity and scientific distance. Like Freud, Schelling instead struggles toward the recovery of a founding trauma—an ever-receding primal scene—suggesting that a metaphysics grounded in the unconscious demands a different model of truth and knowledge altogether. Such a scene, or a crisis as Schelling calls it, requires a rethinking of processes of differentiation that prepare the way for opposition—particularly the oppositions between fantasy and reality, subjectivity and objectivity, and myth and truth.

Schelling's claim in his early lectures on art that mythology is the highest reality, that fantasy is to imagination what intellectual intuition is to reason, offers some insight into Freud's insistence on the world-creating (whether religious, philosophical, or scientific) power of the wish:

> I define creative imagination in relation to fantasy as that in which the productions of art are received and formed, fantasy as that which intuits them externally, casts them out from within itself, as it were, and to that extent also portrays them. The relationship is the same as that between reason and intellectual intuition. Ideas are formed within reason and, in a sense, from the material of reason; intellectual intuition is that which presents them internally. Fantasy is thus the intellectual intuition within art.[26]

In the same way that intellectual intuition defines the deed of self-consciousness—where the self is simultaneously creator and created in a moment eternally repressed from consciousness—fantasy must hold together *artistic* self-creation and its abyssal beginnings. This conception of fantasy in his *Philosophy of Art* lectures comes to carry a metaphysical weight only much later, in Schelling's lectures on mythology; in this latter text, the most fundamental fantasy—mythology—is *real*. There is no deeper meaning to be recovered from mythology because within it (as within infantile subjectivity dominated by unconscious processes) fantasy and reality are not yet distinguished.

As Schelling goes on to argue that the emergence of mythology is simultaneous with the separation of peoples, with the dispersion of languages and worldviews, this analogy between intellectual intuition and fantasy becomes more fully fleshed out. Like the self-positing "I" of intellectual intuition, the primal scene that gives rise to mythological expression and to differentiation more generally must remain outside of time.[27] That which precedes mythology, and which mythology pathologically "remembers," can only be an undifferentiated, timeless unity:

> *Whatever* duration we give to this period of homogeneous humanity is entirely indifferent to the extent that this period in which nothing happens has in any event only the significance of a point of departure, of a pure *terminus ad quo*, starting with which time is counted, but in which itself there is not actual time.[28]

It is only after the rupture that mythology is responding to—the *Entscheidung*—that this trauma takes shape as a transition, a beginning. In some way still to be determined, this Absolute Past of self and god(s) alike must relate to Schelling's claim that "the night and fate, the latter itself standing *over* the gods just as the *former* is the mother of the gods, are the dark background, the hidden and mysterious identity from which all gods have emerged."[29] As with all true beginnings—and isn't mythology always about beginnings?—the gods were not brought forth at some point in time; instead, received through fantasy, and produced in imagination, they make "dimly visible" the bringing forth of time itself—the very process of reality-as-(historical) revelation.

Schelling's initial critique of competing approaches to mythology—primarily, the poetic and the philosophical/scientific—concerns their inadequacy in addressing the "dark power" of religion.[30] He argues that while it might be possible for a poetic or philosophical genius to invent a system of the gods, no such arbitrary creation could result in the intensity required to have a religion for a people, and that addressing the source of this power is essential to understanding mythology. It is in this context that Schelling introduces the concept of *Unheimlichkeit* in his *Historical-Critical Introduction to the Philosophy of Mythology*, suggesting that only the most profound and continuous spiritual "crisis" could explain such a hold on a people:

> [A] well-known and popular way of thinking [is] to presuppose for the later, serious times of our human species an epoch of a clear and serene poesy, a condition that was still free from religious terror and all those *uncanny* feelings by which later humanity was harried, the time of a happy and guiltless atheism.[31]

Schelling then presents his own view on the matter, as he doubts whether it is even conceivable "that the dark and *uncanny* power of the belief in gods [developed] from a weak and artificial beginning."[32] It should already be clear from these passages that the uncanny is integral to the dark potency of religious belief for Schelling—the strength of which is such that it could not have contingently come-to-be. When Schelling goes on to define the uncanny in his lectures on mythology and revelation, it is still attached to a "principle" that remains obscure—an obscurity that, it seems, may be ineradicable:

> The Homeric pantheon tacitly contains a Mystery within it, and is as it were built up over an abyss, which it bedecks as with flowers ... The pure sky that hovers above the Homeric poetry was first able to extend over Greece after the dark and darkening power of that uncanny (*unheimliches*) principle (*for one calls "uncanny" all that which should have remained in secret* [*im Geheimnis*], *in concealment and latency, but which has nonetheless stepped forward*)—that aether which forms a dome over the Homeric world, was first able to spread itself out, after the power of that uncanny principle, which dominated in earlier religions, was precipitated down in the Mystery. The Homeric age was first able to conceive of that purely poetic narrative of the gods after the actually religious principle had been hidden in the interior and thus allowed the spirit to turn freely toward the outside.[33]

The suggestion here is that even "poetic" narrative, and perhaps narrative more generally, is built upon the withdrawal of the "dark and darkening." While Schelling seems to suggest that the uncanny is this darkness that cannot be quite right: after all, what is uncanny must—though it ought not—come to light. That is, the uncanny *is* only insofar as it *returns*; even the most harmonious coherence points to its violent history.

The spiritual crisis that Schelling invokes as the real basis of religious power, the trauma that imbues the beautiful Homeric pantheon with meaning, is crucially linked to the Freudian uncanny: it marks the site-less site of the transition from immersive union to differentiation, from Schelling's relative monotheism to successive polytheism.[34] This crisis provokes a process of individuation, of working out the boundaries that both connect us to and separate us from each other and the world:

> Thus *this* fear, this horror before the loss of all consciousness of unity, held together those who remained united and drove them to maintain at least a partial unity, in order to persist, if not as humanity, then at least as a people. This fear before the total disappearance of unity, and therewith of all truly human consciousness, provided them not only with the first institutions of a religious type but even the first civil institutions, whose goal was no other than to preserve what they had saved of the unity and to secure against future disintegration.[35]

Schelling goes on to more explicitly connect this spiritual crisis to *language*, pointing out that "it is the name that differentiates and separates a people, just as an individual, from the others, but for just this reason at the same time holds them together."[36] Elsewhere, he refers to this transitional space in biblical terms as a "confusion" of language; confusion that extends to the temporal priority between differentiation and crisis:

> [Let] us build a city and a tower, whose summit reaches to the heavens, that we may make a name for ourselves, *for we might perhaps be scattered across the whole earth.* They say this *before* language is confused; they intimate that which stands before them, the crisis which is announced to them. Thus, the *fear* of being dispersed, of no longer being a whole at all, of rather being fully disbanded, motivates it to the undertaking. Stable residence is first considered when humanity is in danger of losing itself entirely and of disintegrating, but with the first stable abodes the separation begins, thus also the repulsion and exclusion, like the tower of Babel, which is supposed to prevent the entire dispersion, becomes the beginning and the occasion of the separation of the peoples.[37,38]

The emergence of a people—which is also the emergence of distinct languages and mythologies—is importantly linked to the time of trauma: *Nachträglichkeit*. Differentiation, Schelling tells us, cannot be easily located as cause or effect of this confusion of language. Only retroactively, through the histories of the gods in successive polytheism, can relative monotheism show itself as what came *before*. And so mythology is in no way an overcoming of the trauma that provoked it—it is instead both a historical record and retroactive creation of this transition. Similarly, the uncanny is not merely the return of the repressed: it is a return to the temporality activated in and through trauma—to a *realization* of non-existence converging with existence, indifference with difference, by way of the dissolution of the ordinary limits of our experience.

Mythology is an enactment of the development of multiplicity from undifferentiated unity. However, the meaning of history and development must be carefully rethought: "When one compares the mythologies of various peoples, it becomes fully incontestable that it is the actual history of its emergence that mythology has preserved in the sequentiality of its gods."[39] Here, mythology is self-reflective—if we can only bear to listen, it tells of its own arrival. The dispersion and historicizing of men and gods that mythology works against (as a unifying process) is, at the same time, effected by mythology (as a differentiating process). This does not mean, though, that myths are narrations *of* actual events. Rather, Schelling questions just what it means for something to be an *actual event*—what it might *mean* for the truth to show itself mythologically, or at all.

One way to approach such a truth is to take up Markus Gabriel's claim that mythology is the meaningless foundation of meaning:

> Mythology is an unprethinkable event in the sense that there is no reason (no thought) anterior to mythology which could transform it into a reasonable product. In its brute meaninglessness, it is the foundation of meaning, even of the meaning of meaninglessness.[40]

Schelling himself uses the term "unprethinkable" in reference to the tower of Babel, pointing out that "such an indelible symbolic meaning, like the one attached to the name Babel, only emerges in that it is derived from an unprethinkable [*unvordenklich*] impression."[41] Like Gabriel, Schelling suggests that the common ground of religion and language, which is to say the ground of reason and meaning, must exceed reason and meaning: brute reality cannot be logically derived or further interpreted, and it is precisely this impenetrability that makes meaning—whether mythological or scientific—possible.

My worry with Gabriel's account concerns the distinction between what he calls *constitutive* mythology and *regulative* mythology; the former is the *unprethinkable* event, and the latter the histories of the gods that constitute the content of Schelling's successive polytheism. Gabriel writes, "whereas regulative mythology makes use of specific metaphors, symbols, personae, and the like, constitutive mythology bases itself on 'absolute metaphors' in Blumenberg's sense … '*fundamental stocks* of philosophical language.'"[42] Gabriel's essay seems to depend upon an abstract mythology, or set of mythemes, that allows for—and thus cannot be contained by—the existence of any particular worldview. At the same time, he wants this constitutive mythology to provide the unprethinkable *thatness* of reality. But drained of its specificity, constitutive mythology becomes nothing more than the generic, groundless ground of Reason. Although I find his argument that meaning *needs* mythology persuasive and important, it seems to me that the constitutive/regulative distinction in no way helps explain Schelling's account of how meaning depends upon theogony; nor does it clarify the connection between the unprethinkable real and its particular mythological expressions, but only serves to further obscure it. Ultimately, Gabriel seems to assume the opposition between *particular* and *universal* in the guise of the *regulative* and the *constitutive*, rather than trace its development. Like the philosophical and poetic approaches Schelling condemns, Gabriel *uses* mythology instead of letting it speak for itself. As we will see in both Schelling and Freud, the emergence of mythology—a bringing forth that *is* the stories of the births and deaths of gods—is an essential moment in the dialectic between the particular and the universal. The myths of creation and destruction are expressions of the traumatic eruption of (self-)consciousness, of the crisis through which the very possibilities of the particular and universal first appear.

Instead of dwelling on Gabriel's *distinction* between constitutive and regulative mythology, which merely begs the question of whether and how universal and particular mythemes come together, we should consider instead the *identity* Schelling posits between language and myth: "One is almost tempted to say: language itself is only a faded mythology; what mythology still preserves in living and concrete differences is preserved in language only in abstract and formal differences."[43]

Schelling suggests that language *is* mythology, just as mythology *is* a language. Communication, as the construction of Babel illustrates, is always an act of connection and separation. The "faded" or immobile quality of ordinary language, perhaps even more so than the bright sky of the Homeric pantheon, keeps the ongoing crisis of coming-to-consciousness at bay. Even the most comfortable abstractions promise an uncanny return of the repressed—a resurrection that, as Freud so carefully attends to, is evident in the ambivalence of the very terms *Heimlich/Unheimlich*. Where Freud points to the deconstruction of opposition associated with the uncanny in terms of truth/fantasy and inner/outer, Schelling focuses on the incipient anxiety of renegotiating surface/depth, the periphery/center.[44]

Indeed, Schelling's overall claim that mythology *means* what it *is*, would suggest that it is not something psychoanalysis can effectively interpret—or at least not in the way Freud is accustomed to. Schelling's account of mythology may instead lead us to how Freud *can* relate to mythology, how his method of interpretation uniquely depends upon it. At a superficial level, we can see this dependence in the centrality of Oedipus—which is already a repetition of the motifs operative in the prophecy, murder, and castration of Uranus/Kronos/Zeus as well as in Freud's own myth of the primal horde. There is nothing for Freud to "interpret" in these events except for their literal, universal truth. However, this is not to say that the themes common to the Oedipal tragedy and Greek mythology are instances of constitutive mythology and its "fundamental stocks of philosophical language" that Gabriel introduces. Rather, the authentically psychoanalytic approach, where interpretation does not quite *apply* to mythology but *emerges* from it, suggests a way to trace the mutual development of language and reality in Schellingian terms.

Symptoms of subjectivity

On Schelling's view, the uncanny is the site where self-identity (*Heimlich*) shows itself as irreducibly not-itself, divided (*Unheimlich*). The Homeric pantheon, Schelling writes, can only appear to us as basking under a "pure sky" because there is *hidden* within it the "religious" and "darkening power" of the uncanny. The uncanny, as the return of the repressed, allows for meaning construed as retrieval from the depths. It is for this reason that Schelling refuses to reduce mythology to allegory: the very possibility of the latter has to be grounded in the former.

Without the intimation of the hidden, without interiority and the limit that shelters/divides, there can be no meaning at all. And it is only through mythology that this depth and surface come-to-be distinguished. Schelling discovers that interpretation is unthinkable without the histories of the gods: it is not only interiority that mythology demarcates, but the past as such, in its hiddenness, and its intimacy. From Uranus, through Kronos to Zeus/Dionysus, Schelling draws together the formation of consciousness with the development of meaning. Initially with Uranus, there is a certain flat naïveté, an unreflective and undifferentiated immersion (unconscious unity, pre-historical and self-enclosed); with the birth of Kronos, the transitional stage between unconscious unity and self-conscious differentiation, *anxiety* sets in. Dislocated by the memory of overcoming the past that defines him, and the desire to forget that he is vulnerable to the same fate, Kronos *is* uncanny. His individuality—individuality itself—is split between needing the past to legitimize himself and denying the past to dissuade the gods to come. The all-consuming, child-devouring present forecloses the past in order to refuse the future.[45] It is only with the arrival of this second god—and the *anxiety* such succession entails—that the first becomes meaningful as a god:

> [T]he one God, reigning over the placid, pre-historical time, was indeed the only one existing up to that point, but not in the sense that no second one *was able* to follow him; rather, only that another had not yet *actually* followed him. To this extent he was essentially already a mythological god, although he only first became such actually when the second actually arrived and made himself into the master of human consciousness.[46]

Only when Kronos subjects Uranus to the past—in his conflicted creation of and separation from it—does mythology, as a history and a symptom, properly begin. The anxiety that Kronos experiences is *real*—it is an anxiety surrounding the emergence of *times*, a consequence of making past that defines us and divides us in trauma.

In *Totem and Taboo*, Freud's first text dealing with the sources of religion and the taboos of civilization, we find a similar claim about the anxiety accompanying the succession of the gods:

> The contrast between "sacred" and "unclean" coincides with a suc-
> cession of two stages of mythology. The earlier of these stages did
> not completely disappear when the second one was reached but per-
> sisted in what was regarded as an inferior and eventually contempti-
> ble form. It is, he [Wundt] says, a general law of mythology that a
> stage which has been passed, for the very reason that it has been
> overcome and driven under by a superior stage, persists in an inferior
> form alongside the latter one, so that the objects of its veneration turn
> into objects of horror.[47]

Here Freud explicitly connects *history* with *anxiety*: the first god inspires
horror because the past is not over—in its very disappearance, this first
god is truly erected and threatens return. Here, the collective consciousness of a people converges with Freud's theory of *Nachträglichkeit* for
the individual—the radical therapeutic premise that trauma is not a stable
event locatable in time, but a disruption, and redefinition of the temporal
order. In conceiving of memory and history as living processes, Freud
destabilizes the past, its *reality* beholden to what can only come later. In
the same work he goes on to discuss Dionysus-Zagreus, Kronos' succes-
sor. While Schelling presents Dionysus as the meaningful gathering of
past and present that can resolve the anxiety of individuation in the
eternal coming-to-be of the future, Freud's version seems a bit darker.
Instead of redemption, he points to the endless cycle of familial brutality:
"Mankind, it was said, were descended from the Titans, who had killed
the young Dionysus-Zagreus and torn him to pieces."[48] The future
(Dionysus), like the present (Kronos), is a *repetition* of the past—and,
more specifically, of its dislocation, and violent sundering. This repetition threatens to undo any real distinction between past and future as each
god suffers the fate of, and thus becomes identified with, his father. But
even Freud's version can be read as productive, or rather reproductive:
we might recognize such a creative repetition in the way that the past
must be both *repeated* and *engendered* for there to be continued development of an individual or a people. In its oscillation between revelation
and concealment, the conflicted pulse of the symptom suggests how we
might understand mythology as both literally true and still interpretable.

   The crisis of consciousness speaks to us *mythologically*. Mythology is
the memory of a founding loss, the trace of the mutual emergence of time
and consciousness—of difference as such. But it is also the repetition of

this primordial separation, as it conceals the lost unity through the very act of historicizing and narrating. In this way, the trauma of transition unites the history of consciousness with the history of the gods. Mythology expresses the constitutional anxiety of the subject, and consciousness as a negotiation between the dual threats of immersive unity and isolating difference. The individual, no less than language and meaning, disappears through the collapse into undifferentiated union as well as through the fetishization of distinction. Schelling's emphasis on *birth*, an attentiveness to birth that is marked by the *castration* of the father and *devouring* of the son, cannot be overlooked in this respect. Birth recalls us to Schelling's overarching concern with an organic holding together, a living temporality that neither destroys what comes before nor vanishes into what comes later; but it also gestures toward the undeniably *horrific* (murderous, incestuous, bloody) aspects of such an (un)natural begetting. The bond that unites Uranus, Kronos, and Dionysus *is* the dialectic of individuation and communion—the intractable identity of illness and cure, of repetition and creation.

Schelling's work on mythology requires a rethinking of the meshwork of temporality, meaning, and anxiety. In tracing the development of human consciousness out of the unconscious, Schelling does not want us to simply find the historical development of subjectivity comparable to, or allegorized in, mythology. Rather, he challenges us to develop forms of meaning and relating that are necessary for facing mythology and origins more generally:

> Certainly, mythology has no reality *outside* of consciousness; but if it only takes its course in the determinations of consciousness, that is, in its representations, then nonetheless this *course of events, this succession of representations themselves* cannot again be such a one that is merely *imagined*; it must have *actually* taken place, must have actually occurred in consciousness. This succession is not fashioned by mythology, but rather—contrariwise—mythology is fashioned by it. For mythology is just precisely the whole of those doctrines of the gods that have actually succeeded each other, and thus it has come into being through this succession.[49]

The connection here between the development of consciousness and mythology is precisely *not* allegorical. But how *do* the gods relate to us?

Just what is Schelling saying when he claims mythology is both fantasy and history?

These questions gesture toward the great hope and the great danger of Schelling's efforts. I suggest that this relation is an *uncanny belonging together*—a connection founded in and expressed by the anxious, transitional space between what *is* and what *is not*. In other words, it is precisely in working out the boundaries between the actual and the imagined, within the border realm of the uncanny, that the gods and consciousness arrive (and continue to arrive) together. At first it seems that the way Freud derives mythology from psychic structures, as the projection of infantile desires and fears onto the world, is at odds with Schelling. This kind of interpretive gesture on Freud's part is apparent in texts like *Future of an Illusion*, where he presents mythology both as a mode of religious experience and as a protection against paralyzing vulnerability and senselessness:

> Impersonal forces and destinies cannot be approached; they must remain eternally remote. But if the elements have passions that rage as they do in our own souls, if death itself is not something spontaneous but the violent act of an evil Will, if everywhere in nature there are Beings around us of a kind that we know in our own society, then we can breathe freely, can feel at home in the uncanny and can deal by psychical means with our senseless anxiety. We are still defenseless, perhaps, but we are no longer helplessly paralyzed; we can at least react. We can apply the same methods against these violent supermen outside that we employ in our own society; we can try to adjure them, to appease them, to bribe them, and, by so influencing them, we may rob them of part of their power.[50]

It appears that what Schelling finds to be *actual* in mythology, Freud deems utter *delusion*, and vice versa.[51] But as I have tried to suggest, the uncanny is precisely the moment at which we are called to address—to return to—just what separates truth from desire, the actual from the imagined. Freud's own fascination with mythology is not limited to finding examples that illustrate the projection and distortion of unconscious fears and wishes; at pivotal moments in the development of his thought, he is unable to clearly distinguish foundational elements of psychoanalysis from the structures and status of myth. Further, these "mythological moments" that Freud can never entirely embrace nor do without tend to concern the relationship between desire and history, between the individual and the species, and between repetition and recreation.[52] Perhaps most memorably, Freud's primal horde, as presented in *Civilization and Its Discontents, Totem and Taboo* and to a certain extent in *Moses and Monotheism*, is itself a myth of origins and the origin of myth: it serves to explain, in various and contradictory ways, the inheritance of guilt, the Oedipal Complex, and religion by way of repression and primary ambivalence. As Freud writes in *Civilization and Its Discontents*, concerning the remorse that follows the murder of the father in the primal horde: "This remorse was the result of the primordial ambivalence of feeling towards the father. His sons hated him, but they loved him, too."[53] It is only out of this "primordial ambivalence" that, in devouring the father, they also *become* the father—the very stuff of generation, connection, and separation: which is to say, of mythology.[54] And yet, this is *what actually happened*. Paradoxically, inescapably, and uncomfortably, Freud—in a manner perhaps this is not too far from Schelling's exhortation in the *Weltalter*—discovers mythology in truth and truth in mythology.

This convergence of truth and myth is more fully explored in Freud's final reworking of the primal horde in *Civilization and Its Discontents*. In an effort to explain the development of civilization, Freud again turns to the sexual, murderous, and familial at the root of psychic life. Hoping to discover in the process the emergence of the super-ego and the origin of guilt and repression, Freud reworks the hypothetical primal horde from *Totem and Taboo* insofar as it fails to adequately explain why the murder of the father results in the guilt of the sons. Here, Freud notes the importance of omnipotent thought—a term familiar to us from its uncanny effects—in terms of whether the primal horde should be understood as fiction or reality:

> A great change takes place only when the authority is internalized through the establishment of a super-ego. The phenomena of conscience then reach a higher stage. Actually, it is not until now that we should speak of conscience or sense of guilt. At this point, too, the fear of being found out comes to an end; the distinction, moreover, between doing something bad and wishing to do it disappears entirely, since nothing can be hidden from the super-ego, not even thoughts.[55]

Freud suggests that the developmental achievement that is the super-ego is in fact a re-enforcement of the mechanism of omnipotent thought. That is, the ambivalence between desire and reality is not surpassed at this stage, but preserved, and even increased. And yet, it is in this text that Freud is most insistent on the reality of this primal scene:

> We cannot get away from the assumption that man's sense of guilt springs from the Oedipal complex and was acquired at the killing of the father by the brothers banded together. On that occasion an act of aggression was not suppressed but carried out.[56]

He argues that while successive generations may feel guilt due to the renunciation of their murderous, sexual impulses (in the form of punishments from the super-ego), the erection of the super-ego, and with it the remorseful idealization of the father, can only be the effect of *real action*.

Freud's insistence is striking: why must it be *real* if there is as yet no distinction between the wish and its fulfillment? The omnipotent thought that holds sway in primitive psychic life, while not perhaps as totalizing as it becomes with the super-ego, makes any question of the reality of the murder irrelevant. However, it is not first and foremost in order to explain the *guilt* of the brothers that Freud needs the act to be a real one; it is to explain the deification of the father that follows. It is thus, the inheritability of the Oedipal Complex—the very possibility of *succession*, to borrow Schelling's term—that leads Freud to assert the reality of the primal scene. Simply put: the father needs to *actually* die in order to become a god.

Freud's late text *Moses and Monotheism* reiterates the *real* need for the death of the father to explain the potency of religious feeling. He treats biblical events in the same way that he treats Greek mythology, pointing to their identity as religious phenomena and their rootedness in real and enduring crises; very much in the style of Schelling. Here it is a question of the emergence of a particular people (his *own* people, the Israelites) and mythology as that which both exposes and propagates an originary trauma: the story of Moses bears within its fault-lines the violence of differentiation and individuation, the trauma that marks all true beginnings.[57] Indeed, Freud emphasizes the transition from polytheism to monotheism as fundamental to the meaning and power of Moses' story. The continued reverence for these narratives, Freud suggests, is a testament to a constitutively hidden force—to the most profound and ambivalent feelings of love and hate that spur our development and awaken our nostalgia. It is worth noting, as Derrida does in *Archive Fever*, that Freud's interpretation of Moses is marked by the language of the uncanny: "Freud characterizes the *impression* which circumcision leaves on those who are uncircumcised: 'a disagreeable, uncanny [*unheimlich*] impression.' "[58] For Freud, the symptom-formation that is Moses is a version of the Oedipal myth—and, even more archaically, the Theogony of Uranus-Kronos-Zeus—at the level of a people: the murder of their leader, their father figure, is repressed, transformed, inherited. Beyond this, like the tragedy of Oedipus or the grandson's game of Fort/Da, the story of Moses is a story of inheritance—of our unconscious and ungrounding ground, the past that we never experienced (before we were born, before we were self-conscious) and inevitably take up in our own way. It is not so much that Freud insists upon a *physiological* structure of inheritance, but rather that he opens up the possibility of a distinctively *psychoanalytic* process of history.[59] We do not inherit, genetically as it were, some set of archetypes, or mythemes; rather, we are born into a reality, as well as a people, that is shaped by and remains vulnerable to the earliest psychic formations.

Hesitantly, Freud sketches a reality that must take into account relationships to the world that we no longer have access to but cannot be rid of. Just as Schelling refuses to relegate religion and mythology to the status of *mere* projections that need to be overcome, Freud also knows that mythology is not just symptomatic of primitive psychic states that can be more rationally interpreted and explained. Indeed, it is precisely the claim to have overcome the past which therapy and the uncanny reveal as fantasy. For Freud, remaining open to primitive modes of engaging with reality, including pre-repressive, ego-building processes like projection, introjection, and identification, is integral to therapeutic success *and* to understanding mythology.[60] Freud comes close to Schelling here, suggesting that the truth we discover is neither a historical fact nor an insight into the psychology of an alien, primitive people; it is a truth that still and always belongs to us, and so we experience the uncanny.

Schelling argues that traditional interpretations of mythology amount to just so many ways of masking the transformative reality of myth—protecting us from our *essential* and *existential* uncanniness. Mythology,

Schelling maintains, enacts the historical development of meaning—and, in doing so, the birth of language and of peoples:

> In any case it is apparent that to the Old Testament way of thinking the emergence of peoples, the confusion of language and polytheism are related concepts and connected phenomena. If we look back from here to what was found earlier, then every people is *first there* as such after it has defined and decided itself in view of its mythology. Thus this mythology cannot emerge for it in the time of the *already completed* division and after it had already become a people; because, moreover, it could equally less emerge for the people as long as the latter was, in the whole of humanity, still at the point of being like an until then invisible part of it, mythology's origin will occur precisely in the *transition*, because the people does not yet exist as a determinate one but precisely at this point is ready to extrude and isolate itself as such.[61]

Notice the connection Schelling makes between mythology and transition: the origin of mythology, its meaning and truth, is located in transition. And what kind of location—destabilizing, dynamic—would this be? We are faced with a mutual productivity where the longing for identity springs from and creates difference. The source of this cision, a spiritual crisis as Schelling calls it, can only be experienced as *having been*, as already past. Consciousness is a demand for the very unity it destroys in coming-to-be. The histories of the gods bear witness to the originary longing and unutterable self-division through which meaning becomes questionable—which is to say, becomes possible. For Schelling, there is no sense in working out the distortions in mythology to uncover *what really happened*. Rather, we need to consider the way in which mythology plays out the transitional structure of reality itself.

That Schelling's interest in the uncanny comes in his late exploration of mythology gives credence to my claim that reality must encompass the unconscious and the archaic.[62] Mythology, as Schelling explains, is not some primitive attempt to explain the world that modern science has made redundant; neither is it a veiled message or allegory that might be translated into laws or moral codes. The meaning of mythology is united with its being in a manner quite unlike the removed knowledge of conscious experience or scientific investigation. By grounding knowledge in the unconscious, and truth in the mythological, Schelling disturbs the distinction between the objective and the subjective. Thus meaning is re-imagined as *process*, as *revelation:* like the gods themselves, truth *is* timeless, but only if we reframe this timelessness, as Schelling does in his *Weltalter*, in terms of repression and historicity. In other words, truth is not essentially and eternally *present*, but instead tied to that vanishing limit between concealment and revelation that, equally, holds together the "darkening power" with the "clear blue" Homeric sky: the uncanny. Schelling writes:

> As the common germ of both gods and men, absolute chaos is night, obscurity. The first forms and figures fantasy allows to be born from within it are also still formless. A world of misshapen and frightful forms must perish before the mild realm of the blessed and enduring gods can enter.[63]

Although these "frightful forms" may perish, the gods still bear the traces; we might even say the *symptoms*, of their bond with "absolute chaos." In order to understand the reality Schelling ascribes to the gods (and the "common germ" that humans share with them) we need to acknowledge that the non-presence of this boundary is integral to the truth of mythology; that concealment is always also the possibility of revelation.

Schelling argues that mythology tells us what it means in the only terms it can: as a history of the gods and the development of consciousness. What comes out of Schelling's account is a theory of meaning that both allows for and presses beyond conceptual thought. Language, in its mythological expression, is not primarily a medium for transmitting ideas; more importantly, it is a reflection of how psyche and world interact *as* reality. The practice of psychoanalysis, at least implicitly, depends upon a similarly developmental and reciprocal theory of world-creation and self-expression. Furthermore, it is a tenet of psychoanalysis that the various levels and forms of self-understanding are not simply cast out in favor of more rational structures; rather, the former maintain, and even increase their effectiveness precisely insofar as they threaten and contradict the latter. Borrowing heavily from Hans Loewald's work, Jonathan Lear explains in *Love and Its Place in Nature* that symptoms (and the unconscious fantasies and desires they express) are always pervaded by infantile theories of selfhood and primal forms of subjectivity:

> The case of Anna O. shows us, right at the beginning of psycho-analysis, that in addition to infecting our memories and current experience, archaic mental life has a "theory" of the mind's own workings. Anna O.'s "theory" of catharsis was not an explicitly conceptualized theory, thus the use of quotes. Her "theory" was expressed at the same archaic level of mental functioning as the rest of her fantasies: she experienced catharsis as corporealized discharge.[64]

Lear continues, explaining how it is that the therapeutic model fits into this account:

> A "theory" of the mental process is part of the person's (perhaps unconscious) experience of that process. Thus the fantasied "theory" becomes part and parcel of the mental process, and in altering the fantasy one alters the mental process itself.[65]

Mythology is thus a theory of the mind, in Lear's sense of the term, insofar as it is an expression of a form of psychic life bound up with the attempt to understand that life. Or, as Schelling would have it, mythological language *is* what it *says*—the symbolic (or symptomatic) is the union of being and meaning, the entanglement of our existence with the sense we make of it:

> Mythology as such and every poetic rendering of it in particular are to be comprehended neither schematically nor allegorically, but rather *symbolically*. This is the case because the requirement of absolute artistic representation is: representation with *complete indifference* such that the universal *is* completely the particular and the particular simultaneously the entire universal, and does not merely mean or signify it. The requirement is poetically resolved in mythology, since each figure in it is to be taken as that which it is, for precisely in this way is each also taken as that which it means or signifies. Meaning here is simultaneously being itself, passed over

into the object itself and one with it. As soon as we allow these beings to *mean* or *signify* something, they themselves are no longer *anything*. Their reality is one with their ideality; that is, their *idea*, their concept is also destroyed to the extent that they are not conceived as actual. Their ultimate charm resides precisely in the fact that they, by simply *being* as they are without reference to anything else—absolute within themselves—simultaneously always allow the meaning itself to be dimly visible.[66]

The gods of mythology, on Schelling's account, cannot be fully acknowledged through a language where concept and being, form and content, remain opposed. That is to say, we cannot understand mythology through the paradigm of some *depth* of meaning to be recovered. Already in this early text, Schelling suggests the existential line of thinking that will culminate in his positive philosophy and its interpretation of mythology: to philosophically engage with mythology, we must confront a destabilizing truth; one which encompasses modes of relating to ourselves and the world that can neither be fully integrated nor refused.

Magical thinking

In considering both the development of mythology and of consciousness in Schelling—or the convergent inheritance of an individual, a people, and reality as such—it is useful to look at psychoanalysis as a therapeutic response to the same line of questioning: How does reality encompass the unconscious? It seems to me that the truth sought in Freudian psychoanalysis, a truth that can only be judged by its therapeutic effect, is indispensable in understanding Schelling's philosophy of mythology. The reality of the unconscious, and the various, and contradictory forms of subjectivity that constitute it, depends upon a *transformative* dimension of meaning. The histories of the gods, no less than the case histories of Freud's analysands, open up disturbingly foreign (and thus potent) forms of subjectivity that remain at work in the mutual development of meaning and being. Myths are not just stories, they are profoundly and disturbingly *our own*—provided we can let them mean what they say.

I turn briefly to Freud's Hungarian protégé, Sándor Ferenczi, as a concrete example of how psychoanalytic therapy depends upon language that remains open to and marked by these various modes of meaningful engagement. In *First Contributions to Psychoanalysis*, he offers a series of developmental moments where the structures of the developing ego parallel the modes by which meaning can be created and appreciated. One such stage is "the period of magic thoughts and magic words":

> Now conscious thought by means of speech signs is the highest accomplishment of the psychic apparatus, and alone makes adjustment to reality possible by retarding the reflex motor discharge and the release from unpleasantness. In spite of this the child knows how to preserve his feeling of omnipotence even in this stage of his development, for his wishes that can be set forth in thoughts are still so few and comparatively uncomplicated that the attentive *entourage* concerned with the child's welfare easily manages to guess most of these thoughts. The mimic expressions that continually accompany thinking (peculiarly so with children) make this kind of thought-reading especially easy for the adults; and when the child actually formulates his wishes in words the *entourage*, ever ready to help, hastens to fulfill them as soon as possible. The child then thinks himself in possession of magic capacities, is thus in the *period of magic thoughts and magic words* ... In superstition, magic, and in religious cults this belief in the irresistible power of certain prayer, cursing, or magic formulas, which one has only to think inwardly or only to speak aloud for them to work, plays an enormous part.[67]

Ferenczi argues for a robust psychoanalytic reality by way of a *productive, primal* language. Such a language reaches back to a nascent self-consciousness, suggesting that the individual emerges out of myriad efforts to make sense of and defend against the dual threats of engulfing union and castrating differentiation. I also draw attention to this particular "magical" language insofar as it is essentially a form of playing with boundaries—the same kind of experience that recurs in the uncanny and the therapeutic (as well as in the aesthetic). For the child, we might say, such a phase is developmentally useful, if not necessary; and while behaving in such a manner might appear pathological in an adult, the process of renegotiating the limits of our agency and vulnerability in psychoanalytic therapy is in fact a re-appropriation of this creative, playful dimension of language.

Schelling, in his philosophy of mythology, similarly returns language to its world-creating capacities. Accordingly, if we want to elucidate

Schelling's account of mythological meaning, we would do well to consider the concrete and mutual development of language, subject, and
world that psychoanalysis finds inextricably bound to fantasy and to the
transitional more generally. Though Schelling has been attacked as an
obscurantist for suggesting that absolute truth defies conceptualization, I
think this concern is misplaced. To the contrary: We need to ask, as
psychoanalysis does, how it is that language does in fact give voice to
repressed non-conceptual truths. We could say that language functions
within psychoanalytic therapy in a manner much closer to the way it
functions in mythology than in ordinary speech: speaking both reveals
and conceals the historical and contradictory truths that constitute the
subject. Language here shows itself in its double aspect—as a tool for
delimiting and defining our experience, but also as a concrete manifestation of our sense of being a subject. In other words, the deceptive
transparency of language echoes the even more fundamentally deceptive
transparency of self-consciousness. In ways intentional and not, the
words we choose, like our actions and bearing in the world, encompass
various modes of subjective experience. Free association is thus not the
deterministic manner in which the unconscious speaks, but an activity
bringing into relief these oscillations between various stages of self-
understanding that constitute our subjectivity. Tempted by the solidity of
words, and prior to that by the clear outlines of our bodies, we erro ne-
ously imagine that knowledge—and self-knowledge along with it—must
be unchanging, self-identical, present.

Schelling's provocative claim that mythology *means* what it *is*, is
importantly related to Freud's discovery that hysterical symptoms *are*
memories. For Schelling, we saw that the symbol binds together being
and meaning, cause and existence. Equally, Freud discovers that *how*
symptoms mean is inextricably connected to *what* they mean. For
instance, bodily manifestations are not only or even primarily a representation of intolerable conflicts (what they mean), but also a defensive
regression to a different mode of subjectivity that understands itself as
bodily (how they mean). As with Schelling's theory of mythology,
meaning is not *concealed* within the symptom. "Interpreting" a symptom,
for Freud, is something other than "translating" it into a more refined,
scientific language; meaning is created in the space between life and language, between our being and the thought of our being.[68] It is not merely
the *particular* unconscious wish/es that are manifested in the symptom,

but also the mode of *self-consciousness*, irreducible to conceptual terms, through which, and by which the symptom appears. Similarly for Schelling, it is the self-consciousness of a people—their sense of reality—that is essentially preserved as mythology. To interpret a symptom—or a mythology—is to gather together our various modes of relating self and world in new, more fulfilling ways.

In juxtaposition with Freud, we can see even more clearly that Schelling's lectures on mythology are a rethinking of history in terms of the pathological. Destabilizing the relationship between being and meaning, and in an effort to engage with the crisis to which mythology is a testament, Schelling develops a *therapeutic* approach. Mythology threatens us with the intimation of our shared, conflicted beginnings; as such, it reveals itself as the symptom of a primordial anxiety, a defense against and eruption of temporality and differentiation for an essentially traumatized subjectivity. But in doing so, it offers the possibility of renewed health and individuality.

If we view Freud's project as a philosophy of therapy, concerned with the way meaning affects our very being, then approaching Schelling's reading of mythology as an interpretation of a symptom does not seem so far-fetched. As Freud writes, "linguistic usage, then, employs the word … *symptom* when a function has undergone some unusual change or when a new phenomenon has arisen out of it."[69] Mythology would thus represent a symptom insofar as consciousness itself develops a new form of expression and embodiment through it. Schelling, like Freud, defines a people, and an individual in light of their pathology—and subjectivity becomes a negotiation between the threat of an immersive unity on the one hand, and of alienating separation on the other.

I hope that by framing Freudian interpretation as a form of historicizing subjectivity, and bringing this to bear on Schelling's philosophy of mythology, we can begin to sketch out what a Schellingian therapy might look like. Schelling's lectures on mythology ask to be read in this way, the proximity to Freud showing up even in his locating mythology—as Freud does with psychoanalysis—outside of the opposition between science and art. In Schelling's lectures, mythology is a defense, and a therapeutic effort—a reaction to and repetition of the anxiety concomitant with creation and differentiation. This appeal to an originary anxiety might help provide ontological grounding for separation anxiety, on the societal and individual levels, that Freud assumes are repetitions of a purely *physiological* overstimulation. As mythology arises in Schelling from a primordial cision, the "unprethinkable" transition into languages and peoples, so does the Freudian symptom conceal and express the trauma of individuation (echoes of which resonate in the anxieties of birth, castration, and death).

In order to flesh out this "ontological" anxiety, I cite Freud in "Inhibition, Symptom and Anxiety," where he reverses a foundational psychoanalytic view of clinical anxiety:

> The anxiety belonging to the animal phobias was an untransformed fear of castration. It was therefore a realistic fear, a fear of a danger which was actually impending or was judged to be a real one. It was anxiety which produced repression and not, as I formerly believed, repression which produced anxiety ... it is always the ego's attitude of anxiety which is the primary thing and which sets repression going.[70]

Notice the strange emphasis on the "realistic" nature of the danger of castration—a danger we might prefer to banish to the realm of "fantasy." Anxiety, Freud now realizes, is powerful enough to produce repression— to authenticate and delimit reality, or rather, to alert us to its inherent instability. Such a constitutive instability is corroborated in the same work, as Freud articulates the trauma this anxiety signals as *loss*:

> The statement I have just made, to the effect that the ego has been prepared to expect castration by having undergone constantly repeated object-losses, places the question of anxiety in a new light. We have hitherto regarded it as an affective signal of danger; but now, since the danger is so often one of castration, it appears to us as a reaction to a loss, to a *separation*.[71]

The danger Freud concerns himself with here is not merely the loss of a particular object or satisfaction, but the loss of the sense of reality through which object and satisfaction became meaningful.[72]

With this deeper sense of separation in mind, and what it may suggest about the connection between trauma and subjectivity, we can better approach the symptom in terms of its peculiar fixation on the past: the desire for a lost unity, which the symptom feigns to recuperate, also

signals an underlying terror of futurity and the overwhelming openness
of historical processes. The pathological repetition that symptom and
mythology share serves to foreclose the danger of otherness, to conceal
the abyssal freedom that constitutes an individual and a people as historical. And yet as an effort to bind this "separation anxiety" within the
limits of symbol and narrative, the myth is always also a real trace of the
trauma that makes the pre-historical, pre-egoic past interpretable again.
Therapeutic engagement with symptoms, then, is effective only insofar
as it returns us to the formlessness of anxiety that the symptom, in its
contained particularity, would deny. Schelling insists that in reading
mythology we are not recovering some concealed truth: the interpretation
of mythology demands a re-appropriation—a re*living*—of the trauma that
continues to threaten our stability and to spur our development. If
mythology is both the history and the enactment of an emerging consciousness, this is because consciousness itself is a symptom of irreducible, conflicting desires for union and separation, projection and
identification, revelation and concealment. In Schelling's example of the
successive polytheism of the Greeks—from Uranus through Kronos to
Zeus—we find a literal expression of Freud's psychic processes of development: the vomiting up of the son is the primordial projection or creation, the swallowing a bodily identification, and castration a physical
separation. History—or the development of the individual through trauma
and anxiety—is a working out of the boundaries between being and
meaning, between the physical and the psychical.

When history and consciousness are conceived of in this way, the pre-
historical and the unconscious need to be understood as essentially
without boundary; anxiety arises in the excess of an undifferentiated
totality that is always also an unbearable need, a self-seeking. This need,
which Freud calls the wish, is the contradictory essence of the unconscious. The wish is directed at eliminating difference—the tension
between desire and satisfaction—yet is itself the primal division. This
central conflict that defines the unconscious, the struggle between non-
differentiation and separation that is already present in the wish, is transformed into the symptoms of an individual and the mythology of a
people. Indeed, the very fact that there *is* mythology signifies that the
unconscious continues to exist within higher levels of organization, and
the pre-historical remains vital to the historical. For psychoanalysis, this
means that the goal of therapy would be the "new development" of a

function—through language and consciousness—for acknowledging our most ancient and unrecognizable subjectivity. The temptation here is to imagine that there are unconscious "thoughts" that are *identical* to their potentially conscious counterparts, only temporarily, or contingently inaccessible. But it is more fitting to say that symptoms—as symbols of conflict both within unconscious wishes and between varying levels of psychic organization—express a primal form of subjectivity. Psychoanalytic therapy is the process of individuation achieved through a return to more primitive forms of relating to ourselves and to reality. Psychoanalysis thus comes ever closer to the role Schelling assigns to philosophy in his lectures on mythology: the living force of the unconscious is essential to self-transformation or becoming an authentic individual, where individuality is understood here as the health of the subject, a permeability and ambivalence rooted in our primal modes of responding to the world and making it our own.

Schelling's account of the meaning of mythology suggests a similar notion of healthy regression, a method of self-narration, and a notion of history that opens truth into the archaic.[73] Mythology is the *truthful* expression of a people, the intimate self-reflection of the birth and development of consciousness from the unconscious. This is in fact quite close to Lear's explanation of cathartic regression in psychoanalysis: the symptomatic return to infantile activities that initially constructed the boundaries between self and reality, processes like projection and identification, also *embody* a primitive theory of selfhood or subjectivity. Therapeutic interpretation is an attunement to the subjectivity from which these meaningful expressions arise. Schelling's interpretation of mythology is thus therapeutic because it brings us into contact with the beginnings of subjectivity and our most tenacious, founding fantasy: that the past remain fixed behind us, ensuring the self-certainty of presence and the continued familiarity of the future. But in reading mythology in this way, as a symptom that expresses conflicted desires, Schelling also exposes us to the disintegrative *danger* of interpretation—to a confrontation with the lack that existence disguises and the grounding anxiety that consciousness harbors within itself.

Acting as signal and disguise, a memory that is also a forgetting, mythology shares the dual structure of the symptom—at once evidence of a deeper illness, and the first painful step toward a cure.[74] And it is because mythology is divided in this way that its interpretation must be *more than* an explanation of its emergence—its history more than the inert result of what came before. Early on, Freud recognizes that merely explaining the significance of a symptom to its sufferer does not ensure therapeutic success. Its meaning must be grasped by the analysand in a particular way—it must become his *own*.[75] The insufficiency of merely "giving" the meaning of a symptom in therapeutic practice suggests two related ramifications that apply to Schelling's reading of mythology: (1) a symptom is *more than* the effect of discrete events that lead to its formation, and (2) in order for it to be *therapeutic*, an interpretation requires *more than* explanation. The symptom (and the interpretation of it) not only belongs to a subjectivity which, by its very nature, is historical; it is also the case that the *form* the symptom takes is itself a mode—albeit a regressive one—of *historicizing*. It is an expression of a subjectivity that goes through the trauma of temporalization, a coagulation of primal anxiety that shapes the past and protects us from the alterity of the future. The symptom is duplicitous once more—simultaneously a narration of and defense against the past. Such strange expression betrays the anxiety at the heart of mythology: a history of emergence that also *is* the emergence of history.

Insofar as mythology is a memory of temporalization itself, it cannot simply belong to the past. It is rather like the symptom, which only *appears* external to the subjectivity it disturbs. Indeed, it is the peculiarity of being experienced by the sufferer as an alien, meaningless affliction that marks the inhibition or perversion of a function as a symptom. In order to relieve the symptom, the sufferer must approach it as a mode of self-understanding. Thus psychoanalytic treatment, no less than Schelling's interpretation of mythology, requires a certain vulnerability: a reopening of the borders of subjectivity so that we might come to acknowledge the symptom as our own, as a meaningful expression of the foreignness and familiarity of the past. Schelling maintains that truly engaging with mythology demands disintegration—a depth of questioning that extends to our most fundamental sense of the limits of self and world. Such interpretive vulnerability does not necessarily signal the corrosion of illness or psychosis. To interpret mythology as a symptom is also to light up the world and our subjectivity in a particular way—to develop a sensitivity to and reverence for the uncanniness of existence. In this way, Schelling's interpretation of mythology inaugurates a radical rethinking of what it means for something to be *true*. Mythology draws us into the reciprocity of subject and interpretation, returning us to the therapeutic unity between our being and the sense we make of it.

Notes

1   Now, however, one could still ask in particular if in mythology's era of emergence *poetry* and *philosophy* as such—that is, in their formal opposition—could really have been present at all; because we have seen, on the contrary, how as soon as a mythology is present and has completely filled consciousness, both initially depart from each other in different directions, from out of mythology as from a mutually held middle-point, albeit even then they separate themselves very slowly.

                                                      (Lecture 3, p. 38)

2 Ibid. p. 41.

3 Lecture 5, p. 74.

4 Ibid. p. 74.

5 I have in mind here Freud's description of secondary revision in his *Interpretation of Dreams*:

> What marks this part of the dream-work out and exposes it to view is its purpose. This function proceeds rather as the poet [Heine] maliciously declares philosophers do: with its snippets and scraps it patches the gaps in the dream's structure. The result of its labours is that the dream loses its appearance of absurdity and incoherence, and approaches the pattern of an intelligible experience.
>
>   (pp. 319–320)

6 Ibid. One of Freud's major claims to a novel approach to dream interpretation depends on the difference between his method and what I have termed "universal symbolism." He writes,

> The other popular method of dream-interpretation [besides the "symbolic" method in which a diviner "takes the dream-content as a whole and seeks to replace it with a different, intelligible, and in certain respects analogous content"] ... might be called the "decoding method," as it treats the dream as a kind of secret writing in which every sign is translated by means of a fixed key into another sign whose significance is known. I have had a dream of a letter, for example, but also of a funeral or the like; I now consult a "dream-book" and discover that 'letter' is to be translated as "ill humour," "funeral" as "betrothal."
>
>   (p. 79)

Freud goes on to explain that his own method, though scientific in nature, is closer to the "symbolic" than to the "decoding" method:

> Patients who had undertaken to inform me of all the thoughts and ideas that beset them on a certain subject told me their dreams, and in this way taught me that a dream can be interpolated into the psychical chain which, starting from a pathological idea, can be traced backwards in the

memory. This suggested that the dream itself might be treated as a symptom, and that the method of interpretations for symptoms might be applied to dreams.

(pp. 80–81)

7 Sigmund Freud, *The Unconscious*. Trans., Graham Frankland (London: Penguin Books, 2005). "The Unconscious," p. 64/*SE* XIV, p. 181.
8 Ibid. p. 195.
9 "Drives and their Fates" in *The Unconscious*, p. 36/*SE* Vol. XIV, p. 147.
10 Ibid. p. 25/p. 132.
11 *Portable Kristeva*, p. 237.
12 Ibid. p. 231.
13 Ibid. p. 39/p. 151.
14 *AW* 1813, p. 120.
15 *STI*, p. 50.
16 Ibid. p. 69.
17 Schelling writes in the *Weltalter* that the goal of his science is to engage with the "boundary": "For the essential thing in scientific progression is to recognize the boundary of each moment and to focus on it sharply" (1813, p. 131).
18 *SE* Vol. XXII, p. 168. *New Introductory Lectures on Psychoanalysis*, p. 209.
19 It is worth noting that it is in Freud's polemic against religion, *Future of an Illusion*, that he implicitly draws science and philosophy closer to religion—precisely insofar as each kind of illusion conceals a wish for the world to make sense: "And thus a store of ideas is created, born from man's need to make his helplessness tolerable and built up from the material of memories of the helplessness of his own childhood and the childhood of the human race" (*SE* Vol. XXI, p. 18).
20 Lecture 1, p. 15.

21   … originally the ego includes everything, later it separates off an external world from itself. Our present ego-feeling is, therefore, only a shrunken residue of a much more inclusive—indeed, an all-embracing—feeling which corresponded to a more intimate bond between the ego and the world about it.

(*Civilization and Its Discontents*, *SE* Vol. XXI, p. 68)

See Chapters 1 and 4 for a more detailed examination of primary narcissism.
22 "At this point, however, a curious psychic transformation occurred in the mind of Kronos's devotees. For precisely in the act of his destroying his antagonist [Uranus], Kronos became intimately identified with him" (Beach, p. 200).
23 Lecture 3, p. 45.
24 *FS*, p. 360.
25 See: Introduction, pp. 38–39 for a discussion of Freud's "navel of the dream" in *The Interpretation of Dreams* that suggests a particularly affecting admission of this impossibility.

26 *Philosophy of Art*, p. 38.
27 As Schelling writes in *System of Transcendental Idealism:*

> For if it is through self-consciousness that all limitation originates, and thus all time as well, this original act cannot itself occur in time; hence, of the rational being as such, one can no more say that it has begun to exist than that it has existed for all time; the self as self is absolutely eternal, that is, outside time altogether.
>
> (p. 48)

28 Lecture 5, p. 75.
29 Lecture 3 p. 41.
30 I call the "philosophical/scientific" views those which:

> say that no gods are meant in mythology at all; neither proper and real nor improper and unreal, no personalities, but rather impersonal objects that are only represented poetically as persons. Personification is the principle of this method of interpretation; either ethically customary or natural properties and phenomena are personified.
>
> (Lecture 2, p. 24)

This includes the possibility of geniuses, whether scientific, political, or philosophical, who cover their (perhaps rudimentary) knowledge of the world with poesy in order to communicate it to society at large.

31 Lecture 1, p. 14.
32 Lecture 3, p. 45.
33 Cited in Beach (1994), p. 228.
34 Although I will deal with successive polytheism in greater detail through the course of this chapter, Schelling initially uses the term as a way to distinguish a historical system of the gods from a merely hierarchical one. In other words, Schelling's interest lies in the genealogy of the gods given in mythology, and in successive polytheism as a recollection and trace of an *actual* genealogy:

> Indeed, it can escape to whom it is pointed out that there is a great difference between the polytheism that emerges when indeed a greater or lesser number of gods is conceived, which are however *subordinated* to *one and the same god* as their highest and master, and that polytheism that emerges when *several* gods are assumed, but each of them is the *highest* and *dominating* in a certain time and for this reason can only *follow* one another. If we think to ourselves, say, that the Greek history of the gods had, instead of the *three* races of gods—which it has follow one upon the other—only one, say that of Zeus, then it would also only know of gods (all of which would be resolved into Zeus, as their common unity) coexisting and simultaneous with each other, it would know only of *simultaneous* polytheism. Now, however, it has *three* systems of gods, and in each one One god is the highest ... Thus these

three gods cannot be simultaneous ones but rather only *mutually exclud-ing*, and for this reason ones *following one another in time*. So long as Uranus dominates, Kronos cannot; and should Zeus attain dominance, Kronos must recede into the past. Thus we will name this polytheism the *successive* polytheism [*successiven Polytheismus*].

(Lecture 6 p. 86)

35 Lecture 5 p. 82.
36 Ibid. p. 83.
37 Ibid. p. 83.
38 Ibid. p. 83.
39 Lecture 6, p. 88.
40 Markus Gabriel and Slavoj Žižek, *Mythology, Madness and Laughter: Sub-jectivity in German Idealism* (New York: Continuum, 2009), p. 64.
41 Lecture 5 p. 76.
42 Gabriel (2009), p. 66.
43 Lecture 3, p. 40.
44 Schelling deals with the relationship between periphery and center at some length in his *Freedom* essay:

> The most appropriate comparison is here offered by disease, which is the true counterpart of evil and sin, as it constitutes that disorder which entered nature through a misuse of freedom. Disease of the whole organ-ism can never exist without the hidden forces of the depths being unloosed; it occurs when the irritable principle which ought to rule as the innermost tie of forces in the quiet deep, activates itself, or when Archaos is provoked to desert his quiet residence at the center of things and steps forth into the surroundings. So, on the other hand, *all radical cure con-sists in the reestablishment of the relation of the periphery to the center, and the transition from disease to health can really only take place through its opposite, that is through the restoration of separate and indi-vidual life to the inner light of being, whence there recurs the division.*

(p. 41; my italics)

45 See Schiller's account of a similar development in "On Naïve and Sentimen-tal Poetry" in *Essays* (pp. 179–260).
46 Lecture 6, p. 97.
47 *SE* Vol. XIII, p. 25.
48 Ibid. p. 153.
49 Lecture 6, p. 89.
50 *SE* Vol. XXI, pp. 16–17.
51 It is worth noting that before Freud classed totemism and mythology together with monotheistic world religions, Schelling's claims for the continuum of religious phenomena—stretching from paganism to Christianity—were relat-ively new and controversial. See: Beach (1994) pp. 4–23 for a discussion of these debates.

52 *BPP*, pp. 94–95/*SE* Vol. XVIII, pp. 57–58.

53 *SE* Vol. XXI, p. 95.

54 In Freud's *A Phylogenetic Fantasy*, he posits not only the killing of the primal father by his sons, but also the castration of the sons by the father: "experiences admonish us, however, to substitute another, more gruesome solution—namely, that he robs them of their manhood—after which they are able to stay in the horde as harmless laborers" (p. 17). This text, a so-called twelfth metapsychological paper, written in 1915, was found among Freud's unpublished drafts in 1983. In large part, this text is important due to Freud's inclusion of a pre-Ice Age period of general happiness and satisfaction; his claim is that, due to the shortages and exigency of the Ice Age, the conflicts within the primal horde appear and—more importantly—become etched into human psychic life.

55 *SE* Vol. XXI, p. 125.

56 Ibid. p. 131.

57 See Yosef Hayim Yerushalmi, *Freud's Moses: Judaism Terminable and Interminable* (New Haven: Yale University Press, 1991). Yerushalmi offers a radical reading of Freud's *Moses*, along with an interpretation of the connection between Judaism and psychoanalysis more generally.

58 Cited from: *SE* Vol. XXIII p. 92. Derrida goes on:

> (I have attempted elsewhere to show, and cannot go into it here, that each time the word *unheimlich* appears in Freud's text—and not only in the essay of this title *Das Unheimlich*—one can localize an uncontrollable undecidability in the axiomatics, the epistemology, the logic, the order of the discourse and of the thetic or theoretic statements; and the same is true, in just as significant a way, of Heidegger.)
>
> (p. 46)

In light of this hint of Derrida's, we notice that in Freud's late work on religion—*Future of an Illusion*—he does in fact return to the language of the uncanny yet again:

> But if the elements have passions that rage as they do in our own souls, if death itself is not something spontaneous but the violent act of an evil Will, if everywhere in nature there are Beings around us of a kind that we know in our own society, then we can breathe freely, can feel at home in the uncanny and can deal by psychical means with our senseless anxiety.
>
> (*SE* Vol. XXI, pp. 16–17)

59 Sigmund Freud, *A Phylogenetic Fantasy*. Trans. Axel Hoffer and Peter T. Hoffer (Cambridge: Harvard University Press, 1987).

60 See: Laplanche and Pontalis, *The Language of Psychoanalysis* for discussions of the development of the terms "introjection," "projection," and "identification" in psychoanalytic theory.

61 Lecture 5, p. 79.
62 See Markus Gabriel's essay "The Mythological Being of Reflection" in *Mythology, Madness and Laughter* for a sustained and fruitful discussion of the central role of mythology in Schelling and for a provocative distinction between *constitutive* and *regulative* mythology (p. 66).
63 Lecture 3, p. 37.
64 Lear (1990) p. 36.
65 Ibid. p. 37.
66 *Philosophy of Art*, pp. 48–49.
67 Ferenczi p. 230.
68 See Jonathan Lear, *Love and Its Place in Nature: A Philosophical Interpretation of Freudian Psychoanalysis* (New York: Farrar, Straus and Giroux, 1990).
69 "Inhibitions, Symptoms and Anxiety," p. 3/*SE* Vol. XX p. 87.
70 Ibid. pp. 108–109.
71 Ibid. p. 130, my italics.
72 See: "Loss of Reality in Neurosis and Psychosis," *SE* Vol. XIX pp. 183–190.
73 See Markus Gabriel's essay "The Mythological Being of Reflection" in *Mythology, Madness and Laughter* for a sustained and fruitful discussion of the central role of mythology in Schelling, and for a provocative distinction between *constitutive* and *regulative* mythology (p. 66).
74 At the metaphysical level, mythologizing is thus a form of cure for certain Kantian limitations. Goudeli says something quite similar:

> His suggestion [in *AW*] seems to be that, when we think of the unconditioned, we do not necessarily reach impenetrable dead ends; instead, we can create stories, myths and surmises, which are certainly full of antinomies and paradoxes, but nonetheless, we can do it endlessly. For man himself is part of the "unconditioned" in the moments of his reenactment of the act of creation, in the special experiences where man regenerates the paradox of life and death that permeates his own mode of being. Man's "nexus of living forces," imagination, reason, creativity are but moments in the paradoxical unity of the history of becoming.
>
> (p. 124)

75 *Studies on Hysteria*, *SE* Vol. II pp. 1–323.

Conclusion
Uncanny freedom

At this point, where existence and interpretation converge, I would like to briefly retrace the path that brought us here, and to do so by way of acknowledging two themes that have been left out: first I will look at the role of the imagination in Schelling, and then go on to consider sublimation in Freud. I believe that these "omissions" are not unrelated. They, too, speak to the dislocated subjectivity I have approached through the border phenomena of fantasy and drive, and through the temporality of tragedy and trauma. Taken together, they help us think through concrete possibilities for revitalizing philosophy and psychoanalysis by way of the uncanny.

The kind of truth that I have tried to suggest is bound up with psychoanalysis and with Schelling's philosophy—and, furthermore, the possibility of becoming available to such a truth—has everything to do with a certain conception of creative imagination or fantasy, particularly in regards to self-understanding. If I have tended to use these terms interchangeably, while focusing more on fantasy, I would like to take the time now to defend that choice. The ambiguity that characterizes imagination in the Kantian tradition, between passivity (receptivity) and activity (productivity), is maintained in the Freudian use of fantasy; furthermore, both imagination [*Einbildung*] and fantasy [*Phantasie*] can suggest a paradoxically immaterial materiality—or, in more Derridean language, a virtual reality. That is, the language denotes the brute physicality of a *picture* [*Bild*] or *appearance* (from the Greek *phantasia*), while at the same time gesturing at the difference between what is emphatically real and what is merely imagined. That is, imagination is differentiated from sensation on account of the *absence* of an empirical object, but is itself an activity of bringing to *presence*. As John Sallis puts it so succinctly in *The Gathering of Reason*:

Consequently, imagination as the power of intuiting an object without its presence, of intuiting an absent object, involves *making present* something which is and remains in another regard *absent*. Even at this elementary level imagination inaugurates a certain play of presence and absence, a gathering into presence. And because it *makes* something present, imagination cannot be merely passive (as sense is); it is an active stem within sensibility, within passivity in general. Inaugurating a play of presence and absence, imagination installs itself as a play of activity and passivity, as activity within passivity.[1]

Sallis's reading of the Kantian imagination is of course compatible with Heidegger's remarks in his *Kantbuch*, where the latter emphasizes the creative power and ambivalent space of the imagination in terms of the formation of "the horizon of objectivity as such."[2] It is worth noting, however, that Heidegger immediately goes on to point out that while the imagination can be productive in this sense, it is so only with respect to the production of a "possible object" and that the realization of such an object is "never accomplished by the imagination itself."[3] Even so, given Sallis's point about the play of the imagination *between* presence and absence, the very notion of production—of relating possibility to its realization—must be revisited. Indeed, this is precisely the space in which Schelling developed his account of intellectual intuition: while imagination cannot by itself will a particular empirical *object* into existence, this does not exclude the possibility of a self-productive *subject*. If we take seriously the idea that there is no "objective" reality beneath our meaningful engagements with it, a claim I have suggested that both Schelling and Freud put forth in their own manners, this productive imagination would have some far-reaching consequences.

So while I would not want to collapse imagination into fantasy, my preference for the latter term in large part derives from its unique place in psychoanalysis. That is, I believe we are better able to grasp Schelling's account of the productive imagination as a departure from the Kantian tradition—as an activity that weaves together the potencies of nature with the personalities of man and God—if we think of it in terms of the unconscious. In ordinary English usage, imagination tends to be tied up with conscious creativity while fantasy, in large part due to our Freudian inheritance, connotes the darker, unconscious desires, complexes and forms of thinking and feeling that place pressure on familiar narrative arcs and traditional logical and temporal structures. Whereas the freedom of the Kantian imagination is generally reduced to a certain form of schematic "spontaneity" that is organized and subdued through the understanding, Schelling confronts us with the uncanny aspect of imagination (which I call *fantasy*) and its vulnerable, excessive freedom.

While much important work has been (and I'm sure will continue to be) done on the philosophy of imagination—including an interrogation of the ambivalence between the appearance and that which appears, unity and multiplicity, and passivity and activity—my own contribution in this book has a slightly different, though hardly unrelated, emphasis.[4] My interest in the convergence of Schelling's metaphysics and Freudian psychoanalysis concerns the uncanny space of the boundary. And insofar as this boundary, like the truth that it embodies, ought to remain non-objective, it would confuse the matter to introduce the problematic of the image as such and to assume the unified subject that the Kantian *Einbildung* can imply. In the German, *Einbildung* suggests a process of unification/formation that conceals the equally powerful process of dislocation/dissolution, where the latter lies as much at the heart of the ambivalent reality I have tried to develop here. Indeed, as Kyriaki Goudeli points out in *Challenges to German Idealism*, the Kantian imagination that Schelling takes up and rearticulates runs aground on precisely this point:

> Furthermore, the requirement of the static, formal identity of the self excludes the possibility of dreams, visions, or any states where the subject does not recognize in them its continuing and absolutely same ego—in fact, states which, as will be seen in the following chapters, may lead to even deeper levels of self-consciousness. Instead, according to Kant, these states do not count at all as synthesized representations but as mere ineffable glances, and ultimately as irrational ones; the formal unity of the self excludes the possibility of any sense of break, loss or change of its pure abiding identity.[5]

The advantage in working with the concept of fantasy, then, comes in part from the broader psychoanalytic implementation of a subjectivity grounded in dislocation—in precisely those moments of break, loss, and "ineffable glances" that Kant could not or would not contend with. Indeed, Freud's wide-ranging applications of the term "fantasy" speak to its dual capacity to cover over and expose the disruptions that constitute and disturb identity—to speak and to withhold the truth while reconfiguring and bringing to light the limits between self and world. The acknowledgment of unconscious fantasies, no less than the interpretation of dreams, is an act of creativity; fantasies are not there fully formed, to be retrieved, and put aside, but exist as a negotiation of the limit between what we have been and how we choose to be. Fantasy, as Freud reminds us, is the ineradicable root and motor of memory and perception. Fantasy is thus *the* act of self/world-constitution, at the most concrete level, while imagination was so for Kant only theoretically.

With respect to this essentially liminal, uncanny character of fantasy, where spatio-temporal reality confronts its Other, Julia Kristeva writes in *Time and Sense*:

> The fantasy makes the unconscious into a narrative. As a result, when the outside-time of the unconscious is named and recounted, it acquires a meaning, a goal, and a value. The fantasy, along with the dream narrative, becomes a narration torn between the atemporality of the unconscious and the forward-moving flight of the story. The fantasy is the novel that Freud asked his patients to bring him. As opposed to the neurotic, who is afraid and ashamed of his fantasies, and the pervert, who acts them out meticulously without being disturbed by what they mean, the analysand is invited to do with words what the pervert does with things (and with people who are reduced to mere things). He is invited to *stage* his unconscious ... [t]he fantasy is at the boundary between the outside-time space of the unconscious (which threatens to consume it by depriving it of words in order to direct it toward drives and acts) and the haste of narration (which is the hero's seduction of his victim and narrator's seduction of his addressee).[6]

Kristeva locates fantasy as a temporalizing moment—as that which appears only in its resistance to the conceptual framing through which it is realized. Its therapeutic import derives as much from the empathetic collaboration between analyst and analysand—their mutual *production*—as it does from its value in developing a personal, interpretive rubric. My intention is thus not to disavow the role of the imagination, in either Schelling or Freud, but rather to insist on a reading that focuses more precisely on its therapeutic and even existential possibilities. The connection between freedom and fantasy that I have attempted to draw out of Freud, in particular, comes down to our ability to acknowledge the fluidity of our past and to rearticulate our founding prophecies. Such an acknowledgment depends upon a conception of a subject whose truth is not concealed in or deluded by fantasy, but rather enlivened, and continually renewed by it. For Schelling as well, the redemptive and tragic possibilities of personality are dependent upon our continued connection to a past that must elude us, and our availability to a radically non-objective truth. This strong sense of freedom—a belief in and exhortation to authentic self-creation—is in no way a naïve, Romantic artifact. It remains essential to any philosophy concerned with lived experience, which is to say, to any philosophy worthy of the name.

Nevertheless, the emphasis on mythology and tragedy can be seen as not only naïve but, in fact, quite dangerous: we need only think of the political manipulation of Nietzsche's *The Birth of Tragedy*, which in many ways articulates the convergence of Schelling's and Freud's thought, to be reminded of what might be unleashed in the inauguration or recollection of *Volk* mythology. We would do well to remember Heidegger's appropriation of Hölderlin's line from *Patmos* in this regard: "But where danger is/grows the saving power also."[7] That is, I believe that both Freud and Schelling rely on a cure that always also endangers us—that disintegration, evil, and illness are necessary moments of freedom, goodness, and health. Salvation, no less than damnation, is subject to finitude. Or as Nietzsche puts it, the Dionysian is in no way fully separable from the Apollinian—our identity is inextricably linked to our utter diffusion, form and reason bound to chaos and desire.[8]

To return briefly to Freud, this precarious balance between reason and desire is perhaps best approached through his late, and relatively obscure paper "The Loss of Reality in Neurosis and Psychosis" (1924).[9] Insofar as I have suggested, following Hans Loewald, that there is a certain neurotic restraint at work in Freud's metapsychology, it is worthwhile to address the role of psychosis in expanding the psychoanalytic worldview. While I do not want to collapse the Apollinian into the neurotic, nor the Dionysian into the psychotic, it is still useful to understand the ways in which these are always and everywhere intertwined—the ways in which reality itself must be comprised of both psychotic and neurotic elements. Freud writes in this paper that:

[b]oth neurosis and psychosis are thus the expression of a rebellion on the part of the id against the external world, of its unwillingness— or, if one prefers, its incapacity—to adapt itself to the exigencies of reality, to *Ananke* [Necessity].[10]

Notably, Freud's language here becomes tragic, as he argues that the necessity characterizing reality is fundamentally at odds with the wild freedom of the id. The dichotomy between neurosis and psychosis that in a sense stabilizes his metapsychology is undone, as Freud recognizes that the irreducible alterity of the id cannot but expand and disturb the order of reality.

What I would really like to point to, however, is not so much the contrast between id and reality, or freedom and necessity, but rather what Freud understands by the "loss of reality." Schelling's understanding of freedom as the choice between good and evil in large part rests on a similar conception of reality lost and gained. One way to view this loss is in terms of limits that define truth and fantasy, inner and outer, self and other. Rather than any particular aspect of reality that might be distorted, denied, and replaced, the loss of reality indicates an utter vulnerability and disintegration. While Freud struggles to maintain a reality that exists independently of its dissolution or transformation, Schelling allows us a way to shore up this reality precisely because of such threats. If we look back at Schelling's account of evil and love in the *Freiheitsschrift*, we see that it is only in the pulsation of disintegration and creation, in the letting go of limits in order to realize them more fully, that love can manifest itself. In other words, it is only in loosening our grip on reality that we come closest to its truth. To cite Nietzsche again, the great thinker of psychotic reality:

He beholds the transfigured world of the stage and nevertheless denies it. He sees the tragic hero before him in epic clearness and beauty, and nevertheless rejoices in his annihilation. He comprehends the action deep down, and yet likes to flee into the incomprehensible. He feels the actions of the hero to be justified, and is nevertheless still more elated when these actions annihilate their agent. He shudders at the sufferings which will befall the hero, and yet anticipates in them a higher, much more overpowering joy. He sees more extensively and profoundly than ever, and yet wishes he were blind.[11]

It is in holding together impinging *presence* with its equally powerful and disruptive *withdrawal* that we glimpse reality. This is the essence of tragic vision, Nietzsche tells us, which can take seriously the world of necessity and appearance while simultaneously embracing its impermanence:

> Those who have never had the experience of having to see at the same time that they also longed to transcend all seeing will scarcely be able to imagine how definitely and clearly these two processes coexist and are felt at the same time, as one contemplates the tragic myth.[12]

Nietzsche's description of how tragedy makes us feel—how it provokes an almost nauseating double vision, an existential *vertigo*—returns us to the *other* missing theme: sublimation. But as with the imagination, it is not quite right to say that sublimation is absent from these pages. Chapter 1 was in fact a reading of the sublime, one that emphasizes the experience of splitting (as Nietzsche does in this passage) so neatly disposed of in Kant. I argued that by attending to Schiller's and Schelling's developments in the elucidation of the sublime, we could better understand a certain trajectory of philosophical thinking where the problem of human freedom becomes bound to the unconscious. One could hardly be blamed for thinking that if psychoanalysis had anything to contribute to the conversation, it would come from Freud's theory of sublimation; that, in this obscure process by which drive energy is transformed into intellectual and creative work, psychoanalysis comes as close as it ever does to freedom. Instead, I situated psychoanalysis within this philosophical tradition by way of the uncanny. I will take some time now to explain that move, and to show how my work on the uncanny can in fact open up Freud's remarkably underdeveloped concept of sublimation. I believe that right now this is an essential task of thinking, as we are confronted with the choice of either radically reimagining our intellectual institutions and practices, or admitting that the humanities are useless, meaningless, and removed from ordinary needs and experience: to reinvent sublimation is therefore to reinvent intellectual *life*.

Sublimation, we know, is the optimal fate of the drives; but, as Freud repeatedly admits, it is also the most mysterious. Borrowing the term from the chemists, he once again holds fast to science where another truth holds sway. In *Three Essays* Freud defines sublimation as the "diversion of sexual instinctual forces from sexual aims and their direction to new ones."[13] In *The Ego and the Id*, sublimation is essential to the process of identification and the formation of the super-ego: "The super-ego arises, as we know, from an identification with the father taken as a model. Every such identification is in the nature of a desexualization or even of sublimation."[14] But Freud never gives us much more than this, always intimating that a thorough treatment of the subject is in the works. As late as *Civilization and Its Discontents*, he can only say of sublimation that:

> A satisfaction of this kind, such as an artist's joy in creating, in giving his phantasies body, or a scientist's in solving problems or discovering truths, has a special quality which we shall certainly one day be able to characterize in metapsychological terms. At present we can only say figuratively that such satisfactions seem "finer and higher."[15]

As with Kant's account of the sublime, where reason asserts superiority over the forces of nature and the needs of the body, the process of sublimation seems to be a *freedom from* the compulsion of the sexual drives. It is essential to the formation and maintenance of civilization, as well as to the integrity of the ego.

But why does the whole process remain so obscure? Here I take up Leo Bersani's reading of sublimation in his incredibly fascinating and powerful book, *The Culture of Redemption*, as a fertile fault-line in Freud that revitalizes psychoanalysis.[16] He argues that the sketchy, and often contradictory, accounts of sublimation express a deep and pervasive problem in Freud: how to delimit the sexual. That is, a real theory of sublimation would require that psychoanalysis take up the problem of the *boundary*—in this case, between the sexual and the non-sexual—as I have tried to do through the uncanny. Bersani's sublimation, with its insistence on our irredeemably "shattered" subjectivity and the limits of interpretability, lends support to my overarching claim that there is a therapeutic need for a psychoanalytic account of freedom. In Schelling's system I found the kind of freedom that psychoanalysis ought to recognize and strive for in practice, one that keeps open, and returns us to our grounding instability. In Bersani's work on sublimation, where the erotic is the name for that which resists all formulation, we can see just how much psychoanalysis has to gain from this kind of metaphysical thinking:

it is life that sticks in the throat of reason. When Bersani insists that sublimation is not a movement away from or beyond the sexual (a metaphorical *refinement*), but rather down into its erotic essence (a literal *distillation*), he brings us closer to life.[17]

The "beginning" of subjectivity—which is to say, of the *unity* of the subject—is fragmentation:

> The pleasurable-unpleasurable tension sexuality—the pain of self-shattering excitement—aims at being maintained, replicated, and even increased. The human subject is originally *shattered into* sexuality ... It is as if a certain split occurred in consciousness, a split that paradoxically is also the first experience of self-integration. In this self-reflexive move, a pleasurably shattered consciousness becomes aware of itself as the object of its desire.[18]

It is this foundational, masochistic moment that Bersani considers a kind of "originary sublimation."[19] As I did in Chapter 3, he follows up on Laplanche's deconstruction of a self-enclosed primary narcissism in favor of a wounded subjectivity. What I find useful and important here, in terms of my own work and the themes I have tried to develop, is the way he characterizes the union of creativity and dissolution. As I attempted to work out at the level of ontology, Bersani describes the temporal confusion of a self-seeking that precedes the self. More importantly, he draws attention to the deception that is already there, tied up from the beginning with truth. Not only do we shatter *ourselves* into existence, but reality as well. And this recurs, or ought to, again and again; what else could creativity—secondary sublimation—mean to us? What else could freedom be?

The claim that philosophy, science, art, and therapy are all ways of breaking down and refashioning the limits of reality is itself a concrete challenge to the dichotomy between subjective and objective (which is so easily reified in the opposition between the humanities and the sciences). The trend has been for academics, and indeed all of us, to focus on narrower and narrower concerns and areas of expertise. We feel, simultaneously, too unqualified and too reasonable to deal with *reality* as such: Helpless, and omnipotent. And so I will consider it no small contribution to return to the "big" questions and concerns that might yet reach beyond professional journals and university classrooms. I would thus like to conclude by posing a few questions that, I hope, might suggest a concrete way forward—toward a philosophical therapy for our time. I have tried to argue that, within Freud's corpus, there is another, uncanny Freudian narrative; that, read alongside Schelling, this uncanny psychoanalysis makes reality as vulnerable, as mysterious, and free, as we ourselves are. But what, then, should we do? Doesn't this only lead to nihilism, to solipsistic despair? Are philosophy and psychoanalysis only narcissistic luxuries? Are science and technology the only truth and comfort?

I began this book still frustrated by Freud's insistence that psychoanalysis does not have a *Weltanschauung* of its own; that, from its rudimentary beginnings, he hoped it would become more accurate, more verifiable—more scientific. As I come to the end, I think about how terribly divided he was: Freud the clinician, and Freud the philosopher, Freud the pragmatist, and Freud the clairvoyant. Yet I myself had never noticed the bizarre way this conflict erupts in one of his final lectures, "The Question of a *Weltanschauung*":

> Philosophy is not opposed to science, it behaves like a science and works in part by the same methods; it departs from it, however, by clinging to the illusion of being able to present a picture of the universe which is without gaps and coherent, though one which is bound to collapse with every fresh advance in our knowledge. It goes astray in its method by overestimating the epistemological value of our logical operations and by accepting other sources of knowledge such as intuition.[20]

Freud's description here of how philosophy falls short of science—and thus of truth—is rather familiar. This is not the first time that he has compared philosophy to a paranoiac's fantasy. Basically, Freud argues that psychoanalysis falls under the scientific *Weltanschauung*, which is superior to all others because it is no *Weltanschauung* at all. If we attempt to "present a picture of the universe which is without gaps and coherent," we are merely "clinging to [an] illusion." Indeed, this is a most succinct version of Schellingian evil: a totalizing system, insensitive to otherness, to real difference. I have tried to argue that freedom—therapeutically and philosophically—is the acknowledgment of our role in creating and dissolving these pictures; that in the uncanny we sense that there is only *apparent* coherence, that we might have constructed the world and ourselves, and we might do so otherwise. I agree with Freud here, and in fact believe this glosses his most important and radical insight about the nature of truth (and, which for me, amounts to the same regarding the uncanny): the rational cannot encompass the real. And so his charge that philosophy "overestimates" logic is clear enough. But why, then, does he also claim that philosophy is not logical enough—that it gives too much weight to such unscientific things as intuition? I think Freud means to say that while reality is not rational, the truth is not just a matter of feeling. Whatever form it takes, clarity is dangerous, and worthy of suspicion.

I have always been drawn to Freud precisely for this suspicion, his genius for drawing us into the elusive gaps and stubborn resistances of our experience. I began this project with the idea that there is something in Schelling's metaphysics that helps us attend to reality as such in the same way Freud helps us attend to ourselves. And I hoped that in the process of writing and thinking about this, I would hit upon something more than a clever comparison or series of connections. My feeling now, more than ever, is that the future of psychoanalysis and of philosophy depends upon an expanded sense of the therapeutic. On the one hand, I think that both education and therapy have become increasingly isolating and isolated activities; and, on the other, these intellectual practices suffer from being far too easily and completely integrated into socially and culturally defined norms of success and happiness. I do not mean to suggest (at least, not only) that philosophy and psychoanalysis make us too comfortable. Comfortable is hardly a word I would use to describe the current age. Whenever I read *Civilization and Its Discontents* with my students they don't, at first, admit to any such discontents; the very idea of repression seems alien (as, I suppose, it always should). But eventually, all the anxiety, and attention deficit disorders come out, the depression, and obsessions. It occurs to me that the very same thing I find so attractive in Freud rubs them the wrong way—the grandness of his theory, the tenacity with which he makes their everyday, private experience into something much more important. He makes their disbelief just another piece of evidence. There is something downright terrifying in the audacity. If my students think Freud makes too much out everything, you can imagine how they read Schelling's speculation about the inchoate drives that erupt into existence, the desire, and longing as the very basis of reality. Despite its pretensions, Metaphysics seems to have nothing to do with reality at all. And this is the crux of the issue we face: nothing could be farther from reality than talk about the nature of reality.

Schelling posits that the only way to know the world is to know it *personally*—that is, in the way we become familiar with our own or another person. And this of course seems absurd, almost mythological. In fact, it is mythological, and this is Schelling's method for helping us recognize what Freud would not: that science *does* present a picture of the world—all the more pernicious and seductive because we have forgotten it is a picture at all. The therapeutic action peculiar to psychoanalysis is self-interpretation—a method for acknowledging our narratives *as* narratives, without for that reason taking them any less seriously. But, through this very practice, we catch a glimpse of the boundary between self and world. Psychoanalysis doesn't just make my world different, it does so by showing me that *I have a world* in the first place. Psychoanalysis both complicates and reinforces Schelling's basic idea: yes, to know reality we need to engage with the world empathetically, intimately. We can feel at home in it, akin to it, precisely because of its strangeness, its disturbing, unruly depths.

Notes

1 Sallis (2005) p. 147.
2 Martin Heidegger, *Kant and the Problem of Metaphysics* (Forgotten Books, 2012), p. 137.
3 Ibid. p. 137.
4 To name just a few: John Sallis, *The Gathering of Reason* (Albany: State University of New York Press, 2005); *Double Truth* (Albany: State University of New York Press, 1995); *The Logic of Imagination: The Expanse of the Elemental* (Bloomington: Indiana University Press, 2012). Richard Kearney, *The Wake of Imagination: Towards a Post-Modern Culture* (New York: Routledge, 1998); *Poetics of Imagining: Modern to Post-Modern* (Edinburgh: Edinburgh University Press, 1998).
5 Goudeli (2002) p. 31.
6 *The Portable Kristeva*, p. 130.
7 Martin Heidegger, *The Question Concerning Technology and Other Essays*, p. 34. Trans. William Lovitt (New York: Harper Perennial, 1977).

8   Of this foundation of all existence—the Dionysian basic ground of the world—not one whit more may enter the consciousness of the human individual than can be overcome again by his Apollinian power of transfiguration. Thus these two art drives must unfold their powers in a strict proportion, according to the law of eternal justice. Where the Dionysian powers rise up as impetuously as we experience them now, Apollo, too,

must already have descended among us, wrapped in a cloud; and the next generation will probably behold his most ample beautiful effects.

(Friedrich Nietzsche, *Basic Writings of Nietzsche*. Ed. Walter Kaufmann [New York: The Modern Library, 2000] p. 144)

9 *SE* Vol. XIX, pp. 182–187.
10 Ibid. p. 185.
11 Friedrich Nietzsche, *The Birth of Tragedy*, p. 131.
12 Ibid. p. 140.
13 *SE* Vol. VII, p. 178.
14 *SE* Vol. XIX, p. 54.
15 *SE* Vol. XXI, p. 79.
16 Leo Bersani, *The Culture of Redemption* (Cambridge: Harvard University Press, 1990).
17 Ibid.

A sublimation is only secondarily (and not even necessarily) an ennobling, or a making sublime; it is, most profoundly, a burning away of the occasion, or at least *the dream of purely burn*. Far from being a transcendence of the sexual, sublimations are thus grounded in unalloyed sexuality.

(p. 37)

18 Ibid. p. 36.
19 Ibid. p. 37.
20 *SE* Vol. XXII, p. 160.

Bibliography

Altman, Matthew C. and Cynthia D. Coe. *The Fractured Self in Freud and German Philosophy*. New York: Palgrave Macmillan, 2013.

Bass, Alan. *Interpretation and Difference*. Stanford: Stanford University Press, 2006.

Beach, Edward A. *The Potencies of God(s)*. Albany: State University of New York Press, 1994.

Behler, Ernst, ed. *Fichte, Jacobi, and Schelling: Philosophy of German Idealism*. New York: Continuum, 2003.

Beiser, Frederick C. *Aesthetics and Subjectivity: From Kant to Nietzsche*. Manchester: Manchester University Press, 2003.

Beiser, Frederick C. *The Fate of Reason: German Philosophy from Kant to Fichte*. Cambridge: Harvard University Press, 1987.

Beiser, Frederick C. *German Idealism: The Struggle Against Subjectivism*. Cambridge: Harvard University Press, 2008.

Beiser, Frederick C. *The Romantic Imperative*. Cambridge: Harvard University Press, 2003.

Beiser, Frederick C. *Schiller as Philosopher: A Re-Examination*. Oxford: Clarendon Press, 2005.

Bersani, Leo. *The Culture of Redemption*. Cambridge: Harvard University Press, 1990.

Bowie, Andrew. *From Romanticism to Critical Theory*. London: Routledge, 1997.

Bowie, Andrew, ed. *Schelling and Modern European Philosophy: An Introduction*. London: Routledge, 1993.

Brown, Norman O. *Life Against Death: The Psychoanalytical Meaning of History*. Hanover: Wesleyan University Press, 1959.

Caruth, Cathy. *Unclaimed Experience: Trauma, Narrative, and History*. Baltimore: Johns Hopkins University Press, 1996.

Cavell, Stanley. *Must We Mean What We Say?* Cambridge: Cambridge University Press, 1976.

Cavell, Stanley. *In Quest of the Ordinary: Lines of Skepticism and Romanticism*. Chicago: The University of Chicago Press, 1988.

Derrida, Jacques. *Dissemination*. Trans. Barbara Johnson. Chicago: The University of Chicago Press, 1981.

Derrida, Jacques. *The Postcard*. Trans. Alan Bass. Chicago: The University of Chicago Press, 1987.

Derrida, Jacques. *Psyche: Inventions of the Other*. Stanford: Stanford University Press, 2007.

Derrida, Jacques. *Resistances of Psychoanalysis*. Trans. Kamuf, Peggy, Pascale-Anne Brault and Michael Naas. Stanford: Stanford University Press, 1998.

Derrida, Jacques. *Specters of Marx*. Trans. Peggy Kamuf. New York: Routledge, 1994.

Esposito, Joseph L. *Schelling's Idealism and Philosophy of Nature*. Lewisburg: Bucknell University Press, 1977.

Fackenheim, Emil L. *The God Within: Kant, Schelling and Historicity*. Toronto: University of Toronto Press, 1996.

Ffytche, Matt. *The Foundation of the Unconscious: Schelling, Freud and the Birth of the Modern Psyche*. Cambridge: Cambridge University Press, 2011.

Fichte, Johann G. *Early Philosophical Writings*. Trans. Daniel Breazeale. Ithaca: Cornell University Press, 1988.

Fichte, Johann G. *Foundations of Natural Right*. Trans. Michael Baur. Cambridge: Cambridge University Press, 2000.

Fichte, Johann G. *The Science of Knowledge*. Trans. Peter Heath and John Lachs. Cambridge: Cambridge University Press, 1970.

Freud, Sigmund. *Beyond the Pleasure Principle*. Standard Edition (vol. XVIII, pp. 1–64). London: Hogarth Press, 1920.

Freud, Sigmund. *Dreams and Telepathy*. Standard Edition (vol. XVIII, pp. 196–221). London: Hogarth Press, 1921.

Freud, Sigmund. *The Ego and the Id*. Standard Edition (vol. XIX, pp. 1–66). London: Hogarth Press, 1923.

Freud, Sigmund. *Formulations Regarding Two Principles of Mental Functioning*. Standard Edition (vol. XII, pp. 215–226). London: Hogarth Press, 1925.

Freud, Sigmund. *Instincts and their Vicissitudes*. Standard Edition (vol. XIV, pp. 114–140). London: Hogarth Press, 1915.

Freud, Sigmund. *The Interpretation of Dreams*. Standard Edition (vol. IV, pp. ix–627). London: Hogarth Press, 1900.

Freud, Sigmund. *New Introductory Lectures to Psychoanalysis*. Standard Edition (vol. XXII, pp. 1–182). London: Hogarth Press, 1933.

Freud, Sigmund. *Psychoanalysis and Telepathy*. Standard Edition (vol. XVIII, pp. 175–193). London: Hogarth Press, 1921.

Freud, Sigmund. *The Psychopathology of Everyday Life*. Standard Edition (vol. VI, pp. vii–296). London: Hogarth Press, 1901.

Freud, Sigmund. *Some Neurotic Mechanisms in Jealousy, Paranoia and Homosexuality.* Standard Edition (vol. XVIII, pp. 222–232). London: Hogarth Press, 1922.

Freud, Sigmund. *Three Case Histories.* New York: Touchstone, 1963.

Freud, Sigmund. *The Uncanny.* Standard Edition (vol. XVII, pp. 218–256). London: Hogarth Press, 1919.

Freydberg, Bernard. *Schelling's Dialogical Freedom Essay.* Albany: State University of New York Press, 2008.

Gabriel, Markus and Slavoj Žižek. *Mythology, Madness and Laughter: Subjectivity in German Idealism.* London: Continuum, 2009.

Gay, Peter. *Freud: A Life For Our Time.* New York: W. W. Norton & Company, Inc., 1988.

Goudeli, Kyriaki. *Challenges to German Idealism.* New York: Palgrave Macmillan, 2002.

Grünbaum, Adolf. *The Foundations of Psychoanalysis: A Philosophical Critique.* Berkeley: University of California Press, 1984.

Hadot, Pierre. *Philosophy as a Way of Life* London: Blackwell Publishing, 1995.

Haymer, Paul C. *Reason and Existence: Schelling's Philosophy of History.* Leiden: E. J. Brill, 1967.

Heidegger, Martin. *Being and Time.* Trans. Joan Stambaugh. Albany: State University of New York, 1953.

Heidegger, Martin. *The Question Concerning Technology and Other Essays.* Trans. William Lovitt. New York: Harper Perennial, 1977.

Heidegger, Martin. *Schelling's Treatise on the Essence of Human Freedom.* Trans. Joan Stambaugh. Athens: Ohio University Press, 1985.

Henrich, Dieter. *Between Kant and Hegel: Lectures on German Idealism.* Cambridge: Harvard University Press, 2003.

Kant, Immanuel. *Critique of Judgment.* Trans. Warner Pluhar. Indianapolis: Hackett Publishing Company, 1987.

Kant, Immanuel. *Critique of Pure Reason.* Trans. Paul Guyer and Allen W. Wood. Cambridge: Cambridge University Press, 1997.

Kant, Immanuel. *Religion Within the Limits of Reason Alone.* Trans. Green, Theodore M. and Hoyt H. Hudson. La Salle: The Open Court Publishing Company, 1934.

Kierkegaard, Soren. *The Concept of Anxiety.* Trans. Reidar Thomte. Princeton: Princeton University Press, 1980.

Krell, David F. *The Tragic Absolute: German Idealism and the Languishing God.* Bloomington: Indiana University Press, 2005.

Kristeva, Julia. *The Portable Kristeva.* Ed. Kelly Oliver. New York: Columbia University Press, 2002.

Kristeva, Julia. *Strangers to Ourselves*. Trans. Leon S. Roudiez. New York: Columbia University Press, 1991.

Lacan, Jacques. *Anxiety 1962–1963 Book X*. Trans. Cormac Gallagher (from unedited French manuscripts).

Lacan, Jacques. *Écrits*. Trans. Bruce Fink. New York: W. W. Norton & Company, 1996.

Laplanche, Jean. *Freud and the Sexual*. Trans. John Fletcher, Jonathan House, and Nicholas Ray. International Psychoanalytic Book, 2011.

Laplanche, Jean. *Life and Death in Psychoanalysis*. Trans. Jeffrey Mehlman. Baltimore: The Johns Hopkins University Press, 1970.

Laplanche, Jean. *New Foundations for Psychoanalysis*. Trans. David Macey. Cambridge: Basil Blackwell, 1987.

Laplanche, Jean and Jean-Bertrand Pontalis. *The Language of Psychoanalysis*. Trans. Donald Nicholson-Smith. London: Hogarth, 1973.

Lear, Jonathan. *Happiness, Death and the Remainder of Life*. Cambridge: Harvard University Press, 2000.

Lear, Jonathan. *Love and its Place in Nature*. New Haven: Yale University Press, 1990.

Loewald, Hans. (1976). *Perspectives on Memory. Collected Papers and Monographs*. Maryland: University Publishing Group, 2000.

Loewald, Hans. (1976). *Psychoanalysis and the History of the Individual. Collected Papers and Monographs*. Maryland: University Publishing Group, 2000.

Loewald, Hans. *Psychoanalysis in Search of Nature: Thoughts on Metapsychology, "Metaphysics," Projection. Annual of Psychoanalysis* (vol. 16, pp. 49–54).

Loewald, Hans. (1960). *On the Therapeutic Action of Psychoanalysis. Collected Papers and Monographs*. Maryland: University Publishing Group, 2000.

Marquard, Odo. *Farewell to Matters of Principle*. Trans. Robert M. Wallace. Oxford: Oxford University Press, 1989.

Marquard, Odo. *Transzendentaler Idealismus—Romantische Naturphilosophie— Psychoanalyse*. Gebundene Ausgabe, 1987.

Marx, Werner. *The Philosophy of F. W. J. Schelling: History, System and Freedom*. Bloomington: Indiana University Press, 1984.

Matthews, Bruce. *Schelling's Organic Form of Philosophy: Life as the Schema of Freedom*. Albany: State University of New York Press, 2011.

McGrath, Sean. *The Dark Ground of Spirit: Schelling and the Unconscious*. New York: Routledge, 2012.

Nicholls, Angus and Martin Liebscher, eds. *Thinking the Unconscious: Nineteenth-Century German Thought*. Cambridge: Cambridge University Press, 2010.

Nietzsche, Freidrich. *Basic Writings of Nietzsche*. Trans. Walter Kaufmann. New York: The Modern Library, 2000.

Norman, Judith and Alistair Welchman, eds. *The New Schelling*. London: Continuum, 2004.

Person, Ethel S., ed. *On Freud's "A Child is Being Beaten."* New Haven: Yale University Press, 1997.

Person, Ethel Spector, Peter Fonagy and Sérvulo Augusto Figueira, eds. *On Freud's "Creative Writers and Daydreaming."* New Haven: Yale University Press, 1995.

Richards, Robert J. *The Romantic Conception of Life: Science and Philosophy in the Age of Goethe*. Chicago: The University of Chicago Press, 2002.

Ricoeur, Paul. *Freud & Philosophy: An Essay on Interpretation*. Trans. Denis Savage. New Haven: Yale University Press, 1970.

Sallis, John. *Chorology: On Beginnings in Plato's* Timaeus. Bloomington: Indiany University Press, 1999.

Sallis, John. *Delimitations: Phenomenology and the End of Metaphysics*. Bloomington: Indiana University Press, 1986.

Sallis, John. *Force of Imagination: The Sense of the Elemental*. Bloomington: Indiana University Press, 2000.

Sallis, John. *The Gathering of Reason*. Albany: State University of New York Press, 2005.

Sallis, John. *The Verge of Philosophy*. Chicago: The University of Chicago Press, 2008.

Schelling, Friedrich W. J. *The Ages of the World* (1813). Trans. Judith Norman. Ann Arbor: The University of Michigan Press, 1997.

Schelling, Friedrich W. J. *The Ages of the World* (1815). Trans. Jason M. Wirth. Albany: State University of New York Press, 2000.

Schelling, Friedrich W. J. *Bruno: Or, On the Natural and Divine Principle of Things*. Trans. Michael G. Vater. Albany: State University of New York Press, 1984.

Schelling, Friedrich W. J. *Clara: Or, On Nature's Connection to the Spirit World*. Trans. Fiona Steinkamp. Albany: State University of New York Press, 2002.

Schelling, Friedrich W. J. *First Outline of a System of the Philosophy of Nature*. Trans. Keith R. Peterson. Albany: State University of New York Press, 2004.

Schelling, Friedrich W. J. *The Grounding of Positive Philosophy*. Trans. Bruce Matthews. Albany: State University of New York Press, 2007.

Schelling, Friedrich W. J. *Historical-Critical Introduction to the Philosophy of Mythology*. Trans. Mason Richey and Markus Zisselsberger. Albany: State University of New York Press, 2007.

Schelling, Friedrich W. J. *On The History of Modern Philosophy*. Trans. Andrew Bowie. Cambridge: Cambridge University Press, 1994.

Schelling, Friedrich W. J. *Ideas for a Philosophy of Nature*. Trans. Errol E. Harris and Peter Heath. Cambridge: Cambridge University Press, 1988.

Schelling, Friedrich W. J. *On the Deities of Samothrace.* Trans. David Farrell Krell and Jason Wirth (unpublished, 2015).

Schelling, Friedrich W. J. *Philosophical Inquiries into the Nature of Human Freedom.* Trans. James Gutmann. La Salle: Open Court, 1936.

Schelling, Friedrich W. J. *Sämmtliche Werke.* Ed. K. F. A. Schelling. 14 vols. Stuttgart: J. G. Cotta'scher Verlag, 1856.

Schelling, Friedrich W. J. *System of Transcendental Idealism.* Trans. Peter Heath. Charlottesville: University Press of Virginia, 1978.

Schelling, Friedrich W. J. *Über das Wesen der menschlichen Freiheit.* Ed. Phillip Reclam. Stuttgart: GmbH & Co., 1964.

Schiller, Friedrich. *Essays.* Eds. Walter Hinderer and Daniel O. Dahlstrom. New York: Continuum, 1993.

Schindler, D. C. *The Perfection of Freedom: Schiller, Schelling, and Hegel between the Ancients and the Moderns.* Eugene: Cascade Books, 2012.

Schmidt, Dennis J. *On Germans and Other Greeks: Tragedy and Ethical Life.* Bloomington: Indiana University Press, 2001.

Snow, Dale E. *Schelling and the End of Idealism.* Albany: State University of New York Press, 1996.

Tritten, Tyler. *Beyond Presence: The Late F. W. J. Schelling's Criticism of Metaphysics.* Boston/Berlin: Walter de Gruyter, Inc., 2012.

White, Alan. *Schelling: An Introduction to the System of Freedom.* New Haven: Yale University Press, 1983.

Wirth, Jason M. *The Conspiracy of Life: Meditations on Schelling and His Time.* Albany: State University of New York Press, 2003.

Wirth, Jason M., ed. *Schelling Now: Contemporary Readings.* Bloomington: Indiana University Press, 2005.

Wirth, Jason M. and Patrick M. Burke, eds. *The Barbarian Principle: Merleau-Ponty, Schelling, and the Question of Nature.* Albany: State University of New York Press, 2013.

Yates, Christopher. *The Poetic Imagination in Heidegger and Schelling.* New York: Bloomsbury, 2013.

Žižek, Slavoj. *The Indivisible Remainder: An Essay on Schelling and Related Matters.* London: Verso, 1996.

Index

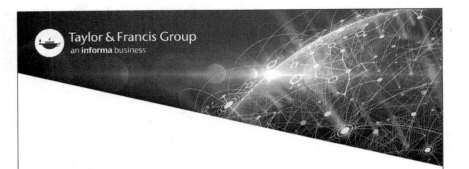